Engineering Problem
Solving with M<small>ATLAB</small>®

MATLAB® Curriculum Series

Cleve Moler, The MathWorks, Inc.
Editor

Engineering Problem Solving with MATLAB®
Second Edition

Delores M. Etter

Department of Electrical and Computer Engineering
University of Colorado, Boulder

An Alan R. Apt Book

Prentice Hall, Upper Saddle River, New Jersey 07458

Library of Congress Cataloging-in-Publication Data
Etter, Delores M.
   Engineering problem solving with MATLAB®
   Delores M. Etter.
      p. cm.
   "An Alan R. Apt book."
   Includes bibliographical references and index
   ISBN 0-13-397688-2
   1. Engineering mathematics—Data processing. 2. MATLAB.
  I. Title.
  TA345.E547 1997   96-22096
  620'.001'51—dc20   CIP

Publisher: Alan Apt
Editor-in-Chief: Marcia Horton
Project Manager: Mona Pompili
Developmental Editor: Sondra Chavez
Copy Editor: Shirley Michaels
Marketing Manager: Joe Hayton
Design Director: Amy Rosen
Designers: Meryl Poweski, Mona Pompili,
     Delores M. Etter
Cover Designer: Rod Hernandez
Production Coordinator: Donna Sullivan
Editoral Assistant: Shirley McGuire
Cover Graphic: MATLAB image of a continuous wavelet transform of sea surface height
   data from the TOPEX Satellite, highlighting soliton waves off the west coast of Africa.
   Provided by Mark Coffey.

In memory of my dearest Mother, Muerladene Janice Van Camp

 © 1997, 1993 by Prentice-Hall, Inc.
Simon & Schuster / A Viacom Company
Upper Saddle River, New Jersey 07458

Printed in the United States of America

10 9 8 7 6 5 4 3 2 1

ISBN   0-13-397688-2

PRENTICE-HALL INTERNATIONAL (UK) LIMITED, *London*
PRENTICE-HALL OF AUSTRALIA PTY. LIMITED, *Sydney*
PRENTICE-HALL CANADA, INC., *Toronto*
PRENTICE-HALL HISPANOAMERICANA, S.A., *Mexico*
PRENTICE-HALL OF INDIA PRIVATE LIMITED, *New Delhi*
PRENTICE-HALL OF JAPAN, INC., *Tokyo*
SIMON & SCHUSTER ASIA PTE. LTD., *Singapore*
EDITORA PRENTICE-HALL DO BRASIL, LTDA., *Rio de Janeiro*

TRADEMARK INFORMATION

MATLAB is a registered
trademark of
The MathWorks, Inc.

Foreword

This is an exciting and unusual textbook. It is exciting because it represents a new approach to an important aspect of engineering education. It is unusual because it combines topics from what are traditionally three or four different courses into a single, introductory course. This new course, intended for freshman or sophomore students in engineering and science, covers

- Elementary applied mathematics
- Basic numerical methods
- Computer programming
- Problem solving methodology

Where do you first see complex numbers? Where do you first learn about 3-by-3 matrices? When do you begin to do useful mathematical computations? How do you combine these ideas into the solution of practical engineering and scientific problems? This book provides answers to such questions early in the collegiate career.

One exercise in the book illustrates this multi-faceted approach:

Write a MATLAB expression for the resistance of three resistors in parallel.

Here, in one problem, we have some basic electrical engineering, some elementary mathematics, and a little bit of computer programming.

Thirteen years ago, Delores Etter wrote two popular textbooks on computer programming and numerical methods. She chose to use Fortran which then was clearly the most widely used language for technical computing. Coincidentally, about this same time MATLAB began to be used outside of the matrix computation community where it originated.

Today, there is a wide variety of languages and environments available for technical computing. Fortran is certainly still important; but so are Pascal, C, and C++. There are sophisticated programmable calculators, spread sheets, and mouse- and menu-based systems. And there are several commercial mathematical languages. In our opinion, MATLAB is the right choice for courses such as this because it is

- Easy to learn and use
- Powerful, flexible, and extensible
- Accurate, robust, and fast
- Widely used in engineering and science
- Backed by a professional software company

At The MathWorks and at Prentice Hall, we are committed to the support of MATLAB's use in education. In the future, you will see new features added to The Student Edition and many new books available in the MATLAB Curriculum Series.

A friend of ours, who is a professor of electrical engineering and an expert on signal processing, says "MATLAB is so good for signal processing because it wasn't designed to do signal processing—it was designed to do mathematics."

Our friend's observation is also the basis for this book. Mathematics, and its embodiment in software, is a foundation for much of modern technology. We believe you will enjoy, and benefit from, this introduction.

Cleve Moler
The MathWorks, Inc.
Natick, Massachusetts

Preface

Engineers and scientists use computers to solve a variety of problems, ranging from the evaluation of a simple function to solving a sytem of equations. MATLAB has become the **technical computing environment** of choice for many engineers and scientists because it is a single interactive system that incorporates **numeric computation**, **symbolic computation**, and **scientific visualization**.

Because the MATLAB computing environment is one that a new engineer is likely to encounter in a job, it is a good choice for an introduction to computing for engineers. This book is appropriate for use as an introductory engineering text or as a supplemental text in an advanced course. It is also useful as a professional reference.

This text was written to introduce engineering problem solving with the following objectives:

- Present a consistent **methodology for solving engineering problems**.
- Describe the exceptional **computational and visualization capabilities of MATLAB**.
- Illustrate the problem-solving process through a variety of **engineering examples and applications**.

To accomplish these objectives, Chapter 1 presents a five-step process that is used consistently for solving engineering problems. The rest of the chapters present the capabilities of MATLAB for solving engineering problems using specific examples from many different engineering disciplines. The text is based on **Version 4** of MATLAB; some of the new features in **Version 5** are discussed in supplemental materials that are available on the Prentice Hall World Wide Web site which is discussed later in this Preface.

TEXT ORGANIZATION

This flexible book is designed for use in a variety of engineering and science course settings from a primary text for introductory students to a supplement for intermediate or advanced courses. The text is divided into three parts—Part I: Fundamental Engineering Computing, Part II: Numerical Techniques, and Part III: Special Topics. Part I presents MATLAB material that is fundamental to basic engineering computing and visualization. The four chapters in Part I focus on the **MATLAB environment** and **MATLAB functions**. Part II contains four chapters that cover common numerical techniques for determining solutions to **systems of linear equations**, for **interpolation** and **curve fitting**, for **numerical integration** and **differentiation**, and for **solving ordinary differential equations**. These chapters are independent of each other, but they do assume that the material in Part I has been covered. Finally, Part III contains three special topics that are very useful in solving more specialized engineering problems: **symbolic mathematics**, **signal processing**, and **control systems**.

It is feasible to cover Chapters 1 through 9 in a one-semester course for a complete presentation of MATLAB's capabilities. If a briefer introduction to MATLAB is desired, we suggest that Chapters 1 through 3 be covered along with selected topics from Chapters 5 through 8. We have also written another text, *Introduction to MATLAB for Engineers and Scientists* (Prentice Hall, 1996, 0-13-519703-1), that is especially designed for a brief (three- to six-week) introduction to the capabilities of MATLAB. The chapters on signal processing and control systems (included in Part III) are specialized chapters that require additional background. These chapters are included to provide reference material for advanced courses.

PREREQUISITES

No prior experience with the computer is assumed. The mathematical background needed for Chapters 1 through 6 is **college algebra** and **trigonometry**; more advanced mathematics is needed for some of the material in later chapters.

PROBLEM-SOLVING METHODOLOGY

The **emphasis on engineering and scientific problem solving** is an important part of this text. Chapter 1 introduces a **five-step process for solving engineering problems** using the computer:

1. State the problem clearly.
2. Describe the input and output information.
3. Work a simple example by hand.
4. Develop an algorithm and convert it to MATLAB.
5. Test the solution with a variety of data.

To reinforce the development of problem solving skills, each of these steps is identified every time a complete solution to an engineering problem is developed.

ENGINEERING AND SCIENTIFIC APPLICATIONS

Throughout the text, emphasis is placed on incorporating real-world engineering and scientific examples and problems with solutions and usable code. This emphasis is centered around a theme of **grand challenges**, which include

*   prediction of weather, climate, and global change
*   computerized speech understanding

- mapping of the human genome
- improvements in vehicle performance
- enhanced oil and gas recovery

Each chapter begins with a photograph and a discussion of some aspect of one of these grand challenges that provides a glimpse of some of the exciting and interesting areas in which engineers might work. The grand challenges are also referenced in many of the other examples and problems.

VISUALIZATION

The visualization of the information related to a problem is a key advantage of using MATLAB for developing and understanding solutions. Therefore, it is important to learn to generate **plots** in a variety of formats to use when analyzing, interpreting, and evaluating data. We begin using plots with the first MATLAB program presented in Chapter 1, and continually expand **plotting capabilities** within the remaining chapters.

SOFTWARE ENGINEERING CONCEPTS

Engineers and scientists are also expected to develop and implement **user-friendly** and **reusable** computer solutions. Therefore, learning software engineering techniques is crucial to successfully developing these computer solutions. **Readability** and **documentation** are stressed in the development of programs. Through MATLAB, users are able to write **portable** code that can be transferred from one computer platform to another. Additional topics that relate to software engineering issues are discussed throughout the text and include the **software life cycle**, **maintenance**, **modularity**, **abstraction**, and **software prototypes**.

THE INTERNET AND THE WORLD WIDE WEB

One of the new sections in this edition discusses the **Internet, electronic mail**, **electronic bulletin boards**, and the **World Wide Web**. Several web sites are listed that contain more information related to this text and to MATLAB.

EXERCISES AND PROBLEMS

Learning any new skill requires practice at a number of different levels of difficulty. **Practice! problems** are short-answer questions that relate to the section of material just presented. Most sections are immediately followed by a set of Practice! problems so readers can determine if they are ready to continue to the next section. Complete solutions to all the Practice! problems are included at the end of the text.

Each chapter ends with a set of **end-of-chapter problems**. These are new problems that relate to a variety of engineering applications with the level of difficulty ranging from straightforward to longer assignments. Engineering data sets are included for many of the problems to use in testing.

STUDENT AIDS

Margin notes are used to help the reader not only identify the important concepts, but also to locate specific topics easily. **Style notes** show how to write MATLAB statements that incorporate good software discipline while **debugging notes** help readers recognize common errors so that they can be avoided. The programming style notes are indicated with the margin note *Style*, and the debugging notes are indicated with a **bug icon**.

Each Chapter Summary reviews the topics covered in the chapter and includes a list of the **Key Terms** from the chapter; a summary of the style notes; and debugging notes; and a **MATLAB Summary** that lists all the special symbols, commands, and functions defined in the chapter. In addition, Appendix A contains a complete summary of MATLAB functions presented in the text, and the last two pages of the text contain commonly-used information.

INSTRUCTOR'S RESOURCES

An **Instructor's Manual** is available that contains complete solutions to all the end-of-chapter problems. Also, transparency masters are included to assist in preparing lecture material.

Additional information related to this text and to MATLAB is available through the World Wide Web. **Script files** and **data files** for examples used in this text, along with additional data files for end-of-chapter problems, are available at **http://www.prenhall.com.** The MathWorks, Inc., maintains a web site for **MATLAB information** at **http://www.mathworks.com.**

ACKNOWLEDGMENTS

I very much appreciate the encouragement of Cleve Moler (Chairman of the MathWorks, Inc.) and Alan Apt (Publisher of Computer Science texts at Prentice Hall) related to the development of my MATLAB texts. I also want to acknowledge the outstanding work of the publishing team, including Marcia Horton, Tom Robbins, Gary June, Joe Hayton, Mona Pompili, Sondra Chavez, Alice Dworkin, and Mike Sutton. This text has been significantly improved by the suggestions and comments of the reviewers of the first edition of *Engineering Problem Solving with MATLAB*. These reviewers included Randall Janka, The MITRE Corporation; Professor John A. Fleming, Texas A&M; Professor Jim Maneval, Bucknell University; Professor Helmuth Worbs, University of Central Florida; Professor Huseyin Abut, San Diego State University; Professor Richard Shiavi, Vanderbilt University; Captain Randy Haupt, U.S. Air Force Academy; Professor Zoran Gajic, Rutgers University; Professor Stengel, Princeton University; Professor William Beckwith, Clemson University; and Professor Juris Vagners, University of Washington.

I also want to express my gratitude to my husband, a mechanical/aerospace engineer, for his help in developing some of the engineering applications problems, and to my daughter, a veterinarian student, for her help in developing some of the DNA-related material and problems. Finally, I want to recognize the important contributions of the students in my introductory engineering courses for their feedback on the explanations, the examples, and the problems.

Delores M. Etter
Department of Electrical/Computer Engineering
University of Colorado, Boulder

Brief Contents

Contents

PART I

Fundamental Engineering Computing

After completing the four chapters in Part I, you will be able to use MATLAB to solve many of the problems that you encounter in your courses and labs. Chapter 1 defines a problem-solving methodology that will be used throughout the text, while Chapter 2 explores the MATLAB environment. In Chapters 3 and 4 we present many useful functions ranging from mathematical functions, to data analysis functions to matrix functions. You will also learn how to write user-written functions and how to generate random numbers. Throughout the discussions and examples, visualization techniques are presented so that you become comfortable using MATLAB to perform computations and to visually display information.

10

Courtesy of NASA/Johnson Space Center.

GRAND CHALLENGE:
Weather Prediction

Weather satellites provide a great deal of information to meteorologists who attempt to predict the weather. Large volumes of historical weather data can also be analyzed and used to test models for predicting weather. In general, meteorologists can do a reasonably good job of predicting the overall weather patterns; however, local weather phenomena such as tornadoes, water spouts, and microbursts are still very difficult to predict. Even predicting heavy rainfall or large hail from thunderstorms is often difficult. Although Doppler radar is useful in locating regions within storms that could contain tornadoes or microbursts, the radar detects the events as they occur and thus gives little time for issuing appropriate warnings to populated areas or aircraft. Accurate and timely prediction of weather and associated weather phenomena is still an elusive goal.

Engineering Problem Solving

OBJECTIVES

Although most of this text is focused on the MATLAB computing environment and its capabilities, we begin by describing some of the recent outstanding engineering achievements, and then we introduce you to a group of grand challenges—problems yet to be solved that will require technological breakthroughs in both engineering and science. One of the grand challenges is weather prediction, discussed in the chapter opening. Because most solutions to engineering problems require computers, we next describe computer systems with a discussion of both computer hardware and computer software. Solving engineering problems effectively also requires a design plan or procedure, so in this chapter we define a problem-solving methodology with five steps for describing a problem and developing a solution. We then return to the problem of weather prediction and discuss some of the different types of weather data that are currently being collected. This data is critical for developing the understanding and intuition needed to create a mathematical model to predict weather. The data is also important because it can be used to test hypothetical models as they are developed. Data analysis in general helps engineers and scientists better understand complex physical phenomena so that they can apply that knowledge to developing solutions to new problems.

1.1   Engineering in the 21st Century

Engineers solve real-world problems using scientific principles from disciplines that include mathematics, physics, chemistry, and computer science. This variety of subjects, and the challenge of real problems, makes engineering interesting and rewarding. In this section we present some of the outstanding engineering achievements of recent years, followed by a discussion of some of the important engineering challenges we face as we go into the next century. Finally, we consider some of the nontechnical skills and capabilities needed by the engineers of the 21st century.

RECENT ENGINEERING ACHIEVEMENTS

Ten outstanding engineering achievements

Since the development of the computer in the late 1950's, a number of very significant engineering achievements have occurred. In 1989, the National Academy of Engineering selected **ten outstanding engineering achievements** from the previous 25 years. These achievements illustrate the multidisciplinary nature of engineering and demonstrate how engineering has improved our lives and expanded the possibilities for the future while providing a wide variety of interesting and challenging careers. We now briefly discuss these ten achievements. Suggested readings at the end of the chapter include more detailed information on these topics.

Microprocessor

The development of the **microprocessor**, a tiny computer smaller than a postage stamp, is one of these top engineering achievements. Microprocessors are used in electronic equipment, household appliances, toys, and games, as well as in automobiles, aircraft, and space shuttles, because they provide powerful, yet inexpensive, computing capabilities. Microprocessors also provide the computing power inside calculators and personal computers.

Moon landing

Several of the top ten achievements relate to the exploration of space. The **moon landing** was probably the most complex and ambitious engineering project ever attempted. Major breakthroughs were required in the design of the Apollo spacecraft, the lunar lander, and the three-stage Saturn V rocket. Even the design

MICROPROCESSOR
Courtesy of Texas Instruments Incorporated

MOON LANDING
Courtesy of National Aeronautics and Space Administration.

of the spacesuit was a major engineering project, resulting in a system that included a three-piece suit and backpack, which together weighed 190 pounds. The computer played a key role not only in the designs of the various systems, but also in the communications required during an individual moon flight. A single flight required the coordination of over 450 people in the launch control center and over 7,000 others on nine ships, in 54 aircraft, and at stations located around the earth.

Application satellites

The space program also provided much of the impetus for the development of **application satellites**, which provide weather information, relay communication signals, map uncharted terrain, and provide environmental updates on the composition of the atmosphere. The Global Positioning System (GPS) is a constellation of 24 satellites that broadcast position, velocity, and time information worldwide. GPS receivers measure the time it takes for a signal to travel from the GPS satellite to the receiver. Using information received from four satellites, a microprocessor in the receiver can determine precise measurements of the receiver's location; the accuracy varies from a few meters to centimeters, depending on the computation techniques used.

Computer-aided design and manufacturing

Another of the top engineering achievements recognizes the contributions of **computer-aided design and manufacturing** (CAD/CAM). CAD/CAM has generated a new industrial revolution by increasing the speed and efficiency of many types of manufacturing processes. CAD allows the design to be done using the computer, which then produces the final schematics, parts lists, and computer simulation results. CAM uses design results to control machinery or industrial robots to manufacture, assemble, and move components.

Jumbo jet

The **jumbo jet** originated from the Air Force C-5A cargo plane that began operational flights in 1969. Much of the success of jumbo jets can be attributed to the high-bypass fanjet, which allows them to fly farther with less fuel and with less noise than previous jet engines. The core of the engine operates like a pure turbojet: Compressor blades pull air into the engine's combustion chamber; the hot expanding gas thrusts the engine forward, and at the same time spins a

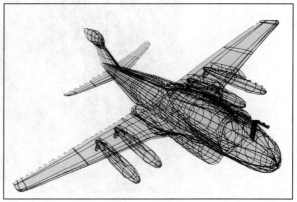

Satellite
Courtesy of National Aeronautics and Space Administration.

Computer-Aided Design
Courtesy of Computervision Corporation.

JUMBO JET   *Courtesy of United Parcel Service.*

turbine, which, in turn, drives the compressor and the large fan on the front of the engine. The spinning fan provides the bulk of the engine's thrust.

Advanced composite materials

The aircraft industry was also first to develop and use **advanced composite materials** which are materials that can be bonded so that one material reinforces the fibers of the other. Advanced composite materials were developed to provide lighter, stronger, and more temperature-resistant materials for aircraft and spacecraft. However, new markets for composites now exist in sporting goods. For example, layers of woven Kevlar fibers increase the strength and reduce the weight of downhill snow skis, and graphite/epoxy golf club shafts are stronger and lighter than conventional steel shafts. Composite materials are also used in the design of prosthetics for artificial limbs.

Computerized axial tomography

The areas of medicine, bioengineering, and computer science were teamed for the development of the CAT (**computerized axial tomography**) scanner

ADVANCED COMPOSITE MATERIALS   *Courtesy of Mike Valeri.*

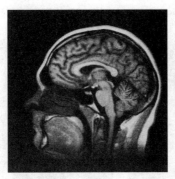

CAT Scan
Courtesy of General Electric.

Genetic Engineering
Courtesy of Matt Meadows.

machine. This instrument can generate three-dimensional images or two-dimensional slices of an object using X-rays that are generated from different angles around the object. Each X-ray measures a density from its angle, and very complicated computer algorithms combine the information from all the X-rays to reconstruct a clear image of the inside of the object. CAT scans are routinely used to identify tumors, blood clots, and brain abnormalities. The U.S. Army is developing a rugged, lightweight CAT scanner that can be transported to medical stations in combat zones.

Genetic engineering **Genetic engineering**, the work of geneticists and engineers, has resulted in many new products, ranging from insulin to growth hormones to infection-resistant vegetables. A genetically engineered product is produced by splicing a gene that produces a valuable substance from one organism into another organism that will multiply itself and the foreign gene along with it. The first commercial genetically engineered product was human insulin, which appeared under the trade name Humulin. Current work includes investigation of genetically altered microbes to clean up toxic waste and to degrade pesticides.

Lasers **Lasers** are light waves that have the same frequency and travel in a narrow beam that can be directed and focused. CO_2 lasers are used to drill holes in materials that range from ceramics to composite materials. Lasers are also used in medical procedures to weld detached retinas, seal leaky blood vessels, vaporize brain tumors, and perform delicate inner-ear surgery. Three-dimensional pictures called holograms are also generated with lasers.

Optical fibers Fiber-optic communications use **optical fibers**, transparent glass threads that are thinner than human hairs. An optical fiber can carry more information than either radio waves or electric waves in copper telephone wires, and it does not produce electromagnetic waves that can cause interference on communication lines. Transoceanic fiber-optic cables provide communication channels between continents. Fiber optics are also used in medical instrumentation to allow surgeons to thread light into the human body for examinations and laser surgery.

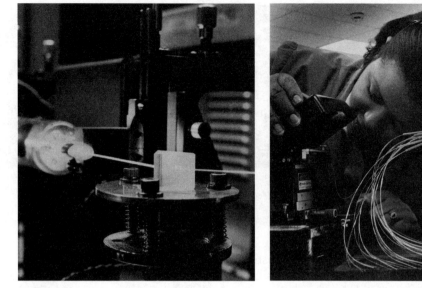

LASERS
Courtesy of Perkin-Elmer.

FIBER OPTICS
Courtesy of Photo Researchers, Inc.

GRAND CHALLENGES FOR THE FUTURE

Grand challenges

Although the recent achievements of engineers have produced dramatic results, there are still many important problems to be solved. In this section we present a group of **grand challenges**—fundamental problems in science and engineering with broad potential impact. The grand challenges were identified by the Office of Science and Technology Policy in Washington, D.C. as part of a research and development strategy for high performance computing. We have selected five of these grand challenges for this text. These challenges are discussed in the chapter opening applications, and problems related to these challenges are solved in examples. The following paragraphs briefly present these grand challenges and outline the types of benefits that will come with their solutions. Just as the computer played an important part in the top ten engineering achievements, it will play an even greater role in solving problems related to these grand challenges.

Prediction of weather, climate, and global change

The **prediction of weather, climate, and global change** requires that we understand the coupled atmosphere and ocean biosphere system. This includes understanding CO_2 dynamics in the atmosphere and ocean, ozone depletion, and climatological changes due to the release of chemicals or energy. This complex interaction also includes solar interactions. A major eruption from a solar storm near a coronal hole (a venting point for the solar wind) can eject vast amounts of hot gases from the sun's surface toward the earth's surface at speeds over a million miles per hour. These hot gases bombard the earth with X-rays and can interfere with communication and cause power fluctuations in power lines. Learning to predict changes in weather, climate, and global change involves collecting large amounts of data and developing new mathematical models that can represent the interdependency of many variables.

Computerized
speech
understanding

Computerized speech understanding could revolutionize our communication systems, but many problems are involved. Teaching a computer to understand words from a small vocabulary spoken by the same person is currently possible. However, to develop systems that are speaker-independent and that understand words from large vocabularies and from different languages is difficult. For example, subtle changes in one's voice, such as those caused by a cold or stress, can affect the performance of speech recognition systems. Also, assuming that the computer can recognize the words, determining their meaning is not simple: Many words are context-dependent and cannot be analyzed separately; and intonation, such as raising one's voice, can change a statement into a question. Although there are still many difficult problems left to address in automatic speech recognition and understanding, exciting possibilities are everywhere. For example, imagine a telephone system that determines the languages being spoken and translates the speech signals so that each person hears the conversation in his or her native language!

Human genome
project

The goal of the **human genome project** is to locate, identify, and determine the function of each of the 50,000 to 100,000 genes that are contained in human DNA (deoxyribonucleic acid), the genetic material found in cells. The deciphering of the human genetic code will lead to many technical advances, including the ability to detect most, if not all, of the more than 4,000 known human genetic diseases, such as sickle-cell anemia and cystic fibrosis. However, deciphering the code is complicated by the nature of genetic information. Each gene is a double-helix strand composed of base pairs (adenine bonded with thymine or cytosine bonded with guanine) arranged in a step-like manner with phosphate groups along the side. These base pairs can occur in any sequential order and represent the hereditary information in the gene. The number of base pairs in human DNA has been estimated to be around three billion. Because DNA directs protein production for all metabolic needs, the proteins produced by a cell may provide a key to the sequence of base pairs in the DNA.

Improvements
in vehicle
performance

Substantial **improvement in vehicle performance** requires more complex physical modeling in the areas of fluid dynamic behavior for three-dimensional flow fields and flow inside engine turbomachinery and ducts. Turbulence in fluid flows impacts the stability and control, thermal characteristics, and fuel performance of aerospace vehicles; modeling this flow is necessary for the analysis of new configurations. Analysis of the aeroelastic behavior of vehicles also affects new designs. Efficiency of combustion systems is also related, because attaining significant improvements in combustion efficiency requires understanding the relationships among the flows of the various substances and the chemistry that causes the substances to react. Vehicle performance is also being addressed through the use of onboard computers and microprocessors. Transportation systems are currently being studied in which cars have computers with small video screens mounted on the dashboard. The driver enters the destination location, and the video screen shows the street names and path to get from the current location to the desired location. A communication network keeps the car's computer aware of any traffic jams so that it can automatically reroute the car if necessary. Other transportation research addresses totally automated driving, with computers and networks handling all the control and information interchange.

Enhanced oil and
gas recovery

Enhanced oil and gas recovery will allow us to locate the estimated 300 billion barrels of oil reserves in the U.S. Current techniques for identifying structures likely to contain oil and gas use seismic techniques that can evaluate structures down to 20,000 feet below the surface. These techniques use a group of sensors (called a sensor array) that is located near the area to be tested. A ground shock signal, sent into the earth, is reflected by the different geological layer boundaries, and is then received by the sensors. Using sophisticated signal processing, the boundary layers can be mapped, and some estimate can be made as to the materials in the various layers, such as sandstone, shale, and water. The ground shock signals can be generated in several ways: A hole can be drilled, and an explosive charge can be exploded in the hole; a ground shock can be generated by an explosive charge on the surface; or a special truck that uses a hydraulic hammer can be used to pound the earth several times per second. Continued research is needed to improve the resolution of the information and to find methods of production and recovery that are economical and ecologically sound.

These grand challenges are only a few of the many interesting problems waiting to be solved by engineers and scientists. Solutions to problems of this magnitude will be the result of organized approaches that combine ideas and technologies. Computers and engineering problem-solving techniques will be key elements in the solution process.

CHANGING ENGINEERING ENVIRONMENT

The engineer of the 21st century will work in an environment that requires many nontechnical skills and capabilities. Although the computer will be the primary computational tool of most engineers, it will also be useful in developing additional nontechnical abilities.

Communication
skills

Engineers need strong **communication skills** for both oral presentations and for preparing written materials. Computers provide the software to assist in writing outlines and developing materials and graphs for presentations and technical reports. Electronic mail (email) and the World Wide Web (WWW) are also very important communication channels that are discussed later in this chapter.

Design/process/
manufacture path

The **design/process/manufacture path**, which consists of taking an idea from concept to product, is one that engineers must understand first-hand. Every step of this process uses computers: design analysis, machine control, robotic assembly, quality assurance, and market analysis. Several problems in the text relate to these topics. For example, in Chapter 6, a program is developed to determine the motion of a robot arm used in assembling circuit boards.

Interdisciplinary
teams

Engineering teams of the future will be **interdisciplinary teams**, just like the engineering teams of today. The discussions of the top ten engineering achievements clearly show the interdisciplinary nature of those achievements. Learning to interact in teams and to develop organizational structures for effective team communication is an important skill for engineers.

World
marketplace

The engineers of the 21st century need to understand the **world marketplace**. This involves understanding different cultures, political systems, and business environments. Courses in these topics and in foreign languages help provide some understanding, and exchange programs with international experiences provide invaluable knowledge in developing a broader world understanding.

Engineers are problem solvers, but problems are not always formulated carefully. An engineer must be able to extract a problem statement from a problem discussion and then determine the important issues related to the problem. This involves not only developing order, but also learning to correlate chaos. It means not only **analyzing** the data, but also **synthesizing** a solution. The integration of ideas can be as important as the decomposition of the problem into manageable pieces. A problem solution may involve not only abstract thinking about the problem, but also experimental learning from the problem environment.

Problem solutions must also be considered in their **societal context**. Environmental concerns should be addressed while alternative solutions to problems are being considered. Engineers must also be conscious of ethical issues in providing test results, quality verifications, and design limitations. It is unfortunate that tragedies like the Challenger explosion are sometimes the impetus for bringing issues of responsibility and accountability into the forefront. Ethical issues are never easy to resolve, and some of the exciting new technological achievements will bring more ethical issues with them. For example, the mapping of the genome will potentially provide ethical, legal, and social implications. Should the gene therapy that allows doctors to combat diabetes also be used to enhance athletic ability? Should prospective parents be given detailed information related to the physical and mental characteristics of an unborn child? What kind of privacy should an individual have over his or her genetic code? Complicated issues arise with any technological advancement because the same capabilities that can do a great deal of good can often be applied in ways that are harmful.

We now begin our study of MATLAB with an introduction to the range of computing systems available to engineers and an introduction to the problem-solving methodology that will be used throughout this text as we use MATLAB to solve engineering problems.

Analyzing
Synthesizing

Societal context

1.2   Computing Systems

Computer

Before we begin discussing MATLAB, a brief discussion on computing is useful, especially for those who have not had prior experience with computers. A **computer** is a machine designed to perform operations that are specified with a set of instructions called a **program**. Computer **hardware** refers to the computer equipment, such as the keyboard, the mouse, the terminal, the hard disk, and the printer. Computer **software** refers to the programs that describe the steps that we want the computer to perform.

COMPUTER HARDWARE

All computers have a common internal organization, as shown in Figure 1.1. The **processor** controls all the other parts. It accepts input values (from a device such as a keyboard) and stores them in the **memory**. It also interprets the instructions

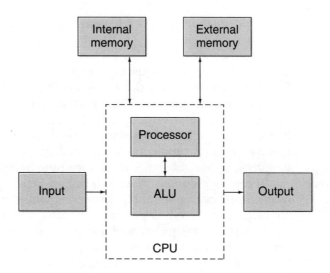

Figure 1.1 *Internal organization of a computer.*

in a computer program. If we want to add two values, the processor will retrieve the values from memory and send them to the **arithmetic logic unit**, or ALU. The ALU performs the addition, and the processor then stores the result in memory. The processing unit and the ALU use internal memory composed of read-only memory (ROM) and random access memory (RAM) in their processing; most data is stored in external memory or secondary memory using hard disk drives or floppy disk drives that are attached to the processor. The processor and ALU together are called the **central processing unit** or CPU. A **microprocessor** is a CPU that is contained in a single integrated circuit chip, which contains millions of components in an area smaller than a postage stamp.

We usually instruct the computer to print the computed values on the terminal screen or on paper using a printer. Dot matrix printers use a matrix (or grid) of pins to produce the shape of a character on paper, whereas a laser printer uses a light beam to transfer images to paper. The computer can also write information to diskettes, which store the information magnetically. A printed copy of information is called a **hard copy**, and a magnetic copy of information is called an **electronic copy** or a soft copy.

Computers come in all sizes, shapes, and forms. (See photos in Figure 1.2.) Personal computers (**PC**s) are small, inexpensive computers that are commonly used in offices, homes, and laboratories. PCs are also referred to as microcomputers, and their design is built around a microprocessor, such as the Intel 486 microprocessor, which can process millions of instructions per second (mips). Minicomputers are more powerful than microcomputers; mainframes are even more powerful computers that are often used in businesses and research laboratories. A **workstation** is a minicomputer or mainframe computer that is small enough to fit on a desktop. **Supercomputers** are the fastest of all computers, and can process billions of instructions per second. As a result of their speed, supercomputers are capable of solving very complex problems that cannot be feasibly solved on other

Central processing unit

PC

ENGINEERING GRAND CHALLENGES

PREDICTION OF WEATHER, CLIMATE, AND GLOBAL CHANGE

To predict weather, climate, and global change, we must understand the complex interactions of the atmosphere and the oceans. These interactions are influenced by many things, including temperature, winds, ocean currents, precipitation, soil moisture, snow cover, glaciers, polar sea ice, and the absorption of ultraviolet radiation by ozone in the earth's atmosphere. As a result of concern over the ozone depletion in the atmosphere, weather balloons (**Photo 1**) were launched in Sweden in 1990 as part of an experiment conducted by engineers and scientists from France, Germany, and the United States to measure the atmospheric ozone and various pollutants near the Arctic pole. **Photo 2** illustrates the total atmospheric ozone concentration in the southern hemisphere in October 1993. These data come from the Total Ozone Mapping Spectrometer instrument on the Russian Meteor-3 satellite; the white region shows a 60% decrease in the ozone levels from 1975.

To be able to predict weather phenomena such as tornadoes, we must understand the combination of events required for them to develop. **Photo 3** shows equipment designed to generate miniature tornadoes; results from experiments such as this one provide new insights to the field of meteorology. ∎

Photo 1   *Weather Balloon*

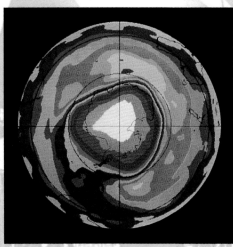

Photo 2   *Ozone Model*

Photo 3   *Tornado Machine*

IMPROVEMENTS IN VEHICLE PERFORMANCE

Significant improvements in vehicle performance will not only affect the modes of transportation available to us, but can also improve the environment by reducing

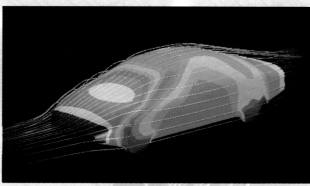

Photo 4 *Car Aerodynamics*

Photo 5 *Wind Tunnel*

Photo 6 *Computer-navigated Car*

pollution and by providing more efficient energy consumption. Computer-aided design techniques allow us to analyze the three-dimensional fluid flow around a vehicle (**Photo 4**). We can also analyze new designs using wind tunnels, which can generate various wind speeds to test the performance of new structures (**Photo 5**). Improvements in transportation will take advantage of engineering breakthroughs in other areas, such as satellite navigation. The Global Positioning System (GPS) satellites can be used to determine the exact position of a GPS receiver, and that information could be used in an onboard computer to direct a driver to a desired location, as shown in **Photo 6**. ■

COMPUTERIZED SPEECH UNDERSTANDING

Computerized speech understanding could revolutionize our communication systems. We still cannot converse normally with computers, but there are applications that use some forms of speech understanding. Educational games such as the one illustrated in **Photo 7** use speech input to teach skills such as language and mathematics; these programs understand words from limited vocabularies. Other computer programs are designed to understand and respond to words from a specific person. For example, motorized wheelchairs can be designed to respond to verbal commands, or computers can take their input from verbal instructions instead of through a keyboard (**Photo 8**).

Photo 7 *Educational Game*

Photo 8 *Speech Input to Computer*

ENHANCED OIL AND GAS RECOVERY

Economical and ecologically sound techniques are needed for the identification and recovery of oil and gas reserves. Sonar signal processing techniques are being developed to identify potential reserves under the ocean, which are then recovered by oil platforms (**Photo 10**). Underground reserves can be located by techniques that map the geological structure, as shown in the computer model in **Photo 11** that was developed using seismic signal processing. This information can be used to determine the materials in the various layers, and thus to indicate areas that are likely to contain oil or gas. Understanding the geological structure and relationships of different regions, such as the Mauna Loa volcano rift shown in **Photo 12**, gives engineers and scientists new information in understanding the earth's structure and the materials of which it is composed. ∎

Photo 10   *Oil Platform*

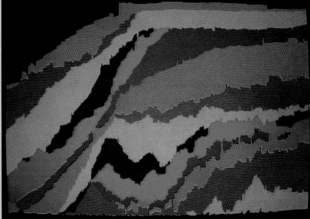

Photo 11   *Computer Model of Earth Layers*

Photo 12   *Geological Experiments in a Volcano*

Photo 9   *Airline Cockpit*

Researchers are currently exploring the use of speech to simplify access to the information contained in the hundreds of gauges and instruments in an airline cockpit (**Photo 9**). For instance, in a future airliner, the pilot may be able to verbally ask for information, such as fuel status, and a computer will respond in synthesized speech with the amount of fuel remaining. ∎

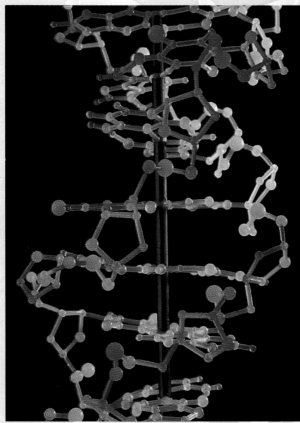

Photo 13   *DNA molecule model*

Photo 14   *Equipment for DNA Sequencing*

HUMAN GENOME PROJECT

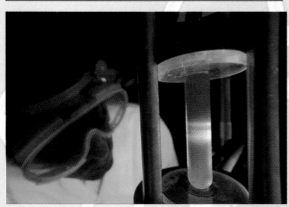

Photo 15   *Bands of DNA*

The goal of the Human Genome Project is to locate, identify, and determine the function of each of the 50,000 to 100,000 genes contained in human DNA (deoxyribonucleic acid). A model of the double-helix DNA molecule is shown in **Photo 13**. Each gene is composed of base pairs arranged in a step-like manner, and it is the identification of the order of these base pairs that provides the key to the human genome. The structure of genes can be studied using equipment such as the electrophoresis machine in **Photo 14**. This machine contains a gel that can separate radioactively tagged DNA fragments using an electric field. **Photo 15** shows an engineer separating bands of DNA for a gene-splicing experiment. ■

Photo credits: 1 *Courtesy of Photo Researchers, Inc.* **2** *Courtesy of Photo Researchers, Inc.* **3** *Courtesy of Rainbow.* **4** *Courtesy of Photo Researchers, Inc.* **5** *Courtesy of National Aeronautics and Space Administration.* **6** *Courtesy of Photo Researchers, Inc.* **7** *Courtesy of FPG International.* **8** *Courtesy of Rainbow.* **9** *Courtesy of FPG International.* **10** *Courtesy of Amoco Corporation.* **11** *Courtesy of Rainbow.* **12** *Courtesy of The Image Works.* **13** *Courtesy of FPG International.* **14** *Courtesy of Photo Researchers, Inc.* **15** *Courtesy of Rainbow.*

Figure 1.2 *Computer hardware.* (**Photo credits:** *a Courtesy of Johnson Space Center.   b Courtesy of The Image Works.   c Courtesy of Apple Computer Inc.   d Courtesy of The Image Works.   e Courtesy of Cray Research.   f Courtesy of IBM.*)

computers. Mainframes and supercomputers require special facilities and a specialized staff to run and maintain the computer systems.

The type of computer needed to solve a particular problem depends on the problem requirements. If the computer is part of a home security system, a microprocessor is sufficient; if the computer is running a flight simulator, a mainframe is probably needed. Computer **networks** allow computers to communicate with each other to share resources and information. For example, ethernet is a commonly used local area network (LAN).

Networks

COMPUTER SOFTWARE

Computer software contains the instructions or commands that we want the computer to perform. There are several important categories of software, including operating systems, software tools, and language compilers. Figure 1.3 illustrates the interaction among these categories of software and the computer hardware. We now discuss each of these software categories in more detail.

Operating system

Operating Systems. Some software, such as the **operating system**, typically comes with the computer hardware when it is purchased. The operating system provides an interface between you (the user) and the hardware by providing a convenient and efficient environment in which you can select and execute the software on your system.

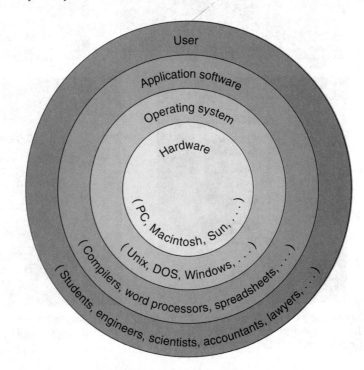

Figure 1.3 *Software interface to the computer.*

Operating systems also contain a group of programs called **utilities** that allow you to perform functions such as printing files, copying files from one diskette to another, and listing the files that you have saved on a diskette. While these utilities are common to most operating systems, the commands themselves vary from computer to computer. For example, to list your files using DOS (a Disk Operating System used mainly with PCs), the command is `dir`; to list your files with UNIX (a powerful operating system frequently used with workstations), the command is `ls`. Some operating systems, such as the Macintosh environment and the Windows environment, simplify the interface with the operating system.

Because MATLAB programs can be run on many different platforms or hardware systems and because a specific computer can use different operating systems, it is not feasible to discuss the wide variety of operating systems that you might use while taking this course. We assume that your professor will provide the specific operating system information that you need to use the computers available at your university; this information is also contained in the operating system manuals.

Word processors

Software Tools. Software tools are programs that have been written to perform common operations. For example, **word processors**, such as Microsoft Word and Word Perfect, are programs that have been written to help you enter and format text. Word processors allow you to move sentences and paragraphs and often have capabilities that allow you to enter mathematical equations and to check your spelling and grammar. Word processors are also used to enter computer programs and store them in files. Sophisticated word processors allow you to produce well-designed pages that combine elaborate charts and graphics with text and headlines. These word processors use a technology called **desktop publishing**, which combines a powerful word processor with a high-quality printer to produce professional-looking documents.

Spreadsheet

Spreadsheet programs are software tools that allow you to work easily with data that can be displayed in a grid of rows and columns. Spreadsheets were initially used for financial and accounting applications, but many science and engineering problems can be solved easily using spreadsheets. Most spreadsheet packages include plotting capabilities, so they can be especially useful in analyzing and displaying information. Excel, Quattro Pro, and Lotus 1-2-3 are popular spreadsheet packages.

Database management

Another popular group of software tools are **database management** programs, such as dBase IV and Paradox. These programs allow you to store a large amount of data, retrieve pieces of the data, and format them into reports. Databases are used by large organizations, such as banks, hospitals, hotels, and airlines. Scientific databases are also used to analyze large amounts of data. Meteorology data is an example of scientific data that requires large databases for storage and analysis.

Computer-aided design

Computer-aided design (CAD) packages, such as AutoCAD, AutoSketch, and CADKEY, allow you to define objects and then manipulate them graphically. For example, you can define an object and then view it from different angles or observe a rotation of the object from one position to another.

Mathematical
computation

MATLAB, Mathematica, MATHCAD, and Maple are powerful **mathematical computation** tools, which also provide extensive capabilities for generating graphs. This combination of computational power and visualization power make them particularly useful tools for engineers. In Chapter 2, we present the computing environment provided by MATLAB.

If an engineering problem can be solved using a software tool, it is usually more efficient to use that tool than to write a program in a computer language to solve the problem. However, many problems cannot be solved using software tools, or a software tool may not be available on the computer system that must be used for solving the problem; thus, we also need to know how to write programs using computer languages. The distinction between a software tool and a computer language is becoming less clear as some of the more powerful tools, such as MATLAB and Mathematica, include their own languages in addition to specialized operations.

Computer Languages. Computer languages can be described in terms of levels. Low-level languages, or machine languages, are the most primitive languages. **Machine language** is tied closely to the design of the computer hardware.

Machine
language

Because computer designs are based on two-state technology (i.e., open or closed circuits, on or off switches, positive or negative charges), machine language is written using two symbols, which are usually represented using the digits 0 and 1. Therefore, machine language is also a **binary** language, and the instructions are written as sequences of 0s and 1s called binary strings. Because machine language is closely tied to the design of the computer hardware, the machine language for a Sun computer is different from the machine language for a Silicon Graphics computer.

Assembly
language

An **assembly language** is also unique to a specific computer design, but its instructions are written in English-like statements instead of binary. Assembly languages usually do not have very many statements; thus, writing programs in assembly language can be tedious. In addition, to use an assembly language, you must know information that relates to the specific computer hardware. Instrumentation that contains microprocessors often requires that the programs operate very fast; thus, the programs are called **real-time programs**. These real-time programs are usually written in assembly language to take advantage of the specific computer hardware in order to perform the steps faster.

High-level
languages

High-level languages are computer languages that have English-like commands and instructions and include languages such as C++, C, Fortran, Ada, Pascal, COBOL, and Basic. Writing programs in high-level languages is certainly easier than writing programs in machine language or in assembly language. However, a high-level language contains a large number of commands and an extensive set of **syntax** (or grammar) rules for using the commands. To illustrate the syntax and punctuation required by both software tools and high-level languages, we compute the area of a circle with a specified diameter in Table 1.1 using several different languages and tools. Notice both the similarities and the differences in this simple computation. Although we included C and C++ as high-level languages, many people like to describe them as mid-level languages because they

---

TABLE 1.1 Comparison of Software Statements

Software	Example Statement
MATLAB	`area = pi*((diameter/2)^2);`
C, C++	`area = 3.141593*(diameter/2)*(diameter/2);`
Fortran	`area = 3.141593*(diameter/2.0)**2`
Ada	`area := 3.141593*(diameter/2)**2;`
Pascal	`area := 3.141593*(diameter/2)*(diameter/2)`
BASIC	`let a = 3.141593*(d/2)*(d/2)`
COBOL	`compute area = 3.141593*(diameter/2)*(diameter/2).`

---

allow access to low-level routines and are often used to define programs that are converted to assembly language.

Languages are also defined in terms of **generations**. The first generation of computer languages is machine language, the second generation is assembly language, and the third generation is high-level language. Fourth generation languages, also referred to as **4GLs**, have not been developed yet and are described only in terms of characteristics and programmer productivity. The fifth generation of languages is called natural languages. To program in a fifth generation language, one would use the syntax of natural speech. Clearly, the implementation of a natural language would require the achievement of one of the grand challenges—computerized speech understanding.

Fortran (FORmula TRANslation) was developed in the mid 1950s for solving engineering and scientific problems. New standards updated the language over the years, and the current standard, Fortran 90, contains strong numerical computation capabilities along with many of the new features and structures in languages such as C. **COBOL** (COmmon Business-Oriented Language) was developed in the late 1950s to solve business problems. **Basic** (Beginner's All-purpose Symbolic Instruction Code) was developed in the mid 1960s as an educational tool and is often included with the system software for a PC. **Pascal** was developed in the early 1970s and is widely used in computer science programs to introduce students to computing. **Ada** was developed at the initiative of the U.S. Department of Defense with the goal of developing a high-level language appropriate to embedded computer systems that are typically implemented using microprocessors. The final design of the language was accepted in 1979, and the language was named in honor of Ada Lovelace who developed instructions for doing computations on an analytical machine in the early 1800s. **C** is a general-purpose language that evolved from two languages, BCPL and B, which were developed at Bell Laboratories in the late 1960s. In 1972, Dennis Ritchie developed and implemented the first C compiler on a DEC PDP-11 computer at Bell Laboratories. The language became very popular for system development because it was hardware independent. Because of its popularity in both industry and in academia, it became clear that a standard definition was needed. A committee of the American National Standards Institute (ANSI) was created in 1983 to provide a machine-independent and unambiguous definition of C. In 1989 the ANSI standard was approved. **C++** is an evolution of the C language that was developed at AT&T Bell Laboratories in the early 1980s by Bjarne Stroustrup. The extensions to the C language provided additional operators and functions that support a new paradigm called object-oriented design and programming.

Executing a Computer Program. A program written in a high-level language such as C must be translated into machine language before the instructions can be executed by the computer. A special program called a **compiler** is used to perform this translation. Thus, in order to be able to write and execute C programs on a computer, the computer's software must include a C compiler.

Compiler

If any errors (often called **bugs**) are detected by the compiler during compilation, corresponding error messages are printed. We must correct our program statements and then perform the compilation step again. The errors identified during this stage are called **compile errors** or compile-time errors. For example, if we want to divide the value stored in a variable called **sum** by 3, the correct expression in C is **sum/3**; if we incorrectly write the expression using the backslash, as in **sum\3**, we will get a compile error. The process of compiling, correcting statements (or **debugging**), and recompiling must often be repeated several times before the program compiles without compile errors. When there are no compile errors, the compiler generates a program in machine language that performs the steps specified by the original C program. The original C program is referred to as the **source program**, and the machine language version is called an **object program**. Thus, the source program and the object program specify the same steps, but the source program is specified in a high-level language, and the object program is specified in machine language.

Execution

Once the program has compiled correctly, additional steps are necessary to prepare the object program for **execution**. This preparation involves **linking** other machine language statements to the object program and then **loading** the program into memory. After this linking/loading, the program steps are executed by the computer. New errors, called execution errors, run-time errors, or **logic errors**, may be identified in this stage; they are also called program bugs. Execution errors often cause termination of a program. For example, the program statements may attempt to perform a division by zero, which generates an execution error. Some execution errors do not stop the program from executing, but they cause incorrect results to be computed. These types of errors can be caused by programmer errors in determining the correct steps in the solutions and by errors in the data processed by the program. When execution errors occur due to errors in the program statements, we must correct the errors in the source program and then begin again with the compilation step. Even when a program appears to execute properly, we must check the answers carefully to be sure that they are correct. The computer will perform the steps precisely as we specify; if we specify the wrong steps, the computer will execute these wrong (but syntactically legal) steps and thus present us with an answer that is incorrect.

The processes of compilation, linking/loading, and execution are outlined in Figure 1.4. The process of converting an assembly language program to binary is performed by an **assembler program**, and the corresponding processes are called assembly, linking/loading, and execution.

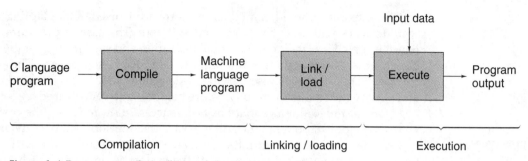

Figure 1.4 *Program compilation/linking/execution.*

Executing a MATLAB Program. In the MATLAB environment, we can develop and execute programs, or scripts, that contain MATLAB commands. We can also execute a MATLAB command, observe the results, and then execute another MATLAB command that interacts with the information in memory, observe its results, and so on. This **interactive environment** does not require the formal compilation, linking/loading, and execution process that was described for high-level computer languages. However, errors in the syntax of a MATLAB command are detected when the MATLAB environment attempts to translate the command, and logic errors can cause execution errors when the MATLAB environment attempts to execute the command.

Interactive environment

Software Life Cycle. In 1955, the cost of a typical computer solution was estimated to be 15% for the software development and 85% for the associated computer hardware. Over the years, the cost of the hardware has decreased dramatically, while the cost of the software has increased. In 1985, it was estimated that these numbers had essentially switched, with 85% of the cost for the software and 15% for the hardware. With the majority of the cost of a computer solution residing in the software development, a great deal of attention has been given to understanding the development of a software solution.

Software life cycle

The development of a software project generally follows definite steps or cycles, collectively called the **software life cycle**. These steps typically include the project definition, the detailed specification, coding and modular testing, integrated testing, and maintenance. Data indicates that the corresponding percentages of effort involved can be estimated as shown in Table 1.2. From these estimates, it is clear that software maintenance is a significant part of the cost of a software system. This **maintenance** includes adding enhancements to the

TABLE 1.2 Software Life Cycle Phases

Life Cycle	Percent of Effort
Definition	3%
Specification	15%
Coding and Modular Testing	14%
Integrated Testing	8%
Maintenance	60%

software, fixing errors identified as the software is used, and adapting the software to work with new hardware and software. The ease of providing maintenance is directly related to the original definition and specification of the solution because these steps lay the foundation for the rest of the project. The problem-solving process that we present in the next section emphasizes the need to define and specify the solution carefully before beginning to code or test it.

Software prototypes

One of the techniques that has been successful in reducing the cost of software development both in time and in cost is the development of **software prototypes**. Instead of waiting until the software system is developed and then letting the users work with it, a prototype of the system is developed early in the life cycle. This prototype does not have all the functions required of the final software, but it allows the user to make desired modifications to the specifications. Making changes earlier in the life cycle is both cost-effective and time-effective. Because of its powerful commands and its graphics capabilities, MATLAB is especially effective in developing software prototypes. Once the MATLAB prototype is performing the desired operations correctly and the users are happy with the user/software interaction, the final solution may be the MATLAB program, or the final solution may be converted to another language for implementation with a specific computer or piece of instrumentation.

As an engineer, it is very likely that you will need to modify or add additional capabilities to existing software. These modifications will be much simpler if the existing software is well-structured and readable and if the documentation is up-to-date and clearly written. Even with powerful tools such as MATLAB, it is important to write well-structured and readable code. For these reasons, we stress developing good habits that make software more readable and self-documenting.

THE INTERNET, EMAIL, AND THE WORLD WIDE WEB

Internet

The **Internet** is a network of computers that evolved from a small experimental research project funded by ARPA (Advanced Research Projects Agency), a government agency, in the mid 1980s. By the mid 1990s the Internet was the world's largest network, connecting over a million computers.

Electronic mail

An **electronic mail** system is software that allows users on a computer network to send messages to other users on the network. Internet users can send electronic messages (**email**) to users all over the world. Sending email and replying to email has become the standard mode of communication in many universities and companies. While using email simplifies many interactions, it also introduces some interesting issues that need to be resolved. For example, people often assume when they delete an email message that it is gone. However, in many cases the message has been stored on other computers or can be retrieved from the original computer's memory; thus, it is still accessible. A privacy issue is also important here: Is email private correspondence, or does a company have the right to read the email of its employees?

Electronic bulletin boards

Electronic bulletin boards are now available on the Internet that allow you to participate in discussion groups. Bulletin boards allow you to not only read notes posted on the bulletin board, but also to post notes to the bulletin boards. There are many bulletin boards with diverse topics that range from technical areas to sports to hobbies. Again, potential for benefit also brings potential for exploitation. A number of lawsuits have been filed over the access of bulletin boards with adult topics by young children using the Internet.

World Wide Web

A number of information browsing services have been developed to make it easy to locate and retrieve information on the Internet. The **World Wide Web** (WWW) is a system that links information stored on many systems. This information contains not only textual information, but also **multimedia** information, such as sound files, images, and animation. To browse information on the WWW, you need access to software that can display these various types of information. Some commonly used browsing software systems are Mosaic, Netscape, and Java. To access a WWW site, you need a **Uniform Resource Locator** (URL).

Uniform
Resource Locator

If you have access to the WWW, you might want to access the MATLAB Web site at **http://www.mathworks.com**. Access to information relative to this text is also available at **http://www.prenhall.com** and **http://ece-www.colorado.edu /faculty/etter.html**.

1.3   An Engineering Problem-Solving Methodology

Problem solving is a key part of engineering courses, and also of courses in computer science, mathematics, physics, and chemistry. Therefore, it is important to have a consistent approach to solving problems. It is also helpful if the approach is general enough to work for all these different areas, so that we do not have to learn a technique for mathematics problems, a different technique for physics problems, and so on. The problem-solving technique that we present works for engineering problems and can be tailored to solve problems in other areas as well; however, it does assume that we are using the computer to help solve the problem.

Problem-solving
methodology

The **problem-solving methodology** that we will use throughout this text has five steps:

1.   State the problem clearly.
2.   Describe the input and output information.
3.   Work the problem by hand (or with a calculator) for a simple set of data.
4.   Develop a MATLAB solution.
5.   Test the solution with a variety of data.

We now discuss each of these steps using data collected from a physics laboratory experiment. Assume that we have collected a set of temperatures from a sensor on a piece of equipment that is being used in an experiment. The temperature measurements are taken every 30 seconds, for 5 minutes, during the experiment. We want to compute the average temperature and we also want to plot the temperature values.

1.   PROBLEM STATEMENT

The first step is to state the problem clearly. It is extremely important to give a clear, concise problem statement to avoid any misunderstandings. For this example, the problem statement is the following:

> Compute the average of a set of temperatures. Then plot the time and temperature values.

2.   INPUT/OUTPUT DESCRIPTION

The second step is to describe carefully the information that is given to solve the problem and then identify the values to be computed. These items represent the input and the output for the problem and collectively can be called input/output or I/O. For many problems, a diagram that shows the input and output is useful. At this point, the program is an "abstraction" because we are not defining the steps to determine the output; instead, we are only showing the information that is used to compute the output.

The **I/O diagram** for this example follows:

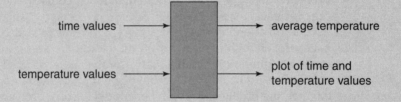

3.   HAND EXAMPLE

The third step is to work the problem by hand or with a calculator, using a simple set of data. This is a very important step and should not be skipped, even for simple problems. This is the step in which you work out the details of the problem solution. If you cannot take a simple set of numbers and compute the output (either by hand or with a calculator), then you are not ready to move on to the next step; you should reread the problem and perhaps consult reference material.

For this problem, the only calculation is computing the average of a set of temperature values. Assume that we use the following data for the hand example:

time (minutes)	temperature (degrees F)
0.0	105
0.5	126
1.0	119

By hand, we compute the average to be (105 + 126 + 119)/3, or 116.6667 degrees F.

4.   MATLAB SOLUTION

Once you can work the problem for a simple set of data, you are ready to develop an **algorithm**—a step-by-step outline of the problem solution. For simple problems such as this one, the algorithm can be immediately written using MATLAB commands; for more complicated problems, it may be necessary to write an outline of the steps and then decompose the steps into smaller steps that can be translated into MATLAB commands. One of the strengths of MATLAB is that its commands match very closely to the steps that we use to solve engineering problems; thus, the process of determining the steps to solve the problem also determines the MATLAB commands.

The next chapter discusses the details of the MATLAB commands used in the following solution, but observe that the MATLAB steps match closely to the solution steps from the hand example:

```
%    Compute average (or mean) temperature
%    and plot the temperature data.
%
time = [0.0, 0.5, 1.0];
temps = [105, 126, 119];
average = mean(temps)
plot(time,temps),title('Temperature Measurements'),...
    xlabel('Time, minutes'),...
    ylabel('Temperature, degrees F'),grid
```

The words that follow percent signs are comments to help us in reading the MATLAB statements. If a MATLAB statement assigns or computes a value, it will also print the value on the screen if the statement does not end in a semicolon. Thus, the values of **time** and **temps** will not be printed because the statements that assign them values end with semicolons; the value of the average will be computed and then printed on the screen because the statement that computes it does not end with a semicolon. Finally, a plot of the time and temperature data will be generated.

5.   TESTING

The final step in our problem-solving process is testing the solution. We should first test the solution with the data from the hand example because we have already computed the solution.

When the previous statements are executed, the computer displays the following output:

```
average =
   116.6667
```

A plot of the data points is also generated. The average matches the one from the hand example, so we now replace the hand data with the data from the physics experiment, giving the following program:

```
%    Compute average (or mean) temperature
%    and plot temperature data.
%
time = [0.0, 0.5, 1.0, 1.5, 2.0, 2.5, 3.0,...
        3.5, 4.0, 4.5, 5.0];
temps = [105, 126, 119, 129, 132, 128, 131,...
         135, 136, 132, 137];
average = mean(temps)
plot(time,temps),title('Temperature Measurements'),...
   xlabel('Time, minutes'),...
   ylabel('Temperature, degrees F'),grid
```

When these commands are executed, the computer displays the following output:

```
average =
   128.1818
```

The plot in Figure 1.5 is also shown on the screen.

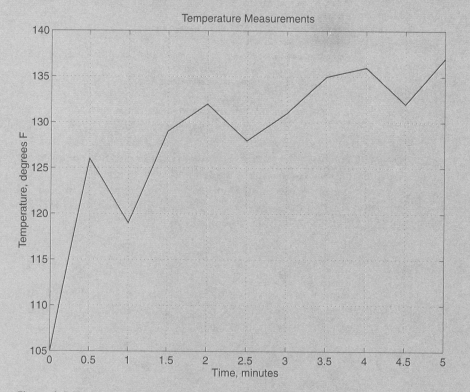

Figure 1.5 *Temperatures collected in physics experiment.*

The steps demonstrated in this example are used in developing the programs in the Problem Solving Applied sections in the chapters that follow.

1.4   Data Collection for Weather Prediction

In each of the following chapters, we include Problem Solving Applied sections that use the new MATLAB statements presented in the chapter to solve a problem related to the grand challenge discussed in the chapter introduction. Although we have shown you a MATLAB program, we do not have the background yet to develop a new program related to weather prediction (the grand challenge discussed in this chapter introduction), but we can discuss the types of weather data that are collected and the preliminary analyses that accompany the search for a solution.

The first step in attempting to develop an equation or a model to predict the weather is to study past weather history. Fortunately, a number of national agencies are interested in collecting and storing weather information. NOAA (National Oceanic and Atmospheric Administration) is a research-oriented organization that studies the oceans and the atmosphere. It also funds environmental research in data analysis, modeling, and experimental work relative to global changes. The National Environmental Satellite, Data, and Information Service collects and distributes information relative to the weather. The **National Climatic Data Center** collects and compiles climatology information from National Weather Service offices across the country. National Weather Service offices also interact with state and local weather forecasters to keep the general public aware of current weather information.

National Climatic
Data Center

The National Climatic Data Center in North Carolina is responsible for maintaining climatological data from National Weather Service offices. This data is available in many forms, including local climatology data by month, by state, and for the world. It also maintains historical climatology data beginning with 1931. Figure 1.6 contains a month summary of local climatology data that was collected by the National Weather Service office at Stapleton International Airport in Denver, Colorado, for the month of January 1991. The summary contains 23 different pieces of weather information collected for each day, including maximum and minimum temperatures, amount of precipitation, peak wind gust, and minutes of sunshine. This data is then analyzed to generate the monthly summary information at the bottom of the form, which includes average temperature, total rainfall, total snowfall, and the number of days that were partly cloudy.

To analyze the data for one month, we might first plot some of the different pieces of data to see if we observe any visible trends in the data. For example, we should be able to observe if the maximum temperature seems to stay the same, increases, decreases, or fluctuates around a common point. Figure 1.7 contains a graph of the maximum temperatures for January 1991. We can see that the temperature has some wide fluctuations or variations, but there is not a steady increase or decrease. We could also analyze temperature data for a year in the same way; Figure 1.8 contains the maximum daily temperatures from January through December 1991. To observe gradual warming trends, it would be important to look at the temperatures over many years. From observing Figures 1.7 and

JAN 1991
DENVER, CO
NAT'L WEA SER OFC
10230 SMITH ROAD

ISSN 0198-7690

LOCAL CLIMATOLOGICAL DATA
Monthly Summary

STAPLETON INTERNATIONAL AP

LATITUDE 39° 45'N   LONGITUDE 104° 52'W   ELEVATION (GROUND) 5282 FEET   TIME ZONE MOUNTAIN   23062

DENVER, CO   JAN 1991

DATE	MAXIMUM	MINIMUM	AVERAGE	DEPARTURE FROM NORMAL	AVERAGE DEW POINT	HEATING (7A)	COOLING (7B)	WEATHER TYPES (8)	SNOW ICE PELLETS ON GROUND (9)	WATER EQUIVALENT (10)	SNOW ICE PELLETS (11)	AVG STATION PRESSURE (12)	RESULTANT DIR (13)	RESULTANT SPEED (14)	AVERAGE SPEED (15)	PEAK GUST SPEED (16)	PEAK GUST DIR (17)	FASTEST 1-MIN SPEED (18)	FASTEST 1-MIN DIR (19)	MINUTES (20)	PERCENT (21)	SUNRISE TO SUNSET (22)	MIDNIGHT TO MIDNIGHT (23)
01	59*	26	43	13	14	22	0		T	0.00	0.0	24.750	19	3.9	6.3	15	S	14	20	552	98	3	4
02	35	12	24	-6	14	41	0		T	0.01	0.1	24.865	04	0.7	5.0	16	N	14	36	467	83	7	6
03	21	14	18	-12	16	47	0	2 8	T	0.05	0.7	24.860	03	1.9	3.4	14	N	10	36	1	0	10	10
04	28	16	22	-8	17	43	0	1 8	T	0.00	0.0	24.560	03	1.1	2.9	10	S	6	14	127	22	9	7
05	42	15	29	0	17	36	0		T	0.00	0.0	24.640	08	4.3	6.3	21	E	13	07	317	56	6	4
06	44	10	27	-2	14	38	0	1	T	0.00	0.0	24.800	04	2.1	3.8	16	N	12	01	494	87	0	0
07	55	8	32	3	8	33	0	1	T	0.00	0.0	24.690	15	2.6	5.3	15	SE	12	21	477	84	7	4
08	49	21	35	6	13	30	0		T	0.00	0.0	24.675	22	0.9	7.3	29	NW	17	19	439	77	2	3
09	37	15	26	-3	16	39	0		0	0.00	0.0	24.700	22	0.4	4.0	12	N	9	36	214	37	10	8
10	50	14	32	3	15	33	0		0	0.00	0.0	24.630	12	3.1	5.1	21	E	14	07	489	85	1	2
11	48	19	34	5	11	31	0		0	0.00	0.0	24.790	24	1.6	6.7	24	NW	15	32	485	84	1	1
12	55	26	41	12	15	24	0		0	0.00	0.0	24.705	24	7.1	9.9	31	W	22	29	437	76	4	3
13	55	32	44*	15	17	21	0		0	T	T	24.610	26	3.7	6.9	40	W	29	29	198	34	10	8
14	46	23	35	6	22	30	0		0	T	T	24.640	04	0.7	6.0	23	NE	14	05	325	56	6	5
15	43	22	33	4	16	32	0		0	0.06	0.8	24.540	09	1.0	6.2	18	NW	13	33	20	3	9	8
16	39	20	30	1	23	35	0	2	2	0.10	2.1	24.770	33	1.3	4.5	21	N	14	01	281	48	7	6
17	42	15	29	0	16	36	0		2	0.00	0.0	24.780	18	2.2	3.8	14	S	8	19	302	52	9	5
18	51	21	36	7	15	29	0		1	0.00	0.0	24.680	18	7.0	7.2	20	S	15	19	582	99	1	0
19	50	18	34	5	20	31	0	1	1	0.23	4.6	24.550	04	4.5	10.0	31	N	23	06	83	14	9	7
20	31	6	19	-10	9	46	0	1	4	0.03	0.3	24.840	16	3.1	4.0	15	SE	7	18	550	94	1	4
21	32	6	19	-10	8	46	0		3	0.00	0.0	24.760	17	3.2	4.4	17	S	10	19	537	91	1	2
22	36	17	27	-2	8	38	0		2	0.00	0.0	24.550	17	5.0	6.5	17	S	14	19	376	64	5	3
23	27	9	18	-12	14	47	0		2	0.07	0.7	24.660	14	1.2	7.9	23	N	16	01	174	29	9	6
24	37	8	23	-7	9	42	0		5	0.02	0.2	24.570	11	1.0	4.7	23	N	18	36	309	52	8	5
25	24	-1	12	-18	6	53	0	1	5	0.07	1.9	24.770	05	2.2	4.3	20	N	15	01	537	90	0	3
26	41	-4*	19	-11	5	46	0		4	0.00	0.0	24.560	22	1.7	4.9	25	W	17	28	552	92	3	1
27	43	19	31	1	11	34	0		4	0.00	0.0	24.390	29	0.9	8.4	38	NW	28	31	460	77	8	5
28	45	7	26	-4	10	39	0	9	4	0.08	2.0	24.380	22	1.4	10.9	37	N	30	36	342	57	7	8
29	17	0	9*	-21	-1	56	0		5	0.04	0.7	24.570	06	2.4	5.1	20	NE	12	01	562	93	1	4
30	47	8	28	-3	6	37	0		5	0.00	0.0	24.660	26	3.5	10.0	33	W	17	29	591	98	1	4
31	53	22	37	6	12	28	0			0.00	0.0	24.830	17	4.7	5.7	17	SW	10	19	120	20	9	8

| SUM 1282 | SUM 442 | | | | TOTAL 1143 | TOTAL 0 | | | TOTAL 0.76 | TOTAL 14.1 | FOR THE MONTH: 24.670 | 17 | 0.8 | 6.0 | 40 | W | 30 | 36 | TOTAL 11400 | % 63 | SUM 164 | SUM 142 |
| AVG 41.4 | AVG 14.3 | AVG 27.9 | DEP -1.6 | AVG 12.7 | DEP 42 | DEP 0 | | | DEP 0.25 | | DATE:13 | | | | DATE:28 | | | | POSSIBLE 18088 | FOR MONTH | AVG 5.3 | AVG 4.6 |

NUMBER OF DAYS

NUMBER OF DAYS					SEASON TO DATE TOTAL 3444	TOTAL 0		PRECIPITATION ≥ .01 INCH 11

PRECIPITATION ≥ .01 INCH ... 11
SNOW, ICE PELLETS ≥ 1.0 INCH ... 4

MAXIMUM TEMP
| ≥ 90° 0 | ≤ 32° 7 |
MINIMUM TEMP
| ≤ 32° 31 | ≤ 0° 3 |

THUNDERSTORMS 1   HEAVY FOG 3   CLEAR 12   PARTLY CLOUDY 8   CLOUDY 11

GREATEST IN 24 HOURS AND DATES
PRECIPITATION 0.26 19-20   SNOW, ICE PELLETS 4.9 19-20

GREATEST DEPTH ON GROUND OF SNOW, ICE PELLETS OR ICE AND DATE 5 30+

Weather types legend: 1 FOG, 2 HEAVY FOG, 3 THUNDERSTORM, 4 ICE PELLETS, 5 HAIL, 6 GLAZE, 7 DUSTSTORM, 8 SMOKE, HAZE, 9 BLOWING SNOW

* EXTREME FOR THE MONTH - LAST OCCURRENCE IF MORE THAN ONE.
T TRACE AMOUNT.
+ ALSO ON EARLIER DATE(S).
HEAVY FOG: VISIBILITY 1/4 MILE OR LESS.
BLANK ENTRIES DENOTE MISSING OR UNREPORTED DATA.

DATA IN COLS 6 AND 12-15 ARE BASED ON 21 OR MORE OBSERVATIONS AT HOURLY INTERVALS. RESULTANT WIND IS THE VECTOR SUM OF WIND SPEEDS AND DIRECTIONS DIVIDED BY THE NUMBER OF OBSERVATIONS. COLS 16 & 17: PEAK GUST - HIGHEST INSTANTANEOUS WIND SPEED. ONE OF TWO WIND SPEEDS IS GIVEN UNDER COLS 18 & 19: FASTEST MILE - HIGHEST RECORDED SPEED FOR WHICH A MILE OF WIND PASSES STATION (DIRECTION IN COMPASS POINTS). FASTEST OBSERVED ONE MINUTE WIND - HIGHEST ONE MINUTE SPEED (DIRECTION IN TENS OF DEGREES). ERRORS WILL BE CORRECTED IN SUBSEQUENT PUBLICATIONS.

I CERTIFY THAT THIS IS AN OFFICIAL PUBLICATION OF THE NATIONAL OCEANIC AND ATMOSPHERIC ADMINISTRATION, AND IS COMPILED FROM RECORDS ON FILE AT THE NATIONAL CLIMATIC DATA CENTER

noaa   NATIONAL OCEANIC AND ATMOSPHERIC ADMINISTRATION   NATIONAL ENVIRONMENTAL SATELLITE, DATA AND INFORMATION SERVICE   NATIONAL CLIMATIC DATA CENTER ASHEVILLE NORTH CAROLINA

Kenneth D Hadeen
DIRECTOR
NATIONAL CLIMATIC DATA CENTER

Figure 1.6 *Local climatological data.*

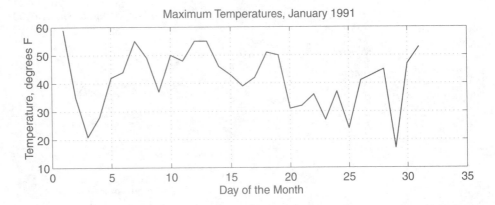

Figure 1.7 *Maximum temperatures for January 1991.*

1.8, it is clear that a straight line (linear model) is not a good model for either set of data; the models for these sets of data are more complicated.

We often are interested in analyzing several different sets of data at the same time to see if there are relationships. For example, we would expect that the maximum temperatures and the average temperatures over a period of time would be related. That is, we expect that days with higher maximum temperatures will also have higher average temperatures. However, we also expect that on some days, the maximum temperature and the average temperature are close together, whereas on other days, the maximum temperature and the average temperature are not close together. Figure 1.9 contains plots of the maximum temperatures and the average temperatures for the month of January 1991 at Stapleton International Airport and illustrates the relationship between the maximum temperatures and the average temperatures. We can perform mathematical computations to measure the relationship, or correlation, between variables.

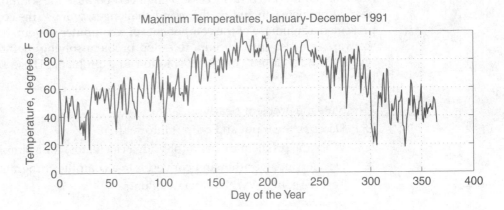

Figure 1.8 *Maximum temperatures for 1991.*

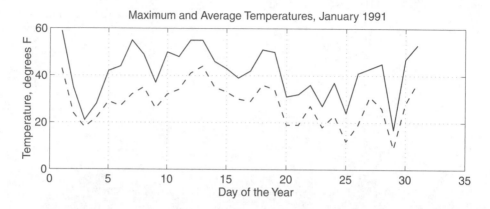

Figure 1.9 *Maximum and average temperatures for January 1991.*

Graphs give us a quick intuitive feel for data trends, but we need more ana-lytical methods for using past history to predict the future. Analytical methods commonly used to model data include developing linear or polynomial models to represent the data. We discuss these types of computations later in the text. MATLAB provides easy access to both the visualization and the analytical methods to analyze data and search for trends. We will discuss both these capabilities of MATLAB later in this text.

CHAPTER SUMMARY

A group of outstanding recent engineering achievements were presented to demonstrate the diversity of engineering applications. A set of grand challenges was then presented to illustrate some of the exciting and difficult problems that currently face engineers and scientists. We also discussed some of the nontechni-cal skills required to be a successful engineer. Because the solutions to most engi-neering problems, including the grand challenges, will use the computer, we also presented a summary of the components of a computer system, from hardware to software. We also introduced a five-step problem-solving methodology that we will use to develop a computer solution to a problem. These five steps are as follows:

1. State the problem clearly.
2. Describe the input and output information.
3. Work the problem by hand (or with a calculator) for a simple set of data.
4. Develop an algorithm and convert it to a computer program.
5. Test the solution with a variety of data.

This process will be used throughout the text as we develop solutions to problems.

KEY TERMS

algorithm
arithmetic logic unit (ALU)
assembler
assembly language
bug
central processing unit (CPU)
compile error
compiler
computer
database management tool
debug
email
execution
grand challenges
hardware
high-level language
I/O diagram
interactive environment
Internet
loader/linker

logic error
machine language
memory
microprocessor
network
object program
operating system
personal computer (PC)
problem-solving methodology
processor
program
software
software life cycle
software maintenance
software prototype
source program
spreadsheet
word processor
World Wide Web

PROBLEMS

The following assignments give you an opportunity to learn more about one of the topics in this chapter. Each report should include at least two references. Good starting points for references include the suggested readings that follow this problem set and the World Wide Web.

1. Write a short report on one of these outstanding engineering achievements:

Moon Landing	Composite Materials
Application Satellites	Jumbo Jets
Microprocessors	Lasers
CAD/CAM	Fiber Optics
CAT Scans	Genetically Engineered Products

2. Write a short report on one of these grand challenges:

Predication of Weather, Climate, and Global Change
Computerized Speech Understanding
Mapping of the Human Genome
Improved Vehicle Performance
Enhanced Oil and Gas Recovery

3. Write a short report on an outstanding engineering achievement that is not included in the list given in this chapter.

4. Write a short report on a topic that you think is a grand challenge that was not included in the list given in this chapter.

5. Write a short report discussing an ethical issue that you think relates to one of the top ten achievements or one of the grand challenges. Present several potential ways in which one might view the issue.

6. Write a short report discussing an ethical or legal issue that you think relates to using email or the World Wide Web. Present several potential ways in which one might view the issue.

7. Write a short report on the history of computing. You can choose to focus on either computer hardware, computer software, or the Internet.

8. Write a short report discussing the equipment used in the collection of climatological data. A good source of information would be a National Weather Service office or a local television weather station.

9. Write a short report discussing the types of climatology data that have been collected over the years. Your university library may contain climatological data in its government records section. Climatological information can also be ordered from the National Climatic Data Center, Federal Building, Asheville, North Carolina 28801-2696.

10. Write a short report comparing several of the network browsers, such as Mosaic, Netscape, and Java.

SUGGESTED READINGS

For further reading on the top ten achievements, the grand challenges, or computing systems, we recommend the following articles from Scientific American.

Barton, John H. "Patenting Life." March 1991.

Berns, Michael W. "Laser Surgery." June 1991.

Beth, Thomas. "Confidential Communication on the Internet." December 1995.

Birge, Robert R. "Protein-Based Computers." March 1995.

Broecker, Wallace. "Chaotic Climate." November 1995.

Bugg, Charles E., William M. Carson, and John A. Montgomery. "Drugs by Design." December 1993.

Brumer, Paul and Moshe Shapiro. "Laser Control of Chemical Reactions." March 1995.

Capecchi, Mario. "Targeted Gene Replacement." March 1994.

Charlson, Robert. J. and Tom M. L. Wigley. "Sulfate Aerosol and Climatic Change." February 1994.

Chou, Tsu-Wei, Roy L. McCullough, and R. Byron Pipes. "Composites." October 1986.

Cohen, Jack S., and Michael E. Hogan. "The New Genetic Medicines." December 1994.

Cooper, George A. "Directional Drilling." May 1994.

Davies-Jones, Robert. "Tornadoes." August 1995.

DeCicco, John and Marc Ross. "Improving Automotive Efficiency." December 1994.

Desurvire, Emmanuelf. "Lightwave Communications: The Fifth Generation." January 1992.

Doolittle, Russell F. and Peer Bork. "Evolutionarily Mobile Modules in Proteins." October 1993.

Drexhage, Martin G. and Cornelius T. Moynihan. "Infrared Optical Fibers." November 1988.

Elitzur, Moshe. "Masers in the Sky." February 1995.

Gasser, Charles S. and Robert T. Fraley. "Transgenic Crops." June 1992.

Farmelo, Graham. "The Discovery of X-Rays." November 1995.

Gibbs, W. Wayt. "Software's Chronic Crisis." September 1994.

Greenberg, Donald P. "Computers and Architecture." February 1991.

Halsey, Thomas C. and James E. Martin. "Electroheological Fluids." October 1993.

Herring, Thomas. "The Global Positioning System." February 1996.

Hess, Wilmot, et al. "The Exploration of the Moon." October 1969.

Hutcheson, G. Dan and Jerry D. Hutcheson. "Technology and Economics in the Semiconductor Industry." January 1996.

Jewell, Jack L., James P. Harbison, and Axel Scherer. "Microlasers." November 1991.

Mahowald, Misha A. and Carver Mead. "The Silicon Retina." May 1991.

Matthews, Dennis L. and Mordecai D. Rosen. "Soft-X-Ray Lasers." December 1988.

Paabo, Svante. "Ancient DNA." November 1993.

Psaltis, Demetri and Fai Mok. "Holographic Memories." November 1995.

Rennie, John. "Grading the Gene Tests." June 1994.

Richelson, Jeffrey T. "The Future of Space Reconnaissance." January 1991.

Ross, Philip E. "Eloquent Remains." May 1992.

Schiller, Jeffrey I. "Secure Distributed Computing." November 1994.

Steinberg, Morris A. "Materials for Aerospace." October 1986.

Triantafyllou, Michael S. and George S. Triantafyllou. "An Efficient Swimming Machine." March 1995.

Veldkamp, Wilfrid B. and Thomas J. McHugh. "Binary Optics." May 1992.

Wallich, Paul. "Silicon Babies." December 1991.

Wallich, Paul. "Wire Pirates." March 1994.

Welsh, Michael J. and Alan E. Smith. "Cystic Fibrosis." December 1995.

2

Courtesy of National Aeronautics and Space Administration.

GRAND CHALLENGE:
Vehicle Performance

Wind tunnels are test chambers built to generate precise wind speeds. Accurate scale models of new aircraft can be mounted on force-measuring supports in the test chamber, and then measurements of the forces on the model can be made at many different wind speeds and angles of the model relative to the wind direction. Some wind tunnels can operate at hypersonic velocities, generating wind speeds of thousands of miles per hour. The size of wind tunnel test sections vary from a few inches across to sizes large enough to accommodate a business jet. At the completion of a wind tunnel test series, many sets of data have been collected that can be used to determine the lift, drag, and other aerodynamic performance characteristics of a new aircraft at its various operating speeds and positions.

MATLAB *Environment*

OBJECTIVES

In this chapter we present the MATLAB environment, which is an interactive environment for numeric computation, data analysis, and graphics. After an introduction to the three types of MATLAB display windows, we discuss ways of representing data as scalars, vectors, or matrices. A number of operators are presented for defining and computing new information. Commands are also presented for printing information and generating plots of information. Finally, we present an example that computes and plots the velocity and acceleration of an aircraft with an advanced turboprop engine.

2.1   Characteristics of the MATLAB Environment

Matrix
Laboratory

The MATLAB software was originally developed to be a "**Matrix Laboratory**." Today's MATLAB, with capabilities far beyond the original MATLAB, is an interactive system and programming language for general scientific and technical computation. Its basic element is a matrix (which we discuss in detail in the next section). Because the MATLAB commands are similar to the expression of engineering steps in mathematics, writing computer solutions in MATLAB is much quicker than using a high-level language such as C or Fortran. In this section, we explain the differences between the student version and the professional version of MATLAB, and we give you some initial workspace information.

STUDENT EDITION VERSION 4

The Student Edition Version 4 is very similar to the Professional Version 4 of MATLAB except for these features:

- Each vector is limited to 8192 elements.
- Each matrix is limited to a total of 8192 elements, with either the number of rows or columns limited to 32.
- Output can be printed using Windows, the Macintosh, and PostScript printing devices.
- Programs cannot dynamically link C or Fortran subroutines.
- A math coprocessor is strongly recommended but is not required.
- A Symbolic Math Toolbox and a Signals and Systems Toolbox are included with the Student Edition.

If you purchase the Student Edition of MATLAB, be sure to complete and return the registration card. As a registered student user, you are entitled to replacement of defective disks at no charge. You also qualify for a discount on upgrades to professional versions of MATLAB, and you will receive update information on MATLAB.

We assume that MATLAB is already installed on the computer that you are using. (If you have purchased the Student Edition of MATLAB, follow the installation instructions in the manual that accompanies the software.) The discussions and programs developed in this text will run properly using either the Student Edition Version or the Professional Version 4.[†] We will assume that the input interaction uses a keyboard and a mouse.

MATLAB WINDOWS

Prompt

To begin MATLAB, select the MATLAB program from a menu in your operating system or enter `matlab` with the keyboard. You should see the MATLAB **prompt** (`>>` or `EDU>>`), which tells you that MATLAB is waiting for you to enter a command. To exit MATLAB, use `quit` or `exit`.

---

†Check the Prentice Hall WWW page for information on Version 5.

Display windows

MATLAB uses three **display windows**: A command window is used to enter commands and data and to print results; a graphics window is used to display plots and graphs; and an edit window is used to create and modify M-files, which are files that contain a program or **script** of MATLAB commands. When you first enter MATLAB, the command window will be the active window. To execute an M-file (such as `hmwk_1.m`), simply enter the name of the file without its extension (as in `hmwk_1`). As commands are executed, appropriate windows will automatically appear; you can activate a window by clicking the mouse within it.

There are several commands for clearing windows. The `clc` command clears the command window, and the `clf` command clears the current figure and thus clears the graph window. The command `clear` does not affect the windows, but it does remove all variables from memory. In general, it is a good idea to start programs with the `clear` and `clf` commands to be sure that the memory has been cleared and that the graph window has been cleared and reset.

MATLAB Expo

If you want to see some of the capabilities of MATLAB, enter the `demo` command. This initiates the **MATLAB Expo**, a graphical demonstration environment that illustrates some of the different types of operations that can be performed with MATLAB. If you enter the `help` command, a help menu appears.

Abort

It is important to know how to **abort** a command in MATLAB. For example, there may be times when your commands cause the computer to print seemingly endless lists of numbers or when the computer seems to go into an endless loop. In these cases, hold down the control key and press *c* to generate a local abort within MATLAB. The control-*c* sequence is sometimes written as ^*c*, but the sequence does not include the ^ character.

2.2   Scalars, Vectors, and Matrices

When solving engineering problems, it is important to be able to visualize the data related to the problem. Sometimes the data is just a single number, such as the radius of a circle. Other times, the data may be a coordinate on a plane, which can be represented as a pair of numbers, with one number representing the x coordinate and the other number representing the y coordinate. In another problem, we might have a set of four xyz coordinates, which represent the four vertices of a pyramid with a triangular base in a three-dimensional space. We can represent all these examples using a special type of data structure called a **matrix**, a set of numbers arranged in a rectangular grid of rows and columns. Thus, a single point can be considered a matrix with one row and one column, an xy coordinate can be considered a matrix with one row and two columns, and a set of four xyz coordinates can be considered a matrix with four rows and three columns. Examples are the following:

Matrix

$$A = [3.5] \qquad B = [1.5 \quad 3.1]$$

$$C = \begin{bmatrix} -1 & 0 & 0 \\ 1 & 1 & 0 \\ 1 & -1 & 0 \\ 0 & 0 & 2 \end{bmatrix}$$

Scalar
Vector

Note that the data within a matrix is written within brackets. When a matrix has one row and one column, we can also refer to the number as a **scalar**. Similarly, when a matrix has one row or one column, we refer to it as a **vector**; to be more specific, we can use the term **row vector** or **column vector**.

When we use a matrix, we need a way to refer to individual elements or numbers in the matrix. A simple method for specifying an element in the matrix uses the row and column number. For example, if we refer to the value in row 4 and column 3 in the matrix C in the previous example, there is no ambiguity—we are referring to the value 2. We use the row and column numbers as **subscripts**; thus, $C_{4,3}$ represents the value 2. To refer to the entire matrix, we use the name without subscripts, as in C. A special font is used for MATLAB matrices and commands. Subscripts are indicated in MATLAB with parentheses, as in `c(4,3)`.

Subscripts

The size of a matrix is specified by the number of rows and columns. Thus, using our previous example, C is a matrix with four rows and three columns, or a 4×3 matrix. If a matrix contains m rows and n columns, then it contains a total of m times n values; thus, C contains 12 values. If a matrix has the same number of rows as columns, it is called a **square matrix**.

Square matrix

Practice!

Answer the following questions about this matrix:

$$G = \begin{bmatrix} 0.6 & 1.5 & 2.3 & -0.5 \\ 8.2 & 0.5 & -0.1 & -2.0 \\ 5.7 & 8.2 & 9.0 & 1.5 \\ 0.5 & 0.5 & 2.4 & 0.5 \\ 1.2 & -2.3 & -4.5 & 0.5 \end{bmatrix}$$

1. What is the size of G?
2. Give the subscript references for all locations that contain the value 0.5.

In MATLAB programs, we assign names to the scalars, vectors, and matrices that we use. The following rules apply to these variable names:

- Variable names must start with a letter.
- Variable names can contain letters, digits, and the underscore character (_).
- Variable names can be of any length, but they must be unique within the first 19 characters.

Style

Because MATLAB is case-sensitive, the names `Time`, `TIME`, and `time` all represent different variables. *Be sure to choose names that help you remember what is being stored in the variable.*

INITIALIZATION

We present four methods for initializing matrices in MATLAB. The first method explicitly lists the values, the second uses the colon operator, the third uses MATLAB functions, and the fourth reads data from the keyboard.

Explicit Lists. The simplest way to define a matrix is to use a list of numbers, as shown in the following example, that defines the matrices **A**, **B**, and **C** that we used in our previous example:

```
A = [3.5];
B = [1.5, 3.1];
C = [-1,0,0; 1,1,0; 1,-1,0; 0,0,2];
```

Assignment statement

These statements are examples of the **assignment statement**, which consists of a variable name followed by an equal sign and the data values to assign to the variable. The data values are enclosed in brackets in row order; semicolons separate the rows, and the values in the rows can be separated by commas or blanks. A value can contain a plus or a minus sign and a decimal point, but it cannot contain a comma.

When we define a matrix, MATLAB will print the value of the matrix on the screen unless we suppress the printing with a semicolon after the definition. In our examples, we will generally include the semicolon to suppress printing. However, when you are first learning to define matrices, it is helpful to see the matrix values. Therefore, you may want to omit the semicolon after a matrix definition until you are confident that you know how to define matrices properly. The **who** and **whos** commands are also very helpful as you use MATLAB. The **who** command lists the matrices that you have defined, and the **whos** command lists the matrices and their sizes.

A matrix can also be defined by listing each row on a separate line, as in the following set of MATLAB commands:

```
C =[-1,0,0
    1,1,0
    1,-1,0
    0,0,2];
```

Ellipsis

If there are too many numbers in a row of the matrix to fit on one line, you can continue the statement on the next line, but a comma and three periods (an **ellipsis**) are needed at the end of the line to indicate that the row is to be continued. For example, if we want to define a row vector **F** with ten values, we could use either of the following statements:

```
F = [1,52,64,197,42,-42,55,82,22,109];
F = [1, 52, 64, 197, 42, -42, ...
     55, 82, 22, 109];
```

MATLAB also allows you to define a matrix using another matrix that has already been defined. For example, consider the following statements:

```
B = [1.5, 3.1];
S = [3.0 B];
```

These commands are equivalent to the following:

```
S = [3.0 1.5 3.1];
```

We can also change values in a matrix or add additional values using a reference to a specific location. Thus, the following command,

```
S(2) = -1.0;
```

changes the second value in the matrix **s** from 1.5 to −1.0.

You can also extend a matrix by defining new elements. If we execute the following command,

```
S(4) = 5.5;
```

then the matrix **s** will have four values instead of three. If we execute the following command,

```
S(8) = 9.5;
```

then the matrix **s** will have eight values, and the values of **s(5)**, **s(6)**, and **s(7)** are automatically set to zero because no values were given for them.

Practice!

Give the sizes of these matrices. Check your answers by entering the commands in MATLAB and then using the **whos** command. In these problems, a matrix definition may refer to a matrix defined in a previous problem.

1. `B = [2; 4; 6; 10]`

2. `C = [5 3 5; 6 2 -3]`

3. `E = [3 5 10 0; 0 0 ...`
    `     0 3; 3 9 9 8]`

4. `T = [4 24 9]`
    `Q = [T 0 T]`

5. `V = [C(2,1); B]`

6. `A(2,1) = -3`

Colon operator

Colon Operator. The **colon operator** is a very powerful operator for creating new matrices. For example, the colon operator can be used to create vectors from a matrix. When a colon is used in a matrix reference in place of a specific subscript, the colon represents the entire row or column. For example, after defining the matrix c, the following commands will store the first column of c in the column vector x, the second column of c in the column vector y, and the third column of c in the column vector z:

```
C = [-1,0,0; 1,1,0; 1,-1,0; 0,0,2];
x = C(:,1);
y = C(:,2);
z = C(:,3);
```

The colon operator can also be used to generate new matrices. If a colon is used to separate two integers, the colon operator generates all the integers between the two specified integers. For example, the following notation generates a vector named H that contains the numbers from 1 to 8:

```
H = 1:8;
```

If colons are used to separate three numbers, then the colon operator generates values between the first and third numbers, using the second number as the increment. For example, the following notation generates a row vector named **time** that contains the numbers from 0.0 to 5.0 in increments of 0.5:

```
time = 0.0:0.5:5.0;
```

The increment can also be negative, as shown in the following example, which generates the numbers 10, 9, 8, . . . 0 in the row vector named **values**:

```
values = 10:-1:0;
```

Submatrix

The colon operator can also be used to select a **submatrix** from another matrix. For example, assume that c has been defined in MATLAB as the following matrix:

$$\begin{bmatrix} -1 & 0 & 0 \\ 1 & 1 & 0 \\ 1 & -1 & 0 \\ 0 & 0 & 2 \end{bmatrix}$$

If we execute the following commands,

```
C_partial_1 = C(:,2:3);
C_partial_2 = C(3:4,1:2);
```

we have defined the following matrices:

$$C\_partial\_1 = \begin{bmatrix} 0 & 0 \\ 1 & 0 \\ -1 & 0 \\ 0 & 2 \end{bmatrix} \qquad C\_partial\_2 = \begin{bmatrix} 1 & -1 \\ 0 & 0 \end{bmatrix}$$

If the colon notation defines a matrix with invalid subscripts, as in `c(5:6,:)`, an error message is displayed.

In MATLAB, it is valid to have a matrix that is empty. For example, the following statements will each generate an **empty matrix**:

Empty matrix

```
a = [];
b = 4:-1:5;
```

Note that an empty matrix is different from a matrix that contains only zeros.

The use of the expression `c(:)` is equivalent to one long column matrix that contains the first column of `c`, followed by the second column of `c`, and so on.

Transpose operator

An operator that is very useful with matrices is the **transpose operator**. The transpose of a matrix `A` is denoted by `A'` and represents a new matrix in which the rows of `A` are transformed into the columns of `A'`. In Chapter 4, we discuss this operator in more detail, but for now we will use the transpose operator only to turn a row vector into a column vector, and a column vector into a row vector. This characteristic can be very useful when printing vectors. For example, suppose that we generate two vectors, `x` and `y`. We then want to print the values so that `x(1)` and `y(1)` are on the same line, `x(2)` and `y(2)` are on the same line, and so on. A simple way to do this is

```
x = 0:4;
y = 5:5:25;
[x' y']
```

The output generated by these statements is

```
0 5
1 10
2 15
3 20
4 25
```

This operator will also be useful in generating some of the tables specified in the problems at the end of this chapter.

Practice!

Give the contents of the following matrices. Then check your answers by entering the MATLAB commands. Use the following matrix `G`:

$$\begin{bmatrix} 0.6 & 1.5 & 2.3 & -0.5 \\ 8.2 & 0.5 & -0.1 & -2.0 \\ 5.7 & 8.2 & 9.0 & 1.5 \\ 0.5 & 0.5 & 2.4 & 0.5 \\ 1.2 & -2.3 & -4.5 & 0.5 \end{bmatrix}$$

1.   `A = G(:,2)`

```
2.    C = 10:15
3.    D = [4:9; 1:6]
4.    F = 0.0:0.1:1.0
5.    T1 = G(4:5,1:3)
6.    T2 = G(1:2:5,:)
```

Special Values and Special Matrices. MATLAB includes a number of predefined constants, special values, and special matrices that are available to our programs. The values that are available to use in MATLAB programs are described in the following list:

pi	Represents π
i, j	Represents the value $\sqrt{-1}$.
Inf	Represents infinity, which typically occurs as a result of a division by zero. A warning message will be printed when this value is computed; if you display a matrix containing this value, the value will print as ∞.
NaN	Represents Not-a-Number and typically occurs when an expression is undefined, as in the division of zero by zero.
clock	Represents the current time in a six-element row vector containing year, month, day, hour, minute, and seconds.
date	Represents the current date in a character string format, such as **20-Jun-96**.
eps	Represents the floating-point precision for the computer being used. This epsilon precision is the smallest amount with which two values can differ in the computer.
ans	Represents a value computed by an expression but not stored in a variable name.

A set of special functions can be used to generate new matrices. The **zeros** function generates a matrix containing all zeros. If the argument to the function is a scalar, as in **zeros(6)**, the function will generate a square matrix using the argument as both the number of rows and the number of columns. If the function has two scalar arguments, as in **zeros(m,n)**, the function will generate a matrix with **m** rows and **n** columns. Because the **size** function returns two scalar arguments that represent the number of rows and the number of columns in a matrix, we can use the **size** function to generate a matrix of zeros that is the same size as another matrix. The following statements illustrate these various cases:

```
A = zeros(3);
B = zeros(3,2);
C = [1 2 3; 4 2 5];
D = zeros(size(C));
```

The matrices generated are the following:

$$A = \begin{bmatrix} 0 & 0 & 0 \\ 0 & 0 & 0 \\ 0 & 0 & 0 \end{bmatrix} \quad B = \begin{bmatrix} 0 & 0 \\ 0 & 0 \\ 0 & 0 \end{bmatrix}$$

$$C = \begin{bmatrix} 1 & 2 & 3 \\ 4 & 2 & 5 \end{bmatrix} \quad D = \begin{bmatrix} 0 & 0 & 0 \\ 0 & 0 & 0 \end{bmatrix}$$

The **ones** function generates a matrix containing all ones, just as the **zeros** function generates a matrix containing all zeros. The arguments for the **ones** function have the same functionality as the arguments for the **zeros** function. The following statements illustrate several various cases:

```
A = ones(3);
B = ones(3,2);
C = [1 2 3; 4 2 5];
D = ones(size(C));
```

The matrices generated are the following:

$$A = \begin{bmatrix} 1 & 1 & 1 \\ 1 & 1 & 1 \\ 1 & 1 & 1 \end{bmatrix} \quad B = \begin{bmatrix} 1 & 1 \\ 1 & 1 \\ 1 & 1 \end{bmatrix}$$

$$C = \begin{bmatrix} 1 & 2 & 3 \\ 4 & 2 & 5 \end{bmatrix} \quad D = \begin{bmatrix} 1 & 1 & 1 \\ 1 & 1 & 1 \end{bmatrix}$$

Identity matrix

An **identity matrix** is a matrix with ones on the main diagonal and zeros elsewhere. For example, the following matrix is an identity matrix with four rows and four columns:

$$\begin{bmatrix} 1 & 0 & 0 & 0 \\ 0 & 1 & 0 & 0 \\ 0 & 0 & 1 & 0 \\ 0 & 0 & 0 & 1 \end{bmatrix}$$

Note that the **main diagonal** is the diagonal containing elements in which the row number is the same as the column number. Therefore, the subscripts for elements on the main diagonal are (1,1), (2,2), (3,3), and so on.

In MATLAB, identity matrices can be generated using the **eye** function. The arguments of the **eye** function are similar to those for the **zeros** function and the **ones** function. Although most applications use a square identity matrix, the definition can be extended to nonsquare matrices. The following statements illustrate these various cases:

```
A = eye(3);
B = eye(3,2);
C = [1 2 3; 4 2 5];
D = eye(size(C));
```

The matrices generated are the following:

$$A = \begin{bmatrix} 1 & 0 & 0 \\ 0 & 1 & 0 \\ 0 & 0 & 1 \end{bmatrix} \qquad B = \begin{bmatrix} 1 & 0 \\ 0 & 1 \\ 0 & 0 \end{bmatrix}$$

$$C = \begin{bmatrix} 1 & 2 & 3 \\ 4 & 2 & 5 \end{bmatrix} \qquad D = \begin{bmatrix} 1 & 0 & 0 \\ 0 & 1 & 0 \end{bmatrix}$$

We recommend that you do not name an identity matrix i because i will not represent $\sqrt{-1}$ in statements that follow. (Complex numbers are discussed in detail in the next chapter.)

User Input. The values for a matrix can also be entered through the keyboard using the **input** command, which displays a text string and then waits for input. The value is then stored in the variable specified. If more than one value is to be entered by the user, they must be enclosed in brackets. If the user strikes the return key without entering input values, an empty matrix is returned. If the command does not end with a semicolon, the values entered for the matrix are printed.

Consider the following command:

```
z = input('Enter values for z in brackets: ');
```

When this command is executed, the text string **Enter values for z in brackets** is displayed on the terminal screen. The user can then enter an expression such as **[5.1 6.3 -18.0]**, which specifies values for **z**. Because this **input** command ends with a semicolon, the values of **z** are not printed when the command is completed.

OUTPUT OPTIONS

There are several ways to present the contents of a matrix. The simplest way is to enter the name of the matrix. The name of the matrix will be repeated, and the values of the matrix will be printed starting with the next line. There are also several commands that can be used to print matrices with more control over the form of the output. The values in a matrix can also be plotted to give a visual representation. We now present some of the details for using these different ways of displaying information.

Default format

Display Format. When elements of a matrix are printed, integers are always printed as integers. Noninteger values are printed using a **default format** (called a short format) that shows four decimal digits. MATLAB allows you to specify other formats (see Table 2.1) that show more significant digits. For example, to specify that we want values to be displayed in a decimal format with 14 decimal digits, we use the command **format long**. The format can be returned to a decimal format with four decimal digits using the command **format short**. Two decimal digits are displayed when the format is specified with **format bank**.

When a value is very large or very small, decimal notation does not work satisfactorily. For example, a value that is used frequently in chemis-

---

TABLE 2.1. Numeric Display Formats

MATLAB Command	Display	Example
format short	default	15.2345
format long	14 decimals	15.23453333333333
format bank	2 decimals	15.23
format short e	4 decimals	1.5235e+01
format long e	15 decimals	1.523453333333333e+01
format +	+, −, blank	+

---

try is Avogadro's constant, whose value to four significant places is 602,300,000,000,000,000,000,000. Obviously we need a more manageable notation for very large values like Avogadro's constant or for very small values like

Scientific notation

0.0000000031. **Scientific notation** expresses a value as a number between 1 and 10 multiplied by a power of l0. In scientific notation, Avogadro's constant becomes 6.023×10^{23}. This form is also referred to as a mantissa (6.023) and an exponent (23). In MATLAB, values in scientific notation are printed with the letter e to separate the mantissa and the exponent, as in **6.023e+23**. If we want MATLAB to print values in scientific notation with five significant digits, we use the command **format short e**. To specify scientific notation with 16 significant digits, we use the command **format long e**. We can also enter values in a matrix using scientific notation, but it is important to omit blanks between the mantissa and the exponent because MATLAB will interpret **6.023 e+23** as two values (**6.023** and **e+23**), whereas **6.023e+23** will be interpreted as one value.

Another format command is **format +**. When a matrix is printed with this format, the only characters printed are plus and minus signs. If a value is positive, a plus sign will be printed; if a value is zero, a space will be skipped; if a value is negative, a negative sign will be printed. This format allows us to view a large matrix in terms of its signs when otherwise we would not be able to see it easily because there might be too many values in a row to fit on a single line.

For long and short formats, a common scale factor is applied to the entire matrix if the elements become very large. This scale factor is printed along with the scaled values.

Finally, the command **format compact** suppresses many of the line feeds that appear between matrix displays and allows more lines of information to be seen together on the screen. In our example output, we will assume that this command has been executed. The command **format loose** will return to the less compact display mode.

Printing Text and Values. The **disp** function can be used to display text enclosed in single quote marks. It can also be used to print the contents of a matrix without printing the matrix name. Thus, if a scalar **temp** contained a temperature value in degrees Fahrenheit, we could print the value on one line plus the units on the next line using these commands:

```
disp(temp); disp('degrees F')
```

If the value of temp is 78, then the output will be the following:

```
 78
degrees F
```

Note that the two **disp** commands were entered on the same line so that they would be executed together.

Formatted Output. The **fprintf** command gives you even more control over the output than you have with the **disp** command. In addition to printing both text and matrix values, you can specify the format to be used in printing the values, and you can specify a skip to a new line. The general form of this command is the following:

```
fprintf(format,matrices)
```

Specifiers

The format contains the text and format specifications to be printed and is followed by the names of the matrices to be printed. Within the format, the **specifiers** **%e**, **%f**, and **%g** are used to show where the matrix values are printed. If **%e** is used, the values will be printed in an exponential notation; if **%f** is used, the values will be printed in a fixed point or decimal notation; if **%g** is used, the values will use either **%e** or **%f**, depending on which is shorter. If the string **\n** appears in the format, the line specified up to that point is printed, and the rest of the information will be printed on the next line. The format usually ends with **\n**.

A simple example of the **fprintf** command is

```
fprintf('The temperature is %f degrees F \n',temp)
```

The corresponding output is

```
The temperature is 78.000000 degrees F
```

If we modify the command to this form

```
fprintf('The temperature is \n %f degrees F \n',temp)
```

then the output is

```
The temperature is
78.000000 degrees F
```

The format specifiers **%f**, **%e**, and **%g** can also contain information to specify the number of decimal places to print and the number of positions to allot for the corresponding value. Consider this command:

```
fprintf('The temperature is %4.1f degrees F \n',temp)
```

The value of `temp` is printed using four positions, one of which is a decimal position:

```
The temperature is 78.0 degrees F
```

The `fprintf` statement allows you to have a great deal of control over the form of the output. We will use it frequently in our examples to help you become familiar with it.

xy plot

Simple *xy* Plots. In this section we show you how to generate a simple *xy* **plot** from data stored in two vectors. Assume that we want to plot the following data collected from an experiment with a remotely controlled model car. The experiment is repeated ten times, and we have measured the distance that the car travels for each trial.

Trial	Distance, ft
1	58.5
2	63.8
3	64.2
4	67.3
5	71.5
6	88.3
7	90.1
8	90.6
9	89.5
10	90.4

Assume that the trial numbers are stored in a vector called **x**, and that the distance values are stored in a vector called **y**. To plot these points, we use the **plot** command, with **x** and **y** as arguments.

```
plot(x,y)
```

The plot in Figure 2.1 is automatically generated. (Slight variations in the scaling of the plot may occur due to the computer type and the size of the graphics window.)

Style

Good engineering practice requires that we include units and a title. Therefore, we include the following commands that add a title, *x* and *y* labels, and a background grid:

```
plot(x,y),title('Laboratory Experiment 1'),...
    xlabel('Trial'),ylabel('Distance, ft'),grid
```

These commands generate the plot in Figure 2.2.

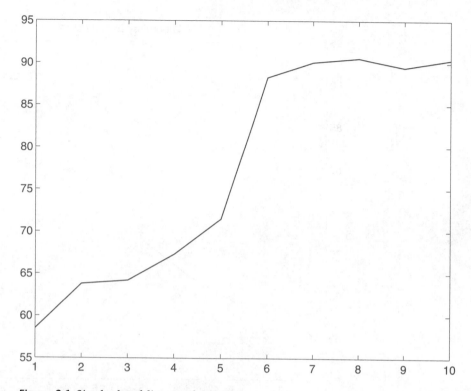

Figure 2.1 *Simple plot of distances for 10 trials.*

If you display a plot and then continue with more computations, MATLAB will generate and display the graph in the graphics window and then return immediately to execute the rest of the commands in the program. Because the plot window is replaced by the command window when MATLAB returns to finish the computations, you may want to use the **pause** command to halt the program temporarily to give you a chance to study the plot. Execution will continue when any key is pressed. If you want to pause for a specified number of seconds, use the **pause(n)** command, which will pause for **n** seconds before continuing. The **print** command will print the contents of the graphics window on the printer attached to the computer.

DATA FILES

Data file

Matrices can also be defined from information that has been stored in a **data file**. MATLAB can interface to two different types of data files—MAT-files and ASCII files. A MAT-file contains data stored in a memory-efficient binary format, and an ASCII file contains information stored in a standard computer text format. MAT-files are preferable for data that is going to be generated and used by MATLAB programs. ASCII files are necessary if the data is to be shared (imported or exported) to programs other than MATLAB programs.

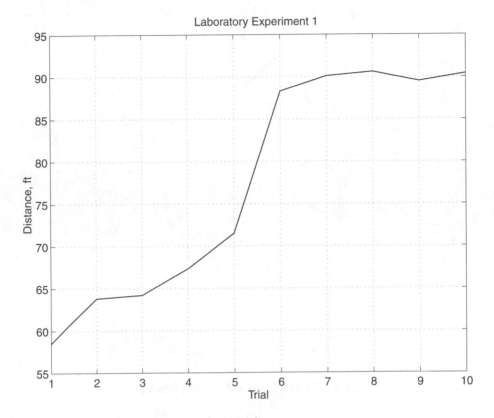

Figure 2.2 *Enhanced plot of distances for 10 trials.*

MAT-files are generated by a MATLAB program using the **save** command, which contains a file name and the matrices to be stored in the file. The **.mat** extension is automatically added to the filename. For example, the following command

```
save data_1 x y;
```

will save the matrices **x** and **y** in a file named **data_1.mat**. To restore these matrices in a MATLAB program, use the command

```
load data_1;
```

An ASCII data file that is going to be used with a MATLAB program should contain only numeric information, and each row of the file should contain the same number of data values. The file can be generated using a word processor program or an editor. It can also be generated by running a program written in a computer language, such as a C program, or it can be generated by a MATLAB program using the following form of the **save** command:

```
save data_2.dat z /ascii;
```

Style

This command causes each row of the matrix z to be written to a separate line in the data file. The `.mat` extension is not added to an ASCII file. *However, as we illustrated in this example, we recommend that ASCII filenames include the extension* `dat` *so that it is easy to distinguish them from MAT-files and M-files.*

Suppose that an ASCII file named `data_3.dat` contains a set of values that represent the time and corresponding distance of a runner from the starting line in a race. Each time and its corresponding distance value are on a separate line of the data file. Thus, the first few lines in the data file might have the following form:

```
0.0     0.0
0.1     3.5
0.2     6.8
```

The `load` command followed by the filename will read the information into a matrix with the same name as the data file. For example, consider this statement:

```
load data_3.dat;
```

The data values will automatically be stored in the matrix `data_3`, which has two columns.

2.3   Scalar and Array Operations

Arithmetic computations are specified by matrices and constants combined with arithmetic operations. In this section, we first discuss operations involving only scalars; then we extend the operations to include element-by-element operations.

SCALAR OPERATIONS

The arithmetic operations between two scalars are shown in Table 2.2. Expressions containing scalars and scalar operations can be evaluated and stored in a specified variable, as in the following statement, which specifies that the values in **a** and **b** are to be added and the sum stored in **x**:

```
x = a + b;
```

This assignment statement should be interpreted as specifying that the value in **a** is added to the value in **b** and the sum is stored in **x**. If we interpret assignment statements in this way, then we are not disturbed by the following valid MATLAB statement:

```
count = count + 1;
```

Clearly this statement is not a valid algebraic statement, but, in MATLAB, it specifies that 1 is to be added to the value in **count**, and the result stored back in **count**.

TABLE 2.2. Arithmetic Operations between Two Scalars

Operation	Algebraic Form	MATLAB
addition	$a + b$	`a + b`
subtraction	$a - b$	`a - b`
multiplication	$a \times b$	`a*b`
division	$\dfrac{a}{b}$	`a/b`
exponentiation	a^b	`a^b`

Therefore, it is equivalent to specifying that the value in **count** should be incremented by 1.

It is important to recognize that a variable can store only one value at a time. For example, suppose that the following MATLAB statements were executed one after another:

```
time = 0.0;
time = 5.0;
```

The value 0.0 is stored in the variable **time** when the first statement is executed and is then replaced by the value 5.0 when the second statement is executed.

When you enter an expression without specifying a variable to store the result, the result or answer is automatically stored in a variable named **ans**. Each time that a new value is stored in **ans**, the previous value is lost.

ARRAY OPERATIONS

Element-by-element

An array operation is performed **element-by-element**. For example, suppose that **A** is a row vector with five elements and **B** is a row vector with five elements. One way to generate a new row vector **c** with values that are the products of corresponding values in **A** and **B** is the following:

```
C(1) = A(1)*B(1);
C(2) = A(2)*B(2);
C(3) = A(3)*B(3);
C(4) = A(4)*B(4);
C(5) = A(5)*B(5);
```

These commands are essentially scalar commands because each command multiplies a single value by another single value and stores the product in a third value. To indicate that we want to perform an element-by-element multiplication between two matrices of the same size, we use an asterisk preceded by a period. Thus, the five statements above can be replaced by the following:

```
C = A.*B;
```

Omitting the period before the asterisk is a serious omission because the statement then specifies a matrix operation, not an element-by-element operation. Matrix operations are discussed in Chapter 4.

For addition and subtraction, array operations and matrix operations are the same, so we do not need to distinguish between them. However, array operations for multiplication, division, and exponentiation are different from matrix operations for multiplication, division, and exponentiation, so we need to include a period to specify an array operation. These rules are summarized in Table 2.3.

TABLE 2.3. Element-by-Element Operations		
Operation	Algebraic Form	MATLAB
addition	$a + b$	a + b
subtraction	$a - b$	a - b
multiplication	$a \times b$	a.*b
division	$\dfrac{a}{b}$	a./b
exponentiation	a^b	a.^b

Element-by-element operations, or array operations, apply not only to operations between two matrices of the same size, but also to operations between a scalar and nonscalar. Thus, the two statements in each set of statements below are equivalent for a matrix **A**:

```
B = 3*A;
B = 3.*A;

C = A/5;
C = A./5;
```

The resulting matrices **B** and **C** will be the same size as **A**.

To illustrate the array operations for vectors, consider the following two row vectors:

$$\mathbf{A} = [2 \quad 5 \quad 6] \qquad \mathbf{B} = [2 \quad 3 \quad 5]$$

If we compute the array product of **A** and **B** using the following statement

```
C = A.*B;
```

then **C** will contain the following values:

$$[4 \quad 15 \quad 30]$$

The array division command,

```
C = A./B;
```

will generate a new vector in which each element of **A** is divided by the corresponding element of **B**. Thus, **c** will contain the following values

[1   1.6667   1.2]

Array exponentiation is also an element-wise operation. For example, consider the following statements:

```
A = [2, 5, 6];
B = [2, 3, 5];
C = A.^2;
D = A.^B;
```

The vectors **c** and **D** are the following:

c = [4   25   36]   D = [4   125   7776]

We can also use a scalar base to a vector exponent, as in

```
C = 3.0.^A;
```

which generates a vector with the following values:

[9   243   729]

This vector could also have been computed with the statement

```
C = (3).^A;
```

If you are not sure that you have written the correct expression, always test it with simple examples like the ones we have used.

The previous examples used vectors, but the same rules apply to matrices with rows and columns, as shown by the following statements:

```
d = [1:5; -1:-1:-5];
p = d.*5;
q = d.^3;
```

The values of these matrices are shown below:

$$d = \begin{bmatrix} 1 & 2 & 3 & 4 & 5 \\ -1 & -2 & -3 & -4 & -5 \end{bmatrix}$$

$$p = \begin{bmatrix} 5 & 10 & 15 & 20 & 25 \\ -5 & -10 & -15 & -20 & -25 \end{bmatrix} \quad q = \begin{bmatrix} 1 & 8 & 27 & 64 & 125 \\ -1 & -8 & -27 & -64 & -125 \end{bmatrix}$$

PRECEDENCE OF ARITHMETIC OPERATIONS

Because several operations can be combined in a single arithmetic expression, it is important to know the order in which operations are performed. Table 2.4 con-

TABLE 2.4. Precedence of Arithmetic Operations	
Precedence	**Operation**
1	parentheses, innermost first
2	exponentiation, left to right
3	multiplication and division, left to right
4	addition and subtraction, left to right

tains the precedence of arithmetic operations in MATLAB. Note that this precedence also follows the standard algebraic precedence.

Assume that we want to compute the area of a trapezoid; the variable **base** contains the length of the base and **height_1** and **height_2** contain the two heights. The area of a trapezoid can be computed using the following MATLAB statement:

```
area = 0.5*base*(height_1 + height_2);
```

Suppose that we omit the parentheses in the expression

```
area = 0.5*base*height_1 + height_2;
```

This statement would be executed as if it were this statement:

```
area = (0.5*base*height_1) + height_2;
```

Note that although the incorrect answer has been computed, there are no error messages printed to alert us to the error. Therefore, it is important to be very careful when converting equations into MATLAB statements. Adding extra parentheses is an easy way to be sure that computations are done in the order that you want.

Style

If an expression is long, break it into multiple statements. For example, consider the following equation:

$$f = \frac{x^3 - 2x^2 + x - 6.3}{x^2 + 0.05005x - 3.14}$$

The value of **f** could be computed using the following MATLAB statements, assuming that **x** is a scalar:

```
numerator = x^3 - 2*x^2 + x - 6.3;
denominator = x^2 + 0.05005*x - 3.14;
f = numerator/denominator;
```

It is better to use several statements that are easy to understand than to use one statement that requires careful thought to figure out the order of operations.

Practice!

Give MATLAB commands to compute the following values. Assume that the variables in the equations are scalars and that they have been assigned values.

1. Correction factor in pressure calculation:

    $$\text{factor} = 1 + \frac{b}{v} + \frac{c}{v^2}$$

2. Slope between two points:

    $$\text{slope} = \frac{y_2 - y_1}{x_2 - x_1}$$

3. Resistance of a parallel circuit:

    $$\text{resistance} = \frac{1}{\dfrac{1}{r_1} + \dfrac{1}{r_2} + \dfrac{1}{r_3}}$$

4. Pressure loss from pipe friction:

    $$\text{loss} = f \cdot p \cdot \frac{1}{d} \cdot \frac{v^2}{2}$$

Practice!

Give the values in the vector **c** after executing the following statements, where **A** and **B** contain the values shown. Check your answers using MATLAB.

$$\mathbf{A} = [2 \quad -1 \quad 5 \quad 0] \qquad \mathbf{B} = [3 \quad 2 \quad -1 \quad 4]$$

1. `C = B + A - 3;`
2. `C = A./B;`
3. `C = 2*A + A.^B;`
4. `C = 2.^B + A;`
5. `C = 2*B/3.*A;`

COMPUTATIONAL LIMITATIONS

The variables stored in a computer have a wide range of values that they can assume. For most computers, the range of values extends from 10^{-308} to 10^{308}, which should be enough to accommodate most computations. However, it is possible for the result of an expression to be outside of this range. For example, suppose that we execute the following commands:

```
x = 2.5e200;
y = 1.0e200;
z = x*y;
```

If we assume the range of values is from 10^{-308} to 10^{308}, then the values of **x** and **y** are within the allowable range. However, the value of **z** should be 2.5e400, and this value exceeds the range. This error is called **exponent overflow** because the exponent of the result of an arithmetic operation is too large to store in the computer's memory. In MATLAB, the result of an exponent overflow is ∞.

Exponent overflow

Exponent underflow is a similar error caused by the exponent of the result of an arithmetic operation being too small to store in the computer's memory. Using the same allowable range, we obtain an exponent underflow with the following commands:

Exponent underflow

```
x = 2.5e-200;
y = 1.0e200;
z = x/y;
```

Again, the values of **x** and **y** are within the allowable range, but the value of **z** should be 2.5e−400. Because the exponent is less than the minimum, we have caused an exponent underflow error to occur. In MATLAB, the result of an exponent underflow is zero.

Division by zero

We know that **division by zero** is an invalid operation. If an expression results in a division by zero in MATLAB, the result of the division is ∞. MATLAB will print a warning message and subsequent computations continue.

2.4   Additional Plotting Capabilities

The most common plot used by engineers and scientists is the *xy* plot. The data that we plot is usually read from a data file or computed in our programs, and stored in vectors which we will call *x* and *y*. We generally assume that the *x* values represent the independent variable and that the *y* values represent the dependent variable. The *y* values can be computed as a function of *x*, or the *x* and *y* values might be measured in an experiment. We now present some additional ways of displaying this information.

LINEAR AND LOGARITHMIC PLOTS

Most plots that we generate assume that the *x* and *y* axes are divided into equally spaced intervals; these plots are called linear plots. Occasionally, we may like to use a logarithmic scale on one or both of the axes. A **logarithmic scale** (base 10) is convenient when a variable ranges over many orders of magnitude because the wide range of values can be graphed without compressing the smaller values.

Logarithmic scale

The MATLAB commands for generating linear and logarithmic plots of the vectors **x** and **y** are the following:

`plot(x,y)`	Generates a linear plot of the values of **x** and **y**.
`semilogx(x,y)`	Generates a plot of the values of **x** and **y** using a logarithmic scale for **x** and a linear scale for **y**.
`semilogy(x,y)`	Generates a plot of the values of **x** and **y** using a linear scale for **x** and a logarithmic scale for **y**.
`loglog(x,y)`	Generates a plot of the values of **x** and **y** using logarithmic scales for both **x** and **y**.

Examples of these plots are shown in Figure 2.3. Later in this section we will show you how to define a group of plots such as the ones shown in this figure.

It is important to recognize that the logarithm of a negative value or of zero does not exist. Therefore, if the data to be plotted in a semilog plot or log–log plot contains negative values or zeros, a warning message will be printed by MATLAB informing you that these data points have been omitted from the data plotted.

Each of these commands can also be executed with one argument, as in `plot(y)`. In these cases, the plots are generated with the values of the subscripts of the vector **y** used as the **x** values.

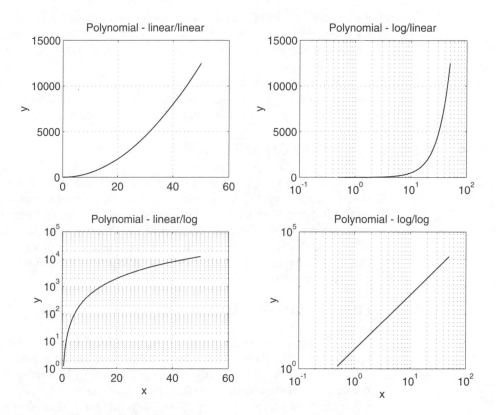

Figure 2.3 *Linear and logarithmic plots.*

MULTIPLE PLOTS

A simple way to plot multiple curves on the same graph is to use multiple arguments in a plot command, as in

```
plot(x,y,w,z)
```

where the variables **x**, **y**, **w**, and **z** are vectors. When this command is executed, the curve corresponding to **x** versus **y** will be plotted, and then the curve corresponding to **w** versus **z** will be plotted on the same graph. The advantage of this technique is that the number of points in the two plots do not have to be the same. MATLAB will automatically select different line types so that you can distinguish between the two plots.

Another way to generate multiple plots on the same graph is to use a single matrix with multiple columns. Each column will be plotted against an **x** vector. For example, the following statements generate a graph containing two functions as shown in Figure 2.4:

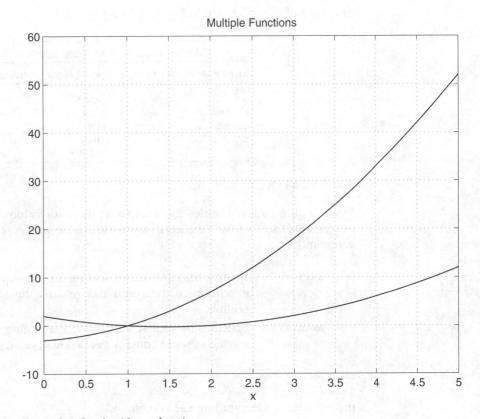

Figure 2.4 *Graph with two functions.*

```
x = 0:0.1:5;
f(:,1) = x'.^2 - 3*x' + 2;
f(:,2) = 2*x'.^2 + x' - 3;
plot(x,f),title('Multiple Functions'),...
    xlabel('x'),grid
```

If the `plot` function does not have a separate `x` vector, as in `plot(f)`, then the columns of `f` are plotted using the row subscripts as x values.

LINE AND MARK STYLE

The command `plot(x,y)` generates a line plot that connects the points represented by the vectors `x` and `y` with line segments. You can also select other line types—dashed, dotted, and dash-dot. You can also select a point plot instead of a line plot. With a point plot, the points represented by the vectors will be marked with a point instead of connected by line segments. You can also select characters other than a point to indicate the points: plus signs, stars, circles, or x-marks. Table 2.5 contains these different options for lines and marks.

The following command illustrates the use of line and mark styles; it generates a solid line plot from the points represented by the vectors `x` and `y` and then plots the points themselves with circles:

```
plot(x,y,x,y,'o')
```

This type of plot is shown in Figure 6.3 on page 170.

| TABLE 2.5. Line and Mark Options | | | |
line type	indicator	point type	indicator
solid	–	point	.
dashed	–	plus	+
dotted	:	star	*
dash-dot	–.	circle	o
		x-mark	x

AXES SCALING

MATLAB automatically scales the axes to fit the data values. However, you can override this scaling with the `axis` command. There are several forms of the `axis` command:

`axis`	Freezes the current axis scaling for subsequent plots. A second execution of the command returns the system to automatic scaling.
`axis(v)`	Specifies the axis scaling using the scaling values in the vector `v` which should contain `[xmin,xmax,ymin,ymax]`.

Style

These commands are especially useful when you want to compare curves from different plots because it can be difficult to visually compare curves plotted with different axes. The `plot` command precedes the corresponding `axis` command.

SUBPLOTS

Subwindows

The **subplot** command allows you to split the graph window into **subwindows**. The possible splits can be two subwindows or four subwindows. Two subwindows can be arranged as either top and bottom or left and right. A four-window split has two subwindows on the top and two on the bottom. The arguments to the **subplot** command are three integers: *m, n, p*. The digits *m* and *n* specify that the graph window is to be split into an *m*-by-*n* grid of smaller windows, and the digit *p* specifies the *p*th window for the current plot. The windows are numbered from left to right, top to bottom. Therefore, the following commands specify that the graph window is to be split into a top plot and a bottom plot, and the current plot is to be placed in the top subwindow:

```
subplot(2,1,1),plot(x,y)
```

Figure 2.3 contains four plots that illustrate the **subplot** command using linear and logarithmic plots. This figure was generated using the following statements:

```
%   Generate plots of a polynomial.
%
x = 0:0.5:50;
y = 5*x.^2;
subplot(2,2,1),plot(x,y),...
    title('Polynomial - linear/linear'),...
    ylabel('y'),grid,...
subplot(2,2,2),semilogx(x,y),...
    title('Polynomial - log/linear'),...
    ylabel('y'),grid,...
subplot(2,2,3),semilogy(x,y),...
    title('Polynomial - linear/log'),...
    xlabel('x'),ylabel('y'),grid,...
subplot(2,2,4),loglog(x,y),...
    title('Polynomial - log/log'),...
    xlabel('x'),ylabel('y'),grid
```

Examples of the **subplot** command are included frequently in this text.

2.5   Problem Solving Applied: Advanced Turboprop Engine

In this section, we perform computations in an application related to the vehicle performance grand challenge. An advanced turboprop engine called the **unducted fan** (UDF) is one of the promising new propulsion technologies being developed for future transport aircraft. Turboprop engines, which have been in use for decades, combine the power and reliability of jet engines with the efficiency of propellers. They are a significant improvement over earlier piston-powered propeller engines. Their application has been limited to smaller commuter-type aircraft, however, because they are not as fast or powerful as the fanjet

Unducted fan

engines used on larger airliners. The UDF engine employs significant advancements in propeller technology which were tested carefully in wind tunnel tests and which have narrowed the performance gap between turboprops and fanjets. New materials, blade shapes, and higher rotation speeds enable UDF-powered aircraft to fly almost as fast as fanjets, with greater fuel efficiency. The UDF is also significantly quieter than the conventional turboprop.

During a test flight of a UDF-powered aircraft, the test pilot has set the engine power level at 40,000 Newtons, which causes the 20,000-kg aircraft to attain a cruise speed of 180 m/s (meters/second). The engine throttles are then set to a power level of 60,000 Newtons, and the aircraft begins to accelerate. As the speed of the plane increases, the aerodynamic drag increases in proportion to the square of the airspeed. Eventually, the aircraft reaches a new cruise speed at which the thrust from the UDF engines is just offset by the drag. The equations used to estimate the velocity and acceleration of the aircraft from the time that the throttle is reset until the plane reaches its new cruise speed (at approximately 120 s) are the following:

$$\text{velocity} = 0.00001 \text{ time}^3 - 0.00488 \text{ time}^2$$
$$+ 0.75795 \text{ time} + 181.3566$$
$$\text{acceleration} = 3 - 0.000062 \text{ velocity}^2$$

Write a MATLAB program that asks the user to enter a beginning time and an ending time (both in seconds) that define an interval of time over which we want to plot the velocity and acceleration of the aircraft. Assume that a time of zero represents the point at which the power level was increased. The ending time should be less than or equal to 120 seconds.

1.   PROBLEM STATEMENT

Compute the new velocity and acceleration of the aircraft after a change in power level.

2.   INPUT/OUTPUT DESCRIPTION

The following diagram shows that the input to the program are starting and ending times and that the output of the program is a plot of the velocity and acceleration values over this window of time.

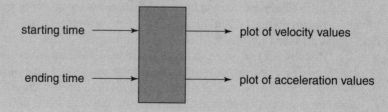

3.   **HAND EXAMPLE**

Because the program is generating a plot for a specified window of time, we will assume that the window is from 0 to 5 seconds. We then compute a few values with a calculator that can be compared to the values from the plot generated by the program.

Time (s)	Velocity (m/s)	Acceleration (m/s^2)
0.0	181.3566	0.9608
3.0	183.5868	0.9103
5.0	185.0256	0.8775

4.   **ALGORITHM DEVELOPMENT**

Generation of the plots of velocity and acceleration values requires the following steps:

1.   Read time interval limits.
2.   Compute corresponding velocity and acceleration values.
3.   Plot new velocity and acceleration.

Because the time interval depends on the input values, it may be very small or large. Therefore, instead of computing velocity and acceleration values at specified points, such as every 0.1 seconds, we will compute 100 points over the specified interval.

```
%    These commands generate and plot velocity and
%    acceleration values in a user-specified interval.
%
start_time = input('Enter start time (in seconds): ');
end_time = input('Enter ending time (max of 120 seconds): ');
%
time_incr = (end_time - start_time)/99;
time = start_time:time_incr:end_time;
velocity = 0.00001*time.^3 - 0.00488*time.^2...
           + 0.75795*time + 181.3566;
acceleration = 3 - 0.000062*velocity.^2;
%
subplot(2,1,1),plot(time,velocity),title('Velocity'),...
   ylabel('meters/second'),grid,...
subplot(2,1,2),plot(time,acceleration),...
   title('Acceleration'),...
   xlabel('Time, s'),ylabel('meters/second^2'),grid
```

5.   TESTING

We first test the program using the data from the hand example. This generates the following interaction:

```
Enter start time (in seconds): 0
Enter ending time (max of 120 seconds): 5
```

The plot generated by the program is shown in Figure 2.5. Because the values computed match the hand example, we can test the program with other time values. If the values had not matched the hand example, we would have had to determine if the error was in the hand example or in the program. The plot generated for the time interval from 0 to 120 seconds is shown in Figure 2.6. Note that the acceleration approaches zero as the velocity approaches its new cruise speed.

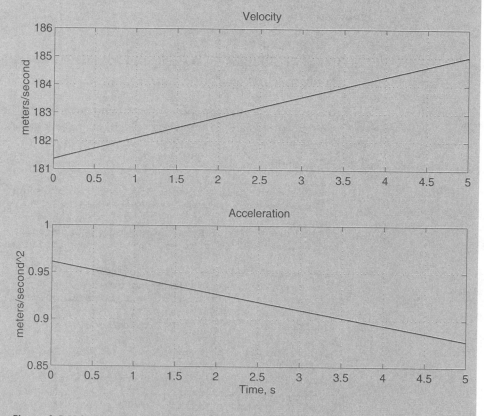

Figure 2.5 *Velocity and acceleration from 0 to 5 seconds.*

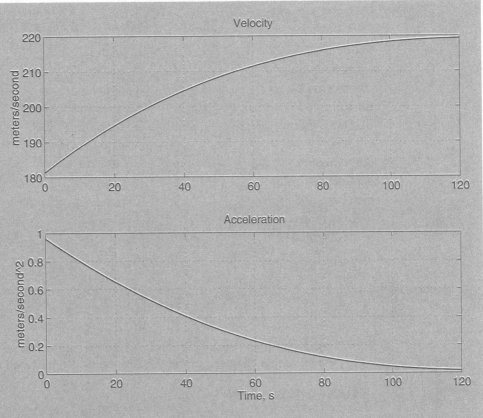

Figure 2.6 *Velocity and acceleration from 0 to 120 seconds.*

In this chapter we introduced you to the MATLAB environment. The primary data structure in MATLAB is a matrix, which can be a single point (a scalar), a list of values (a vector), or a rectangular grid of values with rows and columns. Values can be entered into a matrix using an explicit listing of the values or by using a colon operator that allows us to specify a starting value, an increment, and an ending value for generating the sequence of values. Values can also be loaded into a matrix from MAT-files or ASCII files. We explored the various mathematical operations that are performed in an element-by-element manner. We also demonstrated how to generate simple *xy* plots of data values, illustrated with an application that plotted data from an unducted engine test.

KEY TERMS

abort   matrix
array operation   prompt
colon operator   scalar
data file   scientific notation
display window   script
ellipsis   square matrix
empty matrix   submatrix
exponent overflow   subscript
exponent underflow   transpose operator
identity matrix   vector
main diagonal

MATLAB SUMMARY

This MATLAB summary lists all the special symbols, commands, and functions that were defined in this chapter. A brief description is also included for each one.

SPECIAL CHARACTERS

[ ]	forms matrices
( )	forms subscripts
,	separates subscripts or matrix elements
;	separates commands or matrix rows
%	indicates comments
:	generates matrices
+	scalar and array addition
–	scalar and array subtraction
*	scalar multiplication
.*	array multiplication
/	scalar division
./	array division
^	scalar exponentiation
.^	array exponentiation
'	transpose

COMMANDS AND FUNCTIONS

ans	stores expression values
axis	controls axis scaling

^c	generates a local abort
clc	clears command screen
clear	clears workspace
clf	clears figure
clock	represents current time
date	represents current date
demo	runs demonstrations
disp	displays matrix or text
eps	represents floating-point precision
exit	terminates MATLAB
eye	generates identity matrix
format +	sets format to plus and minus signs only
format compact	sets format to compact form
format long	sets format to long decimal
format long e	sets format to long exponential
format loose	sets format to non-compact form
format short	sets format to short decimal
format short e	sets format to short exponential
fprintf	prints formatted information
grid	inserts a grid in a plot
help	invokes help facility
i	represents the value $\sqrt{-1}$
Inf	represents the value ∞
input	accepts input from the keyboard
j	represents the value $\sqrt{-1}$
load	loads matrices from a file
loglog	generates a log-log plot
NaN	represents the value Not-a-Number
ones	generates matrix of ones
pause	temporarily halts a program
pi	represents the value π
plot	generates a linear xy plot
print	prints the graphics window
quit	terminates MATLAB
save	saves variables in a file
semilogx	generates a log-linear plot
semilogy	generates a linear-log plot
size	determines row and column dimensions
subplot	splits graphics window into subwindows
title	adds a title to a plot
who	lists variables in memory
whos	lists variables and their sizes in memory
xlabel	adds x-axis label to a plot
ylabel	adds y-axis label to a plot
zeros	generates matrix of zeros

Style NOTES

1. Choose names that help you remember what is being stored in a variable.
2. Always include units and a title on a plot for documentation.
3. Use the extension **dat** on data file names to distinguish them from MAT-files and M-files.
4. Use multiple statements to compute long expressions for readability.
5. To compare information on different plots, use the **axis** command to specify the same axes for the plots.

DEBUGGING NOTES

1. Until you are comfortable assigning values to a matrix, omit the semicolon after a matrix definition so that the values are printed.
2. Do not use the names **i** and **j** for variables in a program that also uses complex numbers.
3. Test a complicated expression with simple values to be sure that you understand how it is evaluated.
4. Add extra parentheses, if needed, to be sure that computations are done in the order that you want.
5. Remember that the logarithm of a negative value or of zero does not exist.

PROBLEMS

Conversion Tables. In Problems 1–10, print the specified tables using the transpose operator as needed. Include a table heading and column headings. Choose an appropriate number of decimal places to print.

1. Generate a table of conversions from degrees to radians. The first line should contain the values for 0°, the second line should contain the values for 10°, and so on. The last line should contain the values for 360°. (Recall that π radians = 180°.)
2. Generate a table of conversions from centimeters to inches. Start the centimeters column at 0, and increment by 2 cm. The last line should contain the value 50 cm. (Recall that 1 in. = 2.54 cm.)
3. Generate a table of conversions from mi/hr to ft/s. Start the mi/hr column at 0, and increment by 5 mi/hr. The last line should contain the value 65 mi/hr. (Recall that 1 mi. = 5280 ft.)

Currency Conversions. The following currency conversions apply to problems 4–7:

$1 = 5.045 francs (Fr)

1 yen (Y) = $ .0101239

1.4682 deutsche mark (DM) = $1

4. Generate a table of conversions from francs to dollars. Start the francs column at 5 Fr, and increment by 5 Fr. Print 25 lines in the table.

5. Generate a table of conversions from deutsche marks to francs. Start the deutsche marks column at 1 DM and increment by 2 DM. Print 30 lines in the table.

6. Generate a table of conversions from yen to deutsche marks. Start the yen column at 100 Y, and print 25 lines, with the final line containing the value 10000 Y.

7. Generate a table of conversions from dollars to francs, deutsche marks, and yen. Start the column with $1, and increment by $1. Print 50 lines in the table.

Temperature Conversions. The following problems generate temperature conversion tables. Use the following equations that give relationships between temperatures in degrees Fahrenheit (T_F), degrees Celsius (T_C), degrees Kelvin (T_K), and degrees Rankin (T_R):

$$T_F = T_R - 459.67$$
$$T_F = \frac{9}{5} T_C + 32$$

$$T_R = \frac{9}{5} T_K$$

8. Generate a table with the conversions from Fahrenheit to Kelvin for values from 0° F to 200° F. Allow the user to enter the increment in degrees F between lines.

9. Generate a table with the conversions from Celsius to Rankin. Allow the user to enter the starting temperature and increment between lines. Print 25 lines in the table.

10. Generate a table with conversions from Celsius to Fahrenheit. Allow the user to enter the starting temperature, the increment between lines, and the number of lines for the table.

Courtesy of FPG International.

GRAND CHALLENGE:
Speech Recognition

The modern jet cockpit has literally hundreds of switches and gauges. Several research programs have been looking at the feasibility of using a speech recognition system in the cockpit to serve as a pilot's assistant. The system would respond to verbal requests from the pilot for information such as fuel status or altitude. The pilot would use words from a small vocabulary that the computer had been trained to understand. In addition to understanding a selected set of words, the system would also have to be trained using the speech for the pilot who would be using the system. This training information could be stored on a diskette and inserted into the computer at the beginning of a flight so that the system could recognize the current pilot. The computer system would also use speech synthesis to respond to the pilot's request for information.

MATLAB *Functions*

OBJECTIVES

The operations of adding, subtracting, multiplying, and dividing are the most fundamental operations used by engineers and scientists. However, we also need to perform other routine operations, such as computing the square root of a value, finding the tangent of an angle, or generating a random number. Thus, we present a number of functions for performing computations, working with complex values, and generating random numbers. We also discuss statements and functions that allow you to analyze or modify selected values within a matrix. Although MATLAB contains several hundred functions, there will still be occasions in which you would like to use a function not included in MATLAB; therefore, we demonstrate the steps to write a user-defined function.

3.1   Mathematical Functions

Arithmetic expressions often require computations other than addition, subtraction, multiplication, division, and exponentiation. For example, many expressions require the use of logarithms, trigonometric functions, polynomials, and complex numbers. MATLAB contains a number of functions for performing these additional computations. For example, if we want to compute the sine of an angle and store the result in **b**, we can use the following command:

```
b = sin(angle);
```

The **sin** function assumes that the argument is in radians. If the argument contains a value in degrees, we can convert the degrees to radians within the function reference:

```
b = sin(angle*pi/180);
```

We could also have done the conversion in a separate statement:

```
angle_radians = angle*pi/180;
b = sin(angle_radians);
```

These statements are valid if **angle** is a scalar or a matrix; if **angle** is a matrix, then the function will be applied element-by-element to the values in the matrix.

Now that you have seen an example using a function, we summarize the rules regarding them. A **function** is a reference that represents a matrix. The **arguments** or **parameters** of the function are contained in parentheses following the name of the function. A function may contain no arguments, one argument, or many arguments, depending on its definition. For example, **pi** is a function that has no argument; when we use the function reference **pi**, the value for π automatically replaces the function reference. If a function contains more than one argument, it is very important to give the arguments in the correct order. Some functions also require that the arguments be in specific units. For example, the trigonometric functions assume that the arguments are in radians. In MATLAB, some functions use the number of arguments to determine the output of the function. Also, function names must be lowercase.

A function reference cannot be used on the left side of an equal sign because it represents a value and not a variable. Functions can appear on the right side of an equal sign and in expressions. A function reference can also be part of the argument of another function reference. For example, the following statement computes the logarithm of the absolute value of **x**:

```
log_x = log(abs(x));
```

When one function is used to compute the argument of another function, be sure to enclose the argument of each function in its own set of parentheses. **This nesting** of functions is also called **composition** of functions.

Function

We now discuss several categories of functions that are commonly used in engineering computations. Other functions will be presented throughout the remaining chapters as we discuss relevant subjects. Tables of common functions are included in Appendix A and on the last two pages of the text.

COMMON MATH FUNCTIONS

The common math functions include functions to compute the absolute value of a value or the square root of a value or to round a value. We now list these functions, along with brief descriptions.

abs(x)	Computes the absolute value of **x**.
sqrt(x)	Computes the square root of **x**.
round(x)	Rounds **x** to the nearest integer.
fix(x)	Rounds (or truncates) **x** to the nearest integer toward 0.
floor(x)	Rounds **x** to the nearest integer toward $-\infty$.
ceil(x)	Rounds **x** to the nearest integer toward ∞.
sign(x)	Returns a value of -1 if **x** is less than 0, a value of 0 if **x** equals 0, and a value of 1 otherwise.
rem(x,y)	Returns the remainder of x/y. For example, **rem(25,4)** is 1, and **rem(100,21)** is 16. This function is also called a **modulus** function.
exp(x)	Computes e^x, where e is the base for natural logarithms, or approximately 2.718282.
log(x)	Computes ln **x**, the natural logarithm of **x** to the base e.
log10(x)	Computes $\log_{10}$ **x**, the common logarithm of **x** to the base 10.

Practice!

Evaluate the following expressions, and then check your answer by entering the expressions in MATLAB.

1. `round(-2.6)`
2. `fix(-2.6)`
3. `floor(-2.6)`
4. `ceil(-2.6)`
5. `sign(-2.6)`
6. `rem(15,2)`
7. `floor(ceil(10.8))`
8. `log10(100) + log10(0.001)`
9. `abs(-5:5)`
10. `round([0:0.3:2,1:0.75:4])`

TRIGONOMETRIC AND HYPERBOLIC FUNCTIONS

Trigonometric
functions

The trigonometric functions assume that angles are represented in radians. To convert radians to degrees or degrees to radians, use the following conversions, which use the fact that $180° = \pi$ radians:

```
angle_degrees = angle_radians*(180/pi);
angle_radians = angle_degrees*(pi/180);
```

We now list the trigonometric functions with brief descriptions:

sin(x)	Computes the sine of **x**, where **x** is in radians.
cos(x)	Computes the cosine of **x**, where **x** is in radians.
tan(x)	Computes the tangent of **x**, where **x** is in radians.
asin(x)	Computes the arcsine or inverse sine of **x**, where **x** must be between -1 and 1. The function returns an angle in radians between $-\pi/2$ and $\pi/2$.
acos(x)	Computes the arccosine or inverse cosine of **x**, where **x** must be between -1 and 1. The function returns an angle in radians between 0 and π.
atan(x)	Computes the arctangent or inverse tangent of **x**. The function returns an angle in radians between $-\pi/2$ and $\pi/2$.
atan2(y,x)	Computes the arctangent or inverse tangent of the value y/x. The function returns an angle in radians that will be between $-\pi$ and π, depending on the signs of **x** and **y**.

The other trigonometric functions can be computed using the following equations:

$$\sec(x) = \frac{1}{\cos(x)} \qquad \csc(x) = \frac{1}{\sin(x)} \qquad \cot(x) = \frac{1}{\tan(x)}$$

$$\text{arcsec}(x) = \arccos\left(\frac{1}{x}\right) \text{ for } |x| \geq 1$$

$$\text{arccsc}(x) = \arcsin\left(\frac{1}{x}\right) \text{ for } |x| \geq 1$$

$$\text{arccot}(x) = \arccos\left(\frac{x}{\sqrt{1+x^2}}\right)$$

Practice!

Give MATLAB commands for computing the following values, assuming that all variables are scalars:

1. Uniformly accelerated motion:

    $$\text{motion} = \sqrt{vi^2 + 2 \cdot a \cdot x}$$

2. Electrical oscillation frequency:

    $$\text{frequency} = \frac{1}{\sqrt{\dfrac{2\pi c}{L}}}$$

3. Range for a projectile:

    $$\text{range} = 2vi^2 \cdot \frac{\sin(b) \cdot \cos(b)}{g}$$

4. Length contraction:

    $$\text{length} = k \sqrt{1 - \left(\frac{v}{c}\right)^2}$$

5. Volume of a fillet ring:

    $$\text{volume} = 2\pi x^2 \left(\left(1 - \frac{\pi}{4}\right) \cdot y - \left(0.8333 - \frac{\pi}{4}\right) \cdot x\right)$$

6. Distance of the center of gravity from a reference plane in a hollow cylinder sector:

    $$\text{center} = \frac{38.1972 \cdot (r^3 - s^3) \sin a}{(r^2 - s^2) \cdot a}$$

Hyperbolic functions

The **hyperbolic functions** are functions of the natural exponential function, e^x; the inverse hyperbolic functions are functions of the natural logarithm function, $\ln x$. MATLAB includes several hyperbolic functions, as shown in these brief descriptions:

`sinh(x)`   Computes the hyperbolic sine of **x**, which is equal to $\dfrac{e^x - e^{-x}}{2}$.

cosh(x)	Computes the hyperbolic cosine of **x**, which is equal to $\dfrac{e^{x} + e^{-x}}{2}$.
tanh(x)	Computes the hyperbolic tangent of **x**, which is equal to $\dfrac{\sinh x}{\cosh x}$.
asinh(x)	Computes the inverse hyperbolic sine of **x**, which is equal to $\ln(x + \sqrt{x^2 + 1})$.
acosh(x)	Computes the inverse hyperbolic cosine of **x**, which is equal to $\ln(x + \sqrt{x^2 - 1})$ for **x** greater than or equal to 1.
atanh(x)	Computes the inverse hyperbolic tangent of **x**, which is equal to $\ln\sqrt{\dfrac{1 + x}{1 - x}}$ for $| x | \leq 1$.

Other hyperbolic and inverse hyperbolic functions can be computed using the following equations:

$$\coth x = \frac{\cosh x}{\sinh x} \text{ for } x \neq 0$$

$$\operatorname{sech} x = \frac{1}{\cosh x}$$

$$\operatorname{csch} x = \frac{1}{\sinh x}$$

$$\operatorname{acoth} x = \ln\sqrt{\frac{x + 1}{x - 1}} \text{ for } |x| \geq 1$$

$$\operatorname{asech} x = \ln\left(\frac{1 + \sqrt{1 - x^2}}{x}\right) \text{ for } 0 \leq x \leq 1$$

$$\operatorname{acsch} x = \ln\left(\frac{1}{x} + \frac{\sqrt{1 + x^2}}{|x|}\right)$$

Practice!

Give MATLAB expressions for calculating the following values. (Assume that **x** is a scalar and its value is in the proper range of values for the calculations.)

1. coth **x**   2.   sec **x**

3. csc **x**   4.   acoth **x**

5. asech **x**   6.   acsc **x**

TABLE 3.1 Arithmetic Operations with Complex Numbers

Operation	Result
$c_1 + c_2$	$(a_1 + a_2) + i(b_1 + b_2)$
$c_1 - c_2$	$(a_1 - a_2) + i(b_1 - b_2)$
$c_1 \cdot c_2$	$(a_1 a_2 - b_1 b_2) + i(a_1 b_2 + a_2 b_1)$
$\dfrac{c_1}{c_2}$	$\left(\dfrac{a_1 a_2 + b_1 b_2}{a_2^2 + b_2^2}\right) + i\left(\dfrac{a_2 b_1 - b_2 a_1}{a_2^2 + b_2^2}\right)$
$\lvert c_1 \rvert$	$\sqrt{a_1^2 + b_1^2}$ (magnitude or absolute value of c_1)
$c_1{}^*$	$a_1 - i b_1$ (conjugate of c_1)

(Assume that $c_1 = a_1 + i b_1$ and $c_2 = a_2 + i b_2$.)

COMPLEX NUMBER FUNCTIONS

Complex number

Complex numbers are needed to solve many problems in science and engineering. Recall that a **complex number** has the form $a + ib$ where i is $\sqrt{-1}$, a is the real part of the value, and b is the imaginary part of the value. Table 3.1 reviews the results of arithmetic operations between two complex numbers.

One of the advantages of using MATLAB for engineering computations is its ease in handling complex numbers. A complex number is stored as two real numbers (representing the real part and the imaginary part) in MATLAB. MATLAB commands also assume that **i** represents $\sqrt{-1}$, unless **i** has been given a different value. (MATLAB also recognizes the use of **j** to represent $\sqrt{-1}$. This notation is commonly used in electrical engineering.) Thus, the following command defines a complex variable **x**:

```
x = 1 - i*0.5;
```

When we perform operations between two complex numbers, MATLAB automatically performs the necessary computations, as outlined in Table 3.1. If an operation is performed between a real number and a complex number, MATLAB assumes that the imaginary part of the real number is 0. Be careful not to use the name **i** or **j** for other variables in a program in which you also use complex numbers; the new values will replace the value of $\sqrt{-1}$, and could cause many problems.

Rectangular and Polar Coordinates. We can view the complex number system as a plane with a real and an imaginary axis. Real numbers (those with no imaginary part) represent the x axis, imaginary numbers (those with no real part) represent the y axis, and numbers with both a real part and an imaginary part rep-

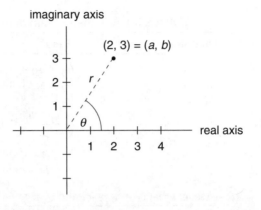

Figure 3.1 *Complex plane.*

resent the rest of the plane. Thus, the real number system (the one with which we are most familiar) is a subset of the complex number system. When we represent a complex number with a real part and an imaginary part, as in 2 + i3, we are using a **rectangular notation**. In Figure 3.1, we see that a complex number could also be described with an angle θ and a radius r relative to the origin. This form is called **polar notation**, and the point 2 + i3 can be represented in polar notation with an angle of .98 radians and a radius of 3.6. From Figure 3.1, it is easy to determine the following relationships for converting between rectangular coordinates and polar coordinates:

Rectangular to polar conversion:

$$r = \sqrt{a^2 + b^2}, \; \theta = \tan^{-1}\frac{b}{a}$$

Polar to rectangular conversion:

$$a = r \cos \theta, b = r \sin \theta$$

MATLAB includes several functions that are specific to complex numbers and their conversions:

conj(x)	Computes the complex **conjugate** of the complex number **x**. Thus, if **x** is equal to $a + i\,b$, then **conj(x)** will be equal to $a - i\,b$.
real(x)	Computes the real portion of the complex number **x**.
imag(x)	Computes the imaginary portion of the complex number **x**.
abs(x)	Computes the absolute value or **magnitude** of the complex number **x**.
angle(x)	Computes the angle using the value of **atan2(imag(x), real(x))**; thus, the angle value is between $-\pi$ and π.

Euler's Formula. To derive some important properties for complex numbers, we need the following **Maclaurin series** representations, which are usually discussed in a calculus course:

$$\sin x = x - \frac{x^3}{3!} + \frac{x^5}{5!} - \cdots \tag{3.1}$$

$$\cos x = 1 - \frac{x^2}{2!} + \frac{x^4}{4!} - \cdots \tag{3.2}$$

$$e^x = 1 + x + \frac{x^2}{2!} + \frac{x^3}{3!} + \cdots \tag{3.3}$$

Now, let x be the imaginary value ib. Then, from Eq. (3.3), we have

$$e^{ib} = 1 + ib + \frac{(ib)^2}{2!} + \frac{(ib)^3}{3!} + \frac{(ib)^4}{4!} + \frac{(ib)^5}{5!} + \cdots$$

$$= 1 + ib - \frac{b^2}{2!} - i\frac{b^3}{3!} + \frac{b^4}{4!} + i\frac{b^5}{5!} + \cdots. \tag{3.4}$$

We now separate the infinite sum in Eq. (3.4) into two parts, giving

$$e^{ib} = \left(1 - \frac{b^2}{2!} + \frac{b^4}{4!} - \cdots\right) + i\left(b - \frac{b^3}{3!} + \frac{b^5}{5!} - \cdots\right) \tag{3.5}$$

Finally, we substitute the infinite sums from Eq. (3.1) and Eq. (3.2) in Eq. (3.5) to obtain

$$e^{ib} = \cos b + i \sin b. \tag{3.6}$$

Euler's formula

Equation (3.6) is a very important formula called **Euler's formula**. We frequently use it and these two additional formulas that can be derived from it:

$$\sin \theta = \frac{e^{i\theta} - e^{-i\theta}}{2i} \tag{3.7}$$

$$\cos \theta = \frac{e^{i\theta} + e^{-i\theta}}{2} \tag{3.8}$$

Using Euler's formula, we can express a complex number in a rectangular coordinate form or in polar form. This relationship is derived as shown:

$$a + ib = (r \cos \theta) + i\,(r \sin \theta)$$
$$= r\,(\cos \theta + i \sin \theta). \tag{3.9}$$

We then use Eq. (3.7) and Eq. (3.8) in Eq. (3.9) to obtain

$$a + ib = r\,e^{i\theta} \tag{3.10}$$

where

$$r = \sqrt{a^2 + b^2},\ \theta = \tan^{-1}\frac{b}{a};\quad a = r \cos \theta,\, b = r \sin \theta$$

Thus, we can represent a complex number in either rectangular form ($a+ib$) or in exponential form ($re^{i\theta}$).

Practice!

Convert the complex values in problems 1–4 to polar form. Then check your answers using MATLAB functions.

1. $3 - i2$ 2. $-i$
3. -2 4. $0.5 + i$

Convert the complex exponential values in problems 5–8 to rectangular form. Check your answers using MATLAB functions.

5. e^i 6. $e^{i0.75\pi}$
7. $0.5e^{i2.3}$ 8. $3.5e^{i3\pi}$

Polar plot

Polar Plots. Data values are sometimes represented by complex values, which can be considered to be an angle and a magnitude. For example, if we are measuring light intensity around a light source, we might represent the information with an angle from a fixed axis and a magnitude that represents the intensity. To plot complex data, we may want to use a **polar plot**, as opposed to plotting the magnitude and phase information separately. The MATLAB command for generating a polar plot of the vectors **theta** and **r** is the following:

polar(theta,r)   Generates a polar plot of the angles **theta** (in radians) versus the magnitudes **r**.

The command **polar(r)** will generate a plot with the indices of the vector **r** used as the θ values.

To illustrate the use of the **polar** function, suppose that we want to generate points on a curve with increasing radius. We could generate angle values from 0 to 2π, and the corresponding radius that increases from 0 to 1. Figure 3.2 contains a polar plot generated with the following statements:

```
theta = 0:2*pi/100:2*pi;
r = theta/(2*pi);
polar(theta,r),title('Polar Plot')
```

POLYNOMIAL FUNCTIONS

Polynomial

A **polynomial** is a function of a single variable that can be expressed in the following general form,

$$f(x) = a_0 x^N + a_1 x^{N-1} + a_2 x^{N-2} + \cdots + a_{N-2} x^2 + a_{N-1} x + a_N$$

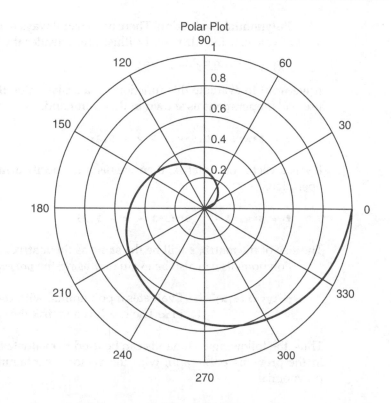

Figure 3.2 *Polar plot with increasing radius.*

Degree

where the variable is x and the **polynomial coefficients** are represented by the values of a_0, a_1, and so on. The **degree** of a polynomial is equal to the largest value used as an exponent. Therefore, the general form for a cubic (degree 3) polynomial is

$$g(x) = a_0 x^3 + a_1 x^2 + a_2 x + a_3$$

and a specific example of a cubic polynomial is

$$h(x) = x^3 - 2x^2 + 0.5x - 6.5.$$

Note that, in the general form, the sum of the coefficient subscript and the variable exponent are equal to the polynomial degree.

Polynomials commonly occur in engineering and science applications because they are often good models to represent physical systems. In this section, we discuss polynomial evaluation and polynomial computations. If you are interested in modeling a set of data using a polynomial model, refer to Chapter 6, which discusses curve fitting.

Polynomial Evaluation. There are several ways to evaluate a polynomial for a set of values using MATLAB. To illustrate, consider the following polynomial:

$$f(x) = 3x^4 - 0.5x^3 + x - 5.2$$

If we want to evaluate this function for a scalar value that is stored in **x**, we can use scalar operations as shown in this command:

```
f = 3*x^4 - 0.5*x^3 + x - 5.2;
```

If **x** is a vector or a matrix, then we need to specify array or element-by-element operations:

```
f = 3*x.^4 - 0.5*x.^3 + x - 5.2;
```

The size of the matrix **f** will be the same as the matrix **x**.

Polynomials can also be evaluated using the **polyval** function:

polyval(a,x)   Evaluates a polynomial with coefficients **a** for the values in **x**. The result is a matrix the same size as **x**.

Thus, the following commands can be used to evaluate the polynomial discussed in the previous paragraph, with the vector **a** containing the coefficients of the polynomial:

```
a = [3,-0.5,0,1,-5.2];
f = polyval(a,x);
```

These commands could also be combined into one command:

```
f = polyval([3,-0.5,0,1,-5.2],x);
```

Suppose that we want to evaluate the following polynomial over the interval [0,5]:

$$g(x) = -x^5 + 3x^3 - 2.5x^2 - 2.5$$

The following **polyval** reference will generate and plot 201 points of the polynomial over the desired interval:

```
x = 0:5/200:5;
a = [-1,0,3,-2.5,0,-2.5];
g = polyval(a,x);
plot(x,g),title('Polynomial Function')
```

Polynomial Operations. If we assume that the coefficients of two polynomials are stored in vectors **a** and **b**, we can then perform polynomial computations using **a** and **b**. For example, to add polynomials, we add the coefficients of like terms. Therefore, the coefficients of the sum of two polynomials is the sum of the coefficients of the two polynomials. Note that the vectors containing the polynomial coefficients must be the same size in order to add them. To illustrate, suppose that we want to perform the following polynomial addition:

$$g(x) = x^4 - 3x^2 - x + 2.4$$

$$h(x) = 4x^3 - 2x^2 + 5x - 16$$

$$s(x) = g(x) + h(x)$$

The MATLAB statements to perform this polynomial addition are

```
g = [1,0,-3,-1,2.4];
h = [0,4,-2,5,-16];
s = g + h;
```

As expected, the value of **s** is [1, 4, −5,4, −13.6].

The coefficients of the polynomial that represents the difference between two polynomials can be computed similarly. The coefficient vector of the difference is computed by subtracting the two polynomial coefficient vectors. Again, the size of the two coefficient vectors would need to be the same.

A scalar multiple of a polynomial can be specified by multiplying the coefficient vector of the polynomial by the scalar. Thus, if we want to specify the following polynomial,

$$g(x) = 3f(x)$$

we can represent $g(x)$ by the coefficient matrix that is a scalar times the coefficient vector of $f(x)$. If $f(x) = 3x^2 - 6x + 1$, then the coefficient vector **g** can be computed as follows:

```
f = [3,-6,1];
g = 3*f;
```

The scalar can, of course, be positive or negative.

Multiplying two polynomials is more complicated than adding or subtracting two polynomials because a number of terms are generated and combined. Similarly, dividing two polynomials is a tedious process because we must multiply and subtract polynomials. MATLAB contains functions to perform polynomial multiplication and division:

conv(a,b)	Computes a coefficient vector that contains the coefficients of the product of polynomials represented by the coefficients in **a** and **b**. The vectors **a** and **b** do not have to be the same size.
[q,r] = deconv(n,d)	Returns two vectors. The first vector contains the coefficients of the quotient and the second vector contains the coefficients of the remainder polynomial.

To illustrate the use of the **conv** and **deconv** functions for polynomial multiplication and division, consider the following polynomial product:

$$g(x) = (3x^3 - 5x^2 + 6x - 2)(x^5 + 3x^4 - x^2 + 2.5)$$

We can multiply these polynomials using the **conv** function as shown below:

```
a = [3,-5,6,-2];
b = [1,3,0,-1,0,2.5];
g = conv(a,b);
```

The values in g are [3, 4, −9, 13, −1, 1.5, −10.5, 15, −5], which represents the following polynomial:

$$g(x) = 3x^8 + 4x^7 - 9x^6 + 13x^5 - x^4 + 1.5x^3 - 10.5x^2 + 15x - 5$$

We can illustrate polynomial division using the previous polynomials:

$$h(x) = \frac{3x^8 + 4x^7 - 9x^6 + 13x^5 - x^4 + 1.5x^3 - 10.5x^2 + 15x - 5}{x^5 + 3x^4 - x^2 + 2.5}$$

This polynomial division is specified by these commands:

```
g = [3,4,-9,13,-1,1.5,-10.5,15,-5];
b = [1,3,0,-1,0,2.5];
[q,r] = deconv(g,b);
```

As expected, the quotient coefficient vector is [3, −5, 6, −2], which represents a quotient polynomial of $3x^3 - 5x^2 + 6x - 2$, and the remainder vector contains zeros.

A number of engineering applications require that the ratio or quotient of two polynomials be expressed as a sum of polynomial fractions. Techniques for partial-fraction expansions of a ratio of two polynomials is discussed in Chapter 10.

Practice!

Assume that the following polynomials have been given:

$$f_1(x) = x^3 - 3x^2 - x + 3$$

$$f_2(x) = x^3 - 6x^2 + 12x - 8$$

$$f_3(x) = x^3 - 8x^2 + 20x - 16$$

$$f_4(x) = x^3 - 5x^2 + 7x - 3$$

$$f_5(x) = x - 2$$

Plot each of the following functions over the interval [0,4]. Use MATLAB functions with polynomial coefficient vectors to evaluate the expressions.

1. $f_1(x)$ 2. $f_2(x) - 2f_4(x)$
3. $3f_5(x) + f_2(x) - 2f_3(x)$ 4. $f_1(x) * f_3(x)$
5. $f_4(x)/(x-1)$ 6. $f_1(x) * f_2(x)/f_5(x)$

Roots of Polynomials. The solution to many engineering problems involve finding the roots of an equation of the form

$$y = f(x)$$

where the **roots** are the values of x for which y is equal to 0. Examples of applications in which we need to find roots of equations include designing the control system for a robot arm, designing springs and shock absorbers for an automobile, analyzing the response of a motor, and analyzing the stability of a digital filter.

If the function $f(x)$ is a polynomial of degree N, then $f(x)$ has exactly N roots. These N roots may contain **multiple roots** or **complex roots**, as will be shown in the following examples. If we assume that the coefficients $(a_0, a_1, \cdots)$ of the polynomial are real values, then any complex roots will always occur in complex conjugate pairs.

If a polynomial is factored into **linear terms**, it is easy to identify the roots of the polynomial by setting each term to 0. For example, consider the following equation:

$$f(x) = x^2 + x - 6$$
$$= (x - 2)(x + 3)$$

Then, if $f(x)$ is equal to 0, we have the following:

$$(x - 2)(x + 3) = 0$$

The roots of the equation, which are the values of x for which $f(x)$ is equal to 0, are then $x = 2$ and $x = -3$. The roots also correspond to the value of x where the polynomial crosses the x axis, as shown in Figure 3.3.

A cubic polynomial has the following general form:

$$f(x) = a_0 x^3 + a_1 x^2 + a_2 x + a_3$$

Because the cubic polynomial has degree 3, it has exactly three roots. If we assume that the coefficients are real, the possibilities for the roots are as follows:

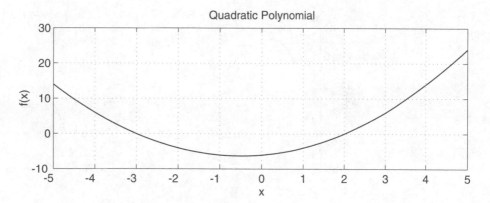

Figure 3.3 *Polynomial with two real roots.*

3 real distinct roots

3 real multiple roots

1 distinct real root and 2 multiple real roots

1 real root and a complex conjugate pair of roots

Examples of functions that illustrate these cases are as follows:

$$f_1(x) = (x - 3)(x + 1)(x - 1)$$
$$= x^3 - 3x^2 - x + 3$$

$$f_2(x) = (x - 2)^3$$
$$= x^3 - 6x^2 + 12x - 8$$

$$f_3(x) = (x + 4)(x - 2)^2$$
$$= x^3 - 12x + 16$$

$$f_4(x) = (x + 2)(x - (2+i))(x - (2-i))$$
$$= x^3 - 2x^2 - 3x + 10$$

Figure 3.4 contains plots of these functions. Note that the real roots correspond to the points where the function crosses the x axis.

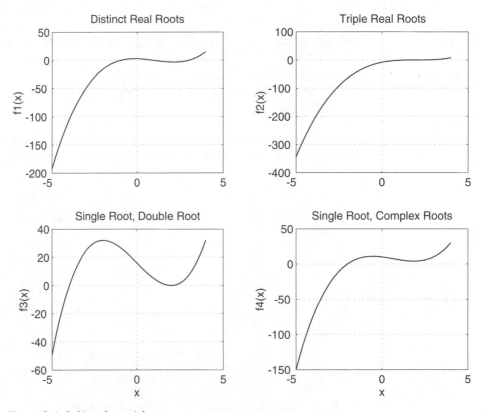

Figure 3.4 *Cubic polynomials.*

It is relatively easy to determine the roots of polynomials of degree 1 or 2 by setting the polynomial equal to 0, and then solving for x. If a second degree polynomial cannot easily be factored, the **quadratic equation** can be used to solve for the two roots. For polynomials of degree 3 and higher, it can be difficult to determine the roots of the polynomials by hand. A number of numerical techniques exist for determining the roots of polynomials. Several techniques, such as the incremental search, the bisection method, and the false-position technique, identify the real roots by searching for points where the function changes sign because this indicates that the function has crossed the x axis. Additional techniques, such as the Newton-Raphson method, can be used to find complex roots.

The MATLAB function for determining the roots of a polynomial is the **roots** function:

roots(a)   Determines the roots of the polynomial represented by the coefficient vector **a**.

The **roots** function returns a column vector containing the roots of the polynomial; the number of roots is equal to the degree of the polynomial. To illustrate the use of this function, assume that we want to determine the roots of this polynomial:

$$f(x) = x^3 - 2x^2 - 3x + 10$$

The commands to compute and print the roots of this polynomial are

```
p = [1,-2,-3,10];
r = roots(p)
```

These two commands could also be combined into one command:

```
r = roots([1,-2,-3,10])
```

The values printed are $2+i$, $2-i$, and -2. We can verify that these values are roots by evaluating the polynomial at the roots and observing that the polynomial values are essentially 0:

```
polyval([1,-2,-3,10],r)
```

If we have the roots of a polynomial and want to determine the coefficients of the polynomial when all the linear terms are multiplied, we can use the **poly** function:

poly(r)   Determines the coefficients of the polynomial whose roots are contained in the vector **r**.

The output of the function is a row vector containing the polynomial coefficients. For example, we can compute the coefficients of the polynomial with roots $-1, 1,$ 3 with the following statement:

```
a = poly([-1,1,3]);
```

The row vector **a** is equal to [1, −3, −1, 3], as expected, because this is one of the example functions mentioned earlier in this section.

Practice!

Determine the real roots for the following polynomials. Then plot the polynomial over an appropriate interval to verify that the polynomial crosses the *x*-axis at the real root locations.

1. $g_1(x) = x^3 - 5x^2 + 2x + 8$
2. $g_2(x) = x^2 + 4x + 4$
3. $g_3(x) = x^2 - 2x + 2$
4. $g_4(x) = x^5 - 3x^4 - 11x^3 + 27x^2 + 10x - 24$
5. $g_5(x) = x^5 - 4x^4 - 9x^3 + 32x^2 + 28x - 48$
6. $g_6(x) = x^5 + 3x^4 - 4x^3 - 26x^2 - 40x - 24$
7. $g_7(x) = x^5 - 9x^4 + 35x^3 - 65x^2 + 64x - 26$
8. $g_8(x) = x^5 - 3x^4 + 4x^3 - 4x + 4$

FUNCTIONS OF TWO VARIABLES

MATLAB contains several functions that are specifically designed to work with evaluating and plotting functions of two variables. We first discuss evaluating functions of two variables; we then discuss three-dimensional plots and contours plots of the resulting functions.

Function Evaluation. Recall that evaluating a function of one variable, such as $f(x)$, involves computing a vector of x values, and then computing a corresponding vector of function values as illustrated in these statements:

```
x = 0:0.1:5;
f = 2*x.^2 - 3*x + 2;
```

Two-dimensional grid   To evaluate a function $f(x,y)$ of two variables, we first define a **two-dimensional grid** in the xy plane. We then evaluate the function at the grid points to determine points on the **three-dimensional surface**. This process is illustrated in Figure 3.5 which shows an underlying grid of xy values with corresponding z values that represent the function values.

A two-dimensional grid in the xy plane is defined in MATLAB by two matrices. One matrix contains the x-coordinates at all the points in the grid, and the

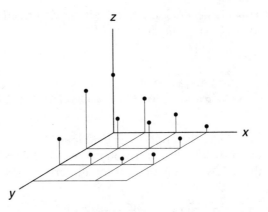

Figure 3.5 *Three-dimensional function.*

other matrix contains the y-coordinates at all the points in the grid. To illustrate, suppose that we want to define a grid in which the x-coordinate varies from -2 to 2 in increments of 1 and the y-coordinate varies from -1 to 2 in increments of 1. This grid is similar to the underlying grid in Figure 3.5. The corresponding matrix of x-grid values is the following:

$$
\begin{array}{rrrrr}
-2 & -1 & 0 & 1 & 2 \\
-2 & -1 & 0 & 1 & 2 \\
-2 & -1 & 0 & 1 & 2 \\
-2 & -1 & 0 & 1 & 2
\end{array}
$$

The corresponding matrix of y-grid values is this matrix:

$$
\begin{array}{rrrrr}
-1 & -1 & -1 & -1 & -1 \\
0 & 0 & 0 & 0 & 0 \\
1 & 1 & 1 & 1 & 1 \\
2 & 2 & 2 & 2 & 2
\end{array}
$$

Thus the point in the upper-left corner of the grid has coordinates $(-2,-1)$ and the point in the lower-right corner of the grid has coordinates (2,2).

The **meshgrid** function generates the two matrices that define the underlying grid for a two-dimensional function.

`[x_grid, y_grid] = meshgrid(x,y)`	Generates two matrices of size $m \times n$, based on values in the vectors **x** and **y** which contain m values and n values, respectively. The **x_grid** matrix contains the values of **x** repeated in each row, and **y_grid** matrix contains the values of **y** repeated in each column.

Thus, to generate the two matrices described on the previous page, we could use the following statements:

```
x = -2:2;
y = -1:2;
[x_grid, y_grid] = meshgrid(x,y);
```

Once the underlying grid matrices have been defined, we can then compute the corresponding function values. To illustrate, assume that we want to evaluate the following function for the underlying grid defined above:

$$z = f(x,y) = \frac{1}{1 + x^2 + y^2}$$

The corresponding function values can be computed and stored in a matrix **z** with four rows and five columns with these statements:

```
z = 1./(1 + x_grid.^2 + y_grid.^2);
```

Since the operations are element-by-element, the value in the **z** matrix with subscripts (1,1) is computed using the values in **x_grid(1,1)** and **y_grid(1,1)**, and so on. Note that no loops were needed to compute all the values in **z**. A common error in computing the values of a two-variable function is to use the vectors **x** and **y**, instead of the underlying grid values in **x_grid** and **y_grid**.

Mesh plot

3-D Plots. There are several ways to plot a three-dimensional surface with MATLAB. In this discussion we present two types of plots—a **mesh plot** and a **surface plot**. A mesh plot has an open mesh as shown in Figure 3.6, and a surface plot has a shaded mesh as shown in Figure 3.7. Several variations of the MATLAB commands for generating these plots are now described:

`mesh(x_pts,y_pts,z)`	Generates an open mesh plot of the surface defined by the matrix **z**. The arguments **x_pts** and **y_pts** can be vectors defining the ranges of values of the *x*- and *y*-coordinates, or they can be matrices defining the underlying grid of *x*- and *y*-coordinates.
`surf(x_pts,y_pts,z)`	Generates a shaded mesh plot of the surface defined by the matrix **z**. The arguments **x_pts** and **y_pts** can be vectors defining the ranges of values of the *x*- and *y*-coordinates, or they can be matrices defining the underlying grid of *x*- and *y*-coordinates.

Mesh Plot

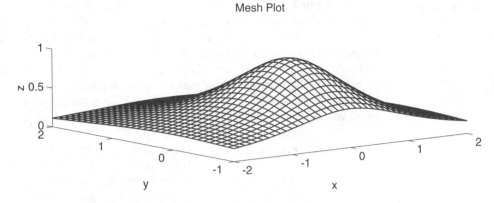

Figure 3.6 *Mesh plot of a function of two variables.*

Surface Plot

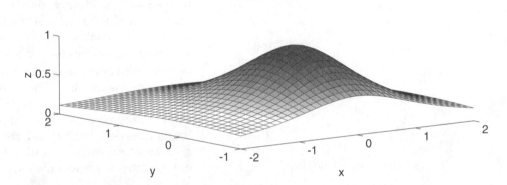

Figure 3.7 *Surface plot of a function of two variables.*

The statements that generated the plots in Figures 3.6 and 3.7 are these:

```
x = -2:0.1:2;
y = -1:0.1:2;
[x_grid,y_grid] = meshgrid(x,y);
z = 1./(1 + x_grid.^2 + y_grid.^2);
subplot(2,1,1),mesh(x_grid,y_grid,z),...
    title('Mesh Plot'),xlabel('x'),...
    ylabel('y'),zlabel('z'),pause
subplot(2,1,1),surf(x_grid,y_grid,z),...
    title('Surface Plot'),xlabel('x'),...
    ylabel('y'),zlabel('z')
```

Note that the arguments **x_grid** and **y_grid** could also have been replaced by **x** and **y**.

After you become comfortable using the **mesh** and **surf** commands, use the **help** function to learn additional options for these commands and about the **view** function (to specify the viewpoint) and the **colormap** function (to specify color scaling).

Contour Plots. A **contour map** is essentially an elevation map that contains a group of lines that connect equal elevations. We can think of a line that connects points of equal elevation as a slice of the countryside at that elevation. If we have a map with many lines showing different elevations, we can determine mountains and valleys from it. A contour map is generated from 3-D elevation data, and can be generated by MATLAB using matrices that define the range of x- and y-coordinates and the elevation (or z coordinate) data. Two variations of the **contour** command and a related variation of the **mesh** command are described below:

contour(x,y,z)	Generates a contour plot of the surface defined by the matrix **z**. The arguments **x** and **y** are vectors defining the ranges of values of the x- and y-coordinates. The number of contour lines and their values are chosen automatically.
contour(x,y,z,v)	Generates a contour plot of the surface defined by the matrix **z**. The arguments **x** and **y** are vectors defining the ranges of values of the x- and y-coordinates. The vector **v** defines the values to use for the contour lines.
meshc(x_pts,y_pts,z)	Generates an open mesh plot of the surface defined by the matrix **z**. The arguments **x_pts** and **y_pts** can be vectors defining the ranges of values of the x- and y-coordinates, or they can be matrices defining the underlying grid of x- and y-coordinates. In addition, a contour plot is generated below the mesh plot.

The following commands generate the plots shown in Figure 3.8 and 3.9, assuming that the matrices **x, y, x_grid, y_grid,** and **z** are defined using the previous MATLAB statements:

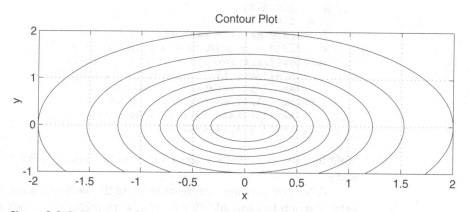

Figure 3.8 *Contour plot of a function of two variables.*

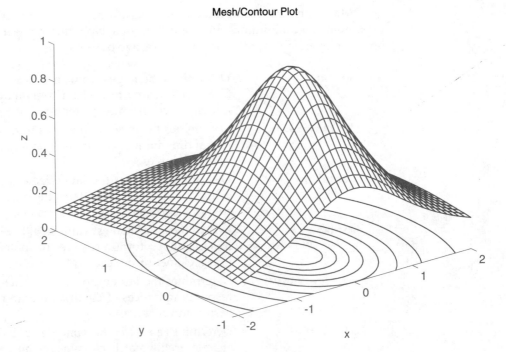

Figure 3.9 *Mesh/contour plot of a function of two variables.*

```
subplot(2,1,1),contour(x,y,z),...
    title('Contour Plot'),xlabel('x'),...
    ylabel('y'),grid,pause,clf
meshc(x_grid,y_grid,z),...
    title('Mesh/Contour Plot'),xlabel('x'),...
    ylabel('y'),zlabel('z')
```

After you become comfortable using the `contour` command, use the `help` function to learn more additional options for this commands and about the `contour3` function (to plot 3-D contour plots).

3.2   Data Analysis Functions

MATLAB contains a number of functions to make it easy to evaluate and analyze data. We first present a number of simple analysis functions, and then we present functions that compute more complicated measures, or **metrics**, related to a data set.

Metrics

SIMPLE ANALYSIS

The following groups of functions are frequently used in evaluating a set of data collected from an experiment.

Maximum and Minimum. This set of functions can be used to determine maximums and minimums and their locations. Note that the **max** and **min** functions can be used to specify one output or two outputs.

max(x)	Determines the largest value in **x**. If **x** is a matrix, this function returns a row vector containing the maximum element from each column.
[y,k] = max(x)	Determines the maximum values from **x** and the corresponding indices of the first maximum value from each column of **x**.
max(x,y)	Determines a matrix the same size as **x** and **y**. Each element in the matrix contains the maximum value from the corresponding positions in **x** and **y**.
min(x)	Determines the smallest value in **x**. If **x** is a matrix, this function returns a row vector containing the minimum element from each column.
[y,k] = min(x)	Determines the minimum values from **x** and the corresponding indices of the first minimum value from each column of **x**.
min(x,y)	Determines a matrix the same size as **x** and **y**. Each element in the matrix contains the minimum value from the corresponding positions in **x** and **y**.

Sums and Products. MATLAB contains functions for computing the sums and products of columns in a matrix and functions for computing the cumulative sums and products within the columns in a matrix.

sum(x)	Determines the sum of the elements in **x**. If **x** is a matrix, this function returns a row vector that contains the sum of each column.
prod(x)	Determines the product of the elements in **x**. If **x** is a matrix, this function returns a row vector that contains the product of each column.
cumsum(x)	Determines a vector of the same size as **x** containing cumulative sums of values from **x**. If **x** is a matrix, the function returns a matrix the same size as **x** containing cumulative sums of values from the columns of **x**.
cumprod(x)	Determines a vector of the same size as **x** containing cumulative products of values from **x**. If **x** is a matrix, the function returns a matrix the same size as **x** containing cumulative products of values from the columns of **x**.

Mean

Mean and Median. The **mean** of a group of values is the average. The Greek symbol μ (mu) is used to represent the mean value, as shown in the following equation that uses summation notation to define the mean:

$$\mu = \frac{\sum_{k=1}^{N} x_k}{N} \tag{3.11}$$

where $\sum_{k=1}^{N} x_k = x_1 + x_2 + \ldots + x_N$.

Median   The **median** is the value in the middle of the group, assuming that the values are sorted. If there is an odd number of values, then the median is the value in the middle position. If there is an even number of values, then the median is the average of the two middle values.

The functions for computing the mean and median are the following:

mean(x)   Computes the mean value (or average value) of the elements of the vector **x**. If **x** is a matrix, this function returns a row vector that contains the mean value of each column.

median(x)   Determines the median value of the elements in the vector **x**. If **x** is a matrix, this function returns a row vector that contains the median value of each column. The values in **x** do not need to be sorted.

Sorting Values. MATLAB contains a function for sorting values into ascending order.

sort(x)   Returns a vector with the values of **x** in ascending order. If **x** is a matrix, this function returns a matrix with each column in ascending order.

Practice!

Determine the matrices represented by the following function references. Then use MATLAB to check your answers. Assume that **w, x,** and **y** are the following matrices:

$$\mathbf{w} = [0 \quad 3 \quad -2 \quad 7] \qquad \mathbf{x} = [3 \quad -1 \quad 5 \quad 7]$$

$$\mathbf{y} = \begin{bmatrix} 1 & 3 & 7 \\ 2 & 8 & 4 \\ 6 & -1 & -2 \end{bmatrix}$$

1.   **max(w)**   2.   **min(y)**
3.   **min(w,x)**   4.   **mean(y)**
5.   **median(w)**   6.   **cumprod(y)**
7.   **sort(2*w+x)**   8.   **sort(y)**

VARIANCE AND STANDARD DEVIATION

Important statistical measurements for a set of data are its variance and standard deviation. Before we give the mathematical definitions, it is useful to develop an intuitive understanding of these values. Consider the values of vectors **data_1** and **data_2** that are plotted in Figure 3.10. If we attempted to draw a line through the middle of the values in the plots, this line would be at approximately 3.0 in both plots. Thus, we would assume that both vectors have approximately the same mean value of 3.0. However, the data in the two vectors clearly have some distinguishing characteristics. The data values in **data_2** vary more from the mean, or deviate more from the mean. Thus, measures of variance and deviation for the values in **data_2** will be greater than the variance and deviation for the val-

Variance

ues in **data_1**. Hence, an intuitive understanding for **variance** (or deviation) relates to the variance of the values from the mean. The larger the variance, the farther the values fluctuate from the mean value.

Mathematically, the variance σ^2 for a set of data values (which we will assume are stored in a vector x) can be computed using the following equation, where σ is the Greek symbol sigma:

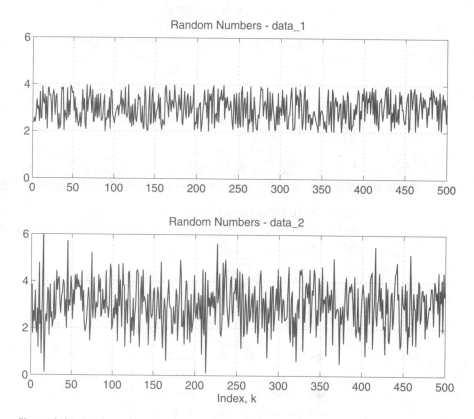

Figure 3.10 *Random sequences.*

$$\sigma^2 = \frac{\sum\limits_{k=1}^{N}(x_k - \mu)^2}{N - 1} \tag{3.12}$$

This equation is a bit intimidating at first, but if you look at it closely, it becomes much simpler. The term $x_k - \mu$ is the difference or deviation of x_k from the mean. This value is squared so that we will always have a positive value. We then add the squared deviations for all the data points. This sum is then divided by $N-1$, which approximates an average. (The equation for the variance sometimes uses a denominator of N, but the form in Equation 3.12 has statistical properties that make it generally more desirable.) Thus, the variance is the average squared deviation of the data from the mean.

Standard deviation

The **standard deviation** is defined as the square root of the variance, or

$$\sigma = \sqrt{\sigma^2} \tag{3.13}$$

MATLAB includes a function to compute the standard deviation.

std(x)   Computes the standard deviation of the values in **x**. If **x** is a matrix, a row vector containing the standard deviation of each column is returned.

To compute the variance, simply square the standard deviation.

HISTOGRAMS

Histogram

A **histogram** is a special type of graph that is particularly relevant to the statistical measurements discussed in this section because it shows the distribution of a set of values. In MATLAB, the histogram computes the number of values falling in ten bins that are equally spaced between the minimum and maximum values from the set of values. For example, if we plot the histograms of the data values in vectors **data_1** and **data_2** from Figure 3.10, we obtain the histograms in Figure 3.11. Note that the information from a histogram is different from the information obtained from the mean and variance. The histogram shows us not only the range of values, but also how they are distributed. For example, the values in **data_1** tend to be equally distributed across the range of values. (In Section 3.7 we will see that these types of values are called uniformly distributed values.) The values in **data_2** are not equally distributed across the range of values. In fact, most of the values are centered around the mean. (In Section 3.7, we will see that this type of distribution is a Gaussian or normal distribution.)

The MATLAB command to generate and plot a histogram is the **hist** command:

hist(x)   Generates a histogram of the values in **x** using 10 bins.
hist(x,n)   Generates a histogram of the values in **x** using **n** bins.

The plots of the **data_1** and **data_2** vectors using 25 bins are shown in Figure 3.12.

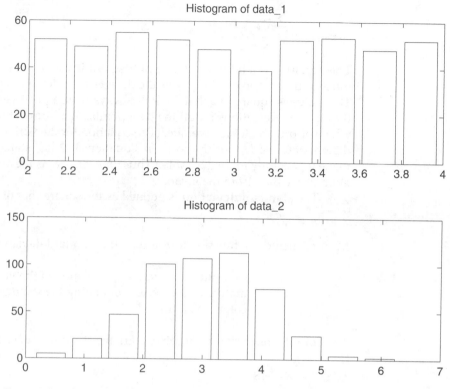

Figure 3.11 *Histograms with 10 bins.*

3.3   Selection Statements and Selection Functions

A **selection** statement allows us to ask a question or test a condition to determine which steps are to be performed next. We first discuss the most common selection statement—an **if** statement—and then discuss the relational and logical operators and functions commonly used with selection statements.

SIMPLE **if** STATEMENT

An example of the **if** statement is shown below:

```
if g < 50
   count = count + 1;
   disp(g);
end
```

Assume that **g** is a scalar. If **g** is less than 50, then **count** is incremented by 1 and **g** is displayed on the screen; otherwise, these two statements are skipped. If **g** is not a scalar, then **count** is incremented by 1 and **g** is displayed only if every element in **g** is less than 50.

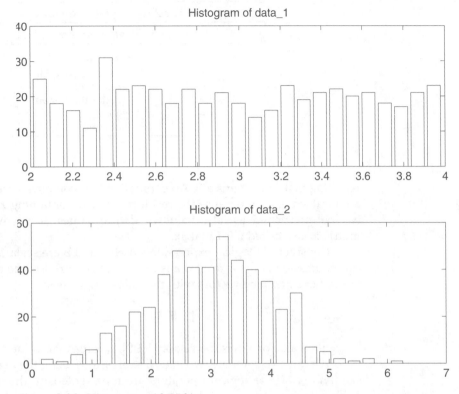

Figure 3.12 *Histograms with 25 bins.*

The general form of a simple **if** statement is the following:

```
if logical expression
    statements
end
```

If the logical expression is true, we execute the statements between the **if** statement and the **end** statement. If the logical expression is false, we jump immediately to the statement following the **end** statement. *It is important to indent the statements within an if structure for readability*

    Because logical expressions are generated from relational operators and log-
ical operators, we now discuss these new operators.

Style

RELATIONAL AND LOGICAL OPERATORS

MATLAB has six **relational operators** for comparing two matrices of equal size,
as shown in Table 3.2. Matrices or matrix expressions are used on both sides of
a relational operator to yield another matrix of the same size. Each entry in
the resulting matrix contains a 1 if the comparison is true when applied to the values in the corresponding positions of the matrices; otherwise, the entry in the

TABLE 3.2 Relational Operators

Relational Operator	Interpretation
<	less than
<=	less than or equal
>	greater than
> =	greater than or equal
= =	equal
~=	not equal

resulting matrix contains a 0. An expression that contains a relational operator is a logical expression because the result is a matrix containing zeros and ones that can be interpreted as false values and true values, respectively; the resulting matrix is also called a **0-1 matrix**.

Consider the logical expression **a<b**. If **a** and **b** are scalars, then the value of this expression is 1 (for true) if **a** is less than **b**; otherwise, the expression is 0 (for false). Let **a** and **b** be vectors with the following values:

$$\mathbf{a} = [2 \ 4 \ 6] \qquad \mathbf{b} = [3 \ 5 \ 1]$$

Then, the value of **a<b** is the vector [1 1 0], whereas the value of **a~=b** is [1 1 1].

We can also combine two logical expressions using the **logical operators** *not*, *and*, and *or*. These logical operators are represented by the symbols shown in Table 3.3.

When two logical expressions are joined by |, entries in the resulting 0-1 matrix are 1 (true) if either or both expressions are true; it is 0 (false) only when both expressions are false. When two logical expressions are joined by **&**, the entire expression is true only if both expressions are true. Table 3.4 lists all possible combinations for the logical operators with two logical expressions.

Logical operators are used with complete logical expressions. For example, **a>b & b>c** is a valid logical expression, but **a>b & c** is not an equivalent expression. Logical expressions can also be preceded by the logical operator *not*. This operator changes the value of the expression to the opposite value; hence, if **a>b** is true, then ~**(a>b)** is false.

A logical expression may contain several logical operators, as in

TABLE 3.3 Logical Operators

Logical Operator	Symbol
not	~
and	&
or		

0-1 matrix

TABLE 3.4 Combinations of Logical Operators

A	B	~A	A | B	A & B
false	false	true	false	false
false	true	true	true	false
true	false	false	true	false
true	true	false	true	true

```
~(b==c | b==5.5)
```

The hierarchy, from highest to lowest is ~, &, and |. Of course, parentheses can be used to change the hierarchy. In the example above, the expressions **b==c** and **b==5.5** are evaluated first. Suppose **b** contains the value 3 and **c** contains the value 5. Then neither expression is true, so the expression **b==c | b==5.5** is false. We then apply the ~ operator, which changes the value of the expression to true. Suppose that we did not have the parentheses around the logical expression, as in

```
~b==c | b==5.5
```

In this case, the expression **~b==c** would be evaluated along with **b==5.5**. For the values given for **b** and **c**, the value of each relational expression is false; thus, the value of the entire logical expression is false. You might wonder how we can evaluate **~b** when the value in **b** is a number. In MATLAB, any values that are nonzero are considered to be true; values of zero are false. As a result, we have to be very careful using relational and logical operators to be sure that the steps being performed are the ones that we want to perform.

Practice!

Determine if the following expressions in problems 1 through 8 are true or false. Then check your answers using MATLAB. Remember that to check your answer, all you need to do is enter the expression and the value represented will be printed. Assume that the following variables have the indicated values:

$a = 5.5$ $b = 1.5$ $k = -3$

1.	`a < 10.0`	2.	`a+b >= 6.5`
3.	`k ~= 0`	4.	`b-k > a`
5.	`~(a == 3*b)`	6.	`-k <= k+6`
7.	`a<10 & a>5`	8.	`abs(k)>3 | k<b-a`

NESTED if STATEMENTS

Here is an example of **nested if** statements that extends the previous example:

```
if g < 50
   count = count + 1;
   disp(g);
   if b > g
      b = 0;
   end
end
```

Again, first assume that **g** and **b** are scalars. Then, if **g<50**, we increment count by 1 and display **g**. In addition, if **b>g**, we set **b** to 0. If **g** is not less than 50, we skip immediately to the statement following the second **end** statement. If **g** is not a scalar, the condition **g<50** is true only if every element of **g** is less than 50. If neither **g** nor **b** is a scalar, **b** is greater than **g** only if every corresponding pair of elements of **g** and **b** are values such that **b** is greater than **g**. If **g** or **b** is a scalar, the other matrix is compared to the scalar element-wise.

else AND elseif CLAUSES

The **else** clause allows us to execute one set of statements if a logical expression is true and a different set if the logical expression is false. To illustrate this statement, assume that we have a variable **interval**. If the value of **interval** is less than 1, we want to set the value of **x_increment** to **interval/10**; otherwise, we want to set the value of **x_increment** to 0.1. The following statement performs these steps:

```
if interval < 1
   x_increment = interval/10;
else
   x_increment = 0.1;
end
```

When we nest several levels of **if-else** statements, it may be difficult to determine which logical expressions must be true (or false) to execute each set of statements. In these cases, the **elseif** clause is often used to clarify the program logic, as illustrated in these statements:

```
if temperature > 100
   disp('Too hot - equipment malfunctioning.')
elseif temperature > 90
   disp('Normal operating range.')
elseif temperature > 50
   disp('Temperature below desired operating range.')
else
   disp('Too cold - turn off equipment.')
end
```

In this example, temperatures between 90 and 100 are in the normal operating range; temperatures outside this range generate an appropriate message.

Practice!

In problems 1 through 4, give MATLAB statements that perform the steps indicated. Assume that the variables are scalars.

1. If the difference between **volt_1** and **volt_2** is larger than 10.0, print the values of **volt_1** and **volt_2**.

2. If the natural logarithm of **x** is greater than or equal to 3, set **time** equal to 0 and increment **count** by 1.

3. If **dist** is less than 50.0 and **time** is greater than 10.0, increment **time** by 2; otherwise increment **time** by 2.5.

4. If **dist** is greater than or equal to 100.0, increment **time** by 2.0. If **dist** is between 50 and 100, increment **time** by 1. Otherwise, increment **time** by 0.5.

LOGICAL FUNCTIONS

MATLAB contains a set of **logical functions** that are very useful. We now discuss each of these functions.

any(x)   Returns a scalar that is 1 (true) if any element in the vector **x** is nonzero; otherwise, the scalar is 0 (false). If **x** is a matrix, this function returns a row vector; an element in this row vector contains a 1 (true) if any element of the corresponding column of **x** is nonzero, and a 0 (false) otherwise.

all(x)   Returns a scalar that is 1 (true) if all elements in the vector **x** are nonzero; otherwise, the scalar is 0 (false). If **x** is a matrix, this function returns a row vector; an element in this row vector contains a 1 (true) if all elements of the corresponding column of **x** are nonzero, and a 0 (false) otherwise.

find(x)   Returns a vector containing the indices of the nonzero elements of a vector **x**. If **x** is a matrix, then the indices are selected from **x(:)**, which is a single-column vector formed from the columns of **x**.

isnan(x)	Returns a matrix with ones where the elements of **x** are **NaN** and zeros where they are not.
finite(x)	Returns a matrix with ones where the elements of **x** are finite and zeros where they are infinite or **NaN**.
isempty(x)	Returns 1 if **x** is an empty matrix and 0 otherwise.

Assume that **A** is a matrix with three rows and three columns of values. Consider the following statement:

```
if all(A)
    disp ('A contains no zeros')
end
```

The string **A contains no zeros** is printed only if all nine values in **A** are non zero.

We now present another example that uses a logical function. Assume that we have a vector containing a group of distance values that represent the distances of a cable car from the nearest tower. We want to generate a vector containing velocities of the cable car at those distances. If the cable car is within 30 feet of the tower, we use this equation to compute the velocity:

$$\text{velocity} = 0.425 + 0.00175d^2$$

If the cable car is farther than 30 feet from the tower, we use the following equation:

$$\text{velocity} = 0.625 + 0.12d - 0.00025d^2$$

We can use the **find** function to find the distance values greater than 30 feet and distance values less than or equal to 30 feet. Because the **find** function identifies the subscripts for each group of values, we can compute the corresponding velocities with these statements:

```
lower = find(d < 30);
velocity(lower) = 0.425 + 0.00175*d(lower).^2;
upper = find(d >= 30);
velocity(upper) = 0.625 + 0.12*d(upper) ...
                  -0.00025*d(upper).^2;
```

If all the values of **d** are less than 30, the vector **upper** will be an empty vector, and the reference to **d(upper)** and **velocity(upper)** will not cause any values to change.

Practice!

Determine the value of the following expressions. Then check your answers by entering the expressions. Assume that the matrix **b** has the indicated values:

$$\mathbf{b} = \begin{bmatrix} 1 & 0 & 4 \\ 0 & 0 & 3 \\ 8 & 7 & 0 \end{bmatrix}$$

1. `any(b)`
2. `find(b)`
3. `all(any(b))`
4. `any(all(b))`
5. `finite(b(:,3))`
6. `any(b(1:2,1:3))`

3.4   Problem Solving Applied: Speech Signal Analysis

Suppose that we want to design a system to recognize the words for the ten digits: "zero," "one," "two," . . ., "nine." One of the first things that we might do is analyze data values collected with a microphone for the ten corresponding sequences (or signals) to see if there are some statistical measurements that would allow us to distinguish these digits. The MATLAB data analysis functions allow us to compute these measurements easily. We could then print a table of the measurements and look for those that allow us to distinguish values. For example, one measurement might allow us to narrow the possible digits to three, and another might allow us to identify the specific digit from the three possible digits.

Utterance

Write a MATLAB program to read and plot an ASCII data file **zero.dat** that contains an **utterance** of the word "zero." The program should also compute the following information: mean, standard deviation, variance, average power, average magnitude, and number of zero crossings. We have already discussed the mean, standard deviation, and variance. The average power is the average squared value; the average magnitude is the average absolute value. The number of zero crossings is the number of times that the values transition from a negative to a positive value or from a positive to a negative value.

1.   PROBLEM STATEMENT

Compute the following statistical measurements for a speech utterance: mean, standard deviation, variance, average power, average magnitude, and number of zero crossings. Also plot the signal.

2.   INPUT/OUTPUT DESCRIPTION

The following I/O diagram shows the file containing the utterance as the input and the various statistical measurements as output.

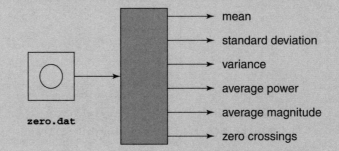

zero.dat

3.   HAND EXAMPLE

For a hand example, assume that an utterance contains the following sequence of values:

$$[2.5 \quad 8.2 \quad -1.1 \quad -0.2 \quad 1.5]$$

Using a calculator, we can compute following values:

$$\text{mean} = \mu \quad = (2.5 + 8.2 - 1.1 - 0.2 + 1.5)/5$$
$$= 2.18$$

$$\text{variance} = ((2.5 - \mu)^2 + (8.2 - \mu)^2 + (-1.1 - \mu)^2 + (-0.2 - \mu)^2$$
$$+ (1.5 - \mu)^2)/4$$
$$= 13.307$$

$$\text{average power} = (2.5^2 + 8.2^2 + (-1.1)^2 + (-0.2)^2 + 1.5^2)/5$$
$$= 15.398$$

$$\text{average magnitude} = (|2.5| + |8.2| + |-1.1| + |-0.2| + |1.5|)/5$$
$$= 2.7$$

$$\text{number of zero crossings} = 2$$

4.   MATLAB SOLUTION

In this solution, we use MATLAB functions to do most of the computations. To compute the number of zero crossings, we generate a vector whose first value is `x(1)*x(2)`, whose second value is `x(2)*x(3)`, and so on, with the last value equal to the product of the next-to-the-last value and the last value. We then use the `find` function to determine the locations of products that are negative, and we use the `length` function to count the number of these products that are negative.

```
%    This program computes a number of statistics
%    for an utterance stored in a data file.
%
load zero.dat;
x = zero;
%
fprintf('Digit Statistics \n\n')
fprintf('mean: %f \n',mean(x))
fprintf('standard deviation: %f \n',std(x))
fprintf('variance: %f \n',std(x)^2)
fprintf('average power: %f \n',mean(x.^2))
fprintf('average magnitude: %f \n',mean(abs(x))
prod = x(1:length(x)-1).*x(2:length(x));
crossings = length(find(prod<0));
fprintf('zero crossings: %.0f \n',crossings)
subplot(2,1,1),plot(x),...
    title('utterance of the word ZERO'),...
    xlabel('Index'),grid
```

5. TESTING

A plot of a datafile containing an utterance of the word "zero" is shown in Figure 3.13. The following set of values was computed for this signal:

```
Digit Statistics
mean: 0.002931
standard deviation: 0.121763
variance: 0.014826
average power: 0.014820
average magnitude: 0.089753
zero crossings: 106
```

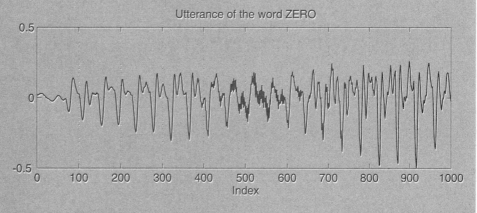

Figure 3.13 *Utterance of the word ZERO.*

We can now run this program with the utterances of different digits to observe the differences in the statistical measurements when different digits are spoken. It is also interesting to run this program using utterances of the same digit that are collected from different people. The wide range of statistics illustrates some of the difficulty in designing speech recognition systems that are speaker independent. Many computer systems have microphones and speakers connected to them. If your computer has this capability, record the utterance "zero," and compare the plot and statistics to the ones shown in this section.

3.5   User-Written Functions

As you use MATLAB to perform more and more computations, you will find calculations that you wish were included as functions in MATLAB. In these cases, you can develop a **user-written function**, and then your program can refer to the function in the same way that it refers to a MATLAB function. A user-written function has very specific rules that must be followed; however, before we list the rules, we consider a simple example.

User-written
function

A **rectangular function**, shown in Figure 3.14, is commonly used in many engineering applications. A common definition for the rectangular function is the following:

$$\text{rect}(x) = \begin{cases} 1, & |x| \leq 0.5 \\ 0, & \text{otherwise} \end{cases}$$

A user-defined function to evaluate this function is shown below:

```
function r = rect(x)
%  RECT     The rectangular function is defined
%           to be 1 on [-0.5,0.5] and 0 elsewhere.
%
r = zeros(size(x));
set1 = find(abs(x)<=0.5);
r(set1) = ones(size(set1));
```

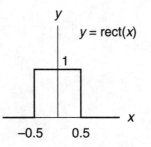

Figure 3.14 *Rectangular function.*

This function should be saved in a file named **rect.m**. Then, MATLAB programs and scripts can refer to this function in the same way that they refer to functions such as **sqrt** and **abs**. An example of using this function is shown below:

```
x = -3:0.1:3;
y = rect(x);
plot(x,y),title('Rect Function'),...
   xlabel('x'),ylabel('y'),grid
```

We now summarize the rules for writing an M-file function. Refer to the **rect** function as you read each rule.

1. The function must begin with a line containing the word **function**, which is followed by the output argument, an equal sign, and the name of the function. The input arguments to the function follow the function name and are enclosed in parentheses. This line distinguishes the function file from a script file.

2. The first few lines should be comments because they will be displayed if help is requested for the function name, as in **help rect**.

3. The only information returned from the function is contained in the output arguments, which are, of course, matrices. Always check to be sure that the function includes a statement that assigns a value to the output argument.

4. The same matrix names can be used in both a function and the program that references it. No confusion occurs as to which matrix is referenced because the function and the program are completely separate. However, any values computed in the function, other than the output arguments, are not accessible from the program.

5. A function that is going to return more than one value should show all values to be returned as a vector in the function statement, as in this example which will return three values:

    ```
    function [dist, vel, accel] = motion(x)
    ```

    All three values need to be computed within the function.

6. A function that has multiple input arguments must list the arguments in the function statement, as shown in this example, which has two input arguments:

    ```
    function error = mse(w,d)
    ```

7. The special variables **nargin** and **nargout** can be used to determine the number of input arguments and the number of output arguments for a function.

The **what** command lists all the M-files and MAT files that are available in the current workspace. The **type** command followed by a file name will display the contents of a file on the screen. If an extension is not included with the file name, the **type** command automatically assumes that the extension is **.m**.

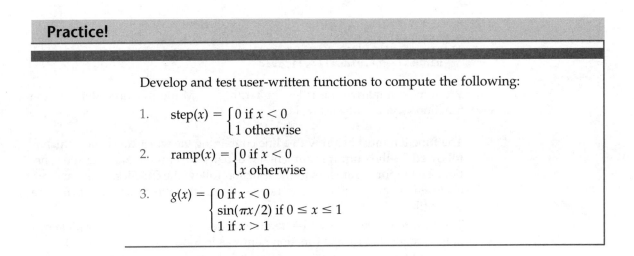

Practice!

Develop and test user-written functions to compute the following:

1. $\text{step}(x) = \begin{cases} 0 \text{ if } x < 0 \\ 1 \text{ otherwise} \end{cases}$

2. $\text{ramp}(x) = \begin{cases} 0 \text{ if } x < 0 \\ x \text{ otherwise} \end{cases}$

3. $g(x) = \begin{cases} 0 \text{ if } x < 0 \\ \sin(\pi x/2) \text{ if } 0 \le x \le 1 \\ 1 \text{ if } x > 1 \end{cases}$

3.6   Random Number Generating Functions

Random numbers

There are many engineering problems that require the use of **random numbers** in the development of a solution. In some cases, the random numbers are used to develop a simulation of a complex problem. The simulation can be tested over and over to analyze the results, and each test represents a repetition of the experiment. We also use random numbers to approximate noise sequences. For example, the static that we hear on a radio is a noise sequence. If we are testing a program that uses an input data file that represents a radio signal, we may want to generate noise and add it to a speech signal or a music signal in order to provide a more realistic signal.

UNIFORM RANDOM NUMBERS

Uniform random numbers

Random numbers are not defined by an equation; instead they can be characterized by the distribution of values. For example, random numbers that are equally likely to be any value between an upper and lower limit are called **uniform random numbers**. The top histogram in Figure 3.10 on page 94 shows the distribution of a set of uniform values between 2 and 4.

Seed value

The **rand** function in MATLAB generates random numbers uniformly distributed over the interval [0,1]. A **seed value** is used to initiate a random sequence of values; this seed value is initially set to 0, but it can be changed with the **seed** function.

`rand(n)`	Generates an **nxn** matrix containing random numbers between 0 and 1.
`rand(m,n)`	Generates an **mxn** matrix containing random numbers between 0 and 1.
`rand('seed',n)`	Sets the value of the seed to **n**.
`rand('seed')`	Returns the current value of the random number generator seed.

The **rand** function generates the same sequence of random values in each work session if the same seed value is used. The following commands generate and print two sets of ten random numbers uniformly distributed between 0 and 1; the difference between the two sets is caused by the different seeds:

```
rand('seed',0)
set1 = rand(10,1);
rand('seed',123)
set2 = rand(10,1);
[set1 set2]
```

The values printed by these commands are the following:

```
0.2190    0.0878
0.0470    0.6395
0.6789    0.0986
0.6793    0.6906
0.9347    0.3415
0.3835    0.2359
0.5194    0.2641
0.8310    0.6044
0.0346    0.4181
0.0535    0.1363
```

Random sequences with values that range between values other than 0 and 1 are often needed. To illustrate, suppose that we want to generate values between −5 and 5. We first generate a random number r (which is between 0 and 1), and then multiply it by 10, which is the difference between the upper and lower bounds $(5-(-5))$. We then add the lower bound (-5), giving a resulting value that is equally likely to be any value between −5 and 5. Thus, if we want to convert a value r that is uniformly distributed between 0 and 1 to a value uniformly distributed between a lower bound a and an upper bound b, we use the following equation:

$$x = (b - a) \cdot r + a \tag{3.14}$$

The sequence **data_1**, plotted in Figure 3.10 on page 94, was generated with this equation:

```
data_1 = 2*rand(1,500) + 2;
```

Thus, the sequence contains 500 values uniformly distributed between 2 and 4. The random number seed was 246.

Practice!

Give the MATLAB statements to generate ten random numbers with the specified range. Check your answers by executing the statements and printing the values generated in the vectors.

1.   Uniform random numbers between 0 and 10.0.
2.   Uniform random numbers between -1 and $+1$.
3.   Uniform random numbers between -20 and -10.
4.   Uniform random numbers between 4.5 and 5.0.
5.   Uniform random numbers between $-\pi$ and π.

GAUSSIAN RANDOM NUMBERS

When we generate a random sequence with a uniform distribution, all values are equally likely to occur. We sometimes need to generate random numbers using distributions in which some values are more likely to be generated than others. For example, suppose that a random sequence represents outdoor temperature measurements taken over a period of time. We would find that temperature measurements have some variation, but typically are not equally likely. For example, we might find that the values vary over only a few degrees, although larger changes could occasionally occur due to storms, cloud shadows, and day-to-night changes.

Gaussian
random numbers

Random sequences that have some values that are more likely to occur than others can often be modeled with **Gaussian random numbers** (also called **normal random numbers**). An example of a distribution of a set of values with a Gaussian distribution is shown in the second plot in Figure 3.10 on page 94. The mean value of this random variable corresponds to the x coordinate of the peak of this distribution, which is approximately 3. From the histogram in Figure 3.12, you can see that most values are close to the mean. Although a uniform random variable has specific upper and lower bounds, a Gaussian random variable is not defined in terms of upper and lower bounds—it is defined in terms of the mean and variance of the values. For Gaussian random numbers, it can be shown that approximately 68% of the values will fall within one standard deviation of the mean, 95% will fall within two standard deviations of the mean, and 99% will fall within three standard deviations of the mean. These statistics are useful in working with Gaussian random numbers.

MATLAB will generate Gaussian values with a mean of zero and a variance of 1.0 if we specify a normal distribution. The functions for generating Gaussian values are as follows:

randn(n)   Generates an **n**x**n** matrix containing Gaussian (or normal) random numbers with a mean of 0 and a variance of 1.

randn(m,n)   Generates an **m**x**n** matrix containing Gaussian (or normal) random numbers with a mean of 0 and a variance of 1.

To modify Gaussian values with a mean of 0 and a variance of 1 to another Gaussian distribution, multiply the values by the standard deviation of the desired distribution and add the mean of the desired distribution. Thus, if r is a random number with a mean of 0 and a variance of 1.0, the following equation will generate a new random number with a standard deviation of a and a mean of b:

$$x = a \cdot r + b \tag{3.15}$$

The sequence **data_2**, plotted in Figure 3.10 on page 94, was generated with this equation:

```
data_2 = randn(1,500) + 3;
```

Thus, the sequence contains 500 Gaussian random variables with a standard deviation of 1 and a mean of 3. The random number seed used was 95.

Practice!

Use MATLAB to generate 1,000 values with the specified characteristics. Calculate the mean and variance of the 1,000 values, and compare to the specified values. Also plot the histogram of the values using 25 bins.

1.   Gaussian random numbers with a mean of 1.0 and a variance of 0.5.
2.   Gaussian random numbers with a mean of −5.5 and a standard deviation of 0.25.
3.   Gaussian random numbers with a mean of −5.5 and a standard deviation of 1.25.

3.7   Matrix Manipulation Functions

MATLAB contains a number of functions that manipulate the contents of a matrix. We will discuss each of these functions, and give an example to illustrate.

ROTATION

A matrix can be rotated in a counterclockwise direction using the **rot90** function:

rot90(A)   Rotates the matrix **A** 90° in a counter clockwise direction.

rot90(A,n)   Rotates the matrix **A** **n**·90° in a counter clockwise direction.

Let the matrix **A** be the following:

$$A = \begin{bmatrix} 2 & 1 & 0 \\ -2 & 5 & -1 \\ 3 & 4 & 6 \end{bmatrix}$$

If we execute the commands

```
B = rot90(A);
C = rot90(A,2);
```

then the values of **B** and **C** are

$$B = \begin{bmatrix} 0 & -1 & 6 \\ 1 & 5 & 4 \\ 2 & -2 & 3 \end{bmatrix} \quad C = \begin{bmatrix} 6 & 4 & 3 \\ -1 & 5 & -2 \\ 0 & 1 & 2 \end{bmatrix}$$

FLIPPING

Two functions are used to flip a matrix:

fliplr(A)   Flips the matrix **A** left-to-right.

flipud(A)   Flips the matrix **A** up-to-down.

For example, consider the following MATLAB commands:

```
A = [1,2; 4,8; -2,0];
B = fliplr(A);
C = flipud(B);
```

After executing these commands, the matrices **A**, **B**, and **C** contain the following values:

$$A = \begin{bmatrix} 1 & 2 \\ 4 & 8 \\ -2 & 0 \end{bmatrix} \quad B = \begin{bmatrix} 2 & 1 \\ 8 & 4 \\ 0 & -2 \end{bmatrix} \quad C = \begin{bmatrix} 0 & -2 \\ 8 & 4 \\ 2 & 1 \end{bmatrix}$$

RESHAPING

The **reshape** function allows you to reshape a matrix into a different number of rows and columns:

reshape(A,m,n)   Reshapes the matrix **A** into **m** rows and **n** columns.

The number of elements in the original matrix and in the reshaped matrix must be the same, or an error message will be printed. The numbers are selected in column order from the old matrix and are then used to fill the new matrix. Consider the following MATLAB statements:

```
A = [2 5 6 -1; 3 -2 10 0];
B = reshape(A,4,2);
C = reshape(A,8,1);
```

After executing these statements, the values in matrices **A**, **B**, and **C** are the following:

$$
A = \begin{bmatrix} 2 & 5 & 6 & -1 \\ 3 & -2 & 10 & 0 \end{bmatrix} \quad B = \begin{bmatrix} 2 & 6 \\ 3 & 10 \\ 5 & -1 \\ -2 & 0 \end{bmatrix} \quad C = \begin{bmatrix} 2 \\ 3 \\ 5 \\ -2 \\ 6 \\ 10 \\ -1 \\ 0 \end{bmatrix}
$$

EXTRACTION

Main diagonal

The functions **diag, triu,** and **tril** allow you to extract elements from a matrix. The definition of all three functions use the definition of the **main diagonal**, which is the diagonal that starts in the upper left corner of a matrix and contains the values with equal row and column subscripts, such as $a_{1,1}$, $a_{2,2}$, and $a_{3,3}$. Even non-square matrices have main diagonals. For example, in the previous example, the elements on the main diagonal of **A** are 2,−2; the elements on the main diagonal of **B** are 2,10; and the element on the main diagonal of **C** is 2.

*k*th diagonal

Diagonals other than the main diagonal can also be defined. For example, we can define a *k*th **diagonal**. When *k* is 0, the *k*th diagonal is the main diagonal. When *k* is positive, the *k*th diagonal is a diagonal parallel to and above the main diagonal. For *k*=1, the *k*th diagonal is the set of elements above those in the main diagonal. For *k*=2, the *k*th diagonal is the set of elements in the second diagonal above the main diagonal. If *k* is less than 0, then the *k*th diagonal is a set of elements on a diagonal below the main diagonal. Thus, for *k*=−1, the *k*th diagonal is the first diagonal below the main diagonal.

The **diag** function is used to extract diagonal values from a matrix:

`diag(A)`   Extracts the main diagonal elements and stores them in a column vector if **A** is a matrix. If **A** is a vector, the function will generate a square matrix with **A** as the diagonal.

`diag(A,k)`   Extracts the **k**th diagonal elements of **A** and stores them in a column vector.

For example, these statements,

```
P = [1 2 3; 2 4 6; -1 2 0];
A = diag(P,1);
```

will generate a vector with the following elements:

$$P = \begin{bmatrix} 1 & 2 & 3 \\ 2 & 4 & 6 \\ -1 & 2 & 0 \end{bmatrix} \quad A = \begin{bmatrix} 2 \\ 6 \end{bmatrix}$$

The **triu** function generates a new matrix that is sometimes referred to as an **upper triangular matrix**:

`triu(A)`   Generates a square matrix of values from **A** with zeros below the main diagonal.

`triu(A,k)`   Generates a square matrix of values from **A** with zeros below the **k**th diagonal.

Consider these statements:

```
A = [1:2:7; 3:3:12; 4:-1:1; 1:4];
B = triu(A);
C = triu(A,-1);
D = triu(A,3);
```

The resulting matrices are

$$A = \begin{bmatrix} 1 & 3 & 5 & 7 \\ 3 & 6 & 9 & 12 \\ 4 & 3 & 2 & 1 \\ 1 & 2 & 3 & 4 \end{bmatrix} \quad B = \begin{bmatrix} 1 & 3 & 5 & 7 \\ 0 & 6 & 9 & 12 \\ 0 & 0 & 2 & 1 \\ 0 & 0 & 0 & 4 \end{bmatrix}$$

$$C = \begin{bmatrix} 1 & 3 & 5 & 7 \\ 3 & 6 & 9 & 12 \\ 0 & 3 & 2 & 1 \\ 0 & 0 & 3 & 4 \end{bmatrix} \quad D = \begin{bmatrix} 0 & 0 & 0 & 7 \\ 0 & 0 & 0 & 0 \\ 0 & 0 & 0 & 0 \\ 0 & 0 & 0 & 0 \end{bmatrix}$$

The **tril** function is similar to the **triu** function, but the **tril** function generates **lower triangular matrices**:

`tril(A)`	Generates a square matrix of values from **a** with zeros above the main diagonal.
`tril(A,k)`	Generates a square matrix of values from **a** with zeros above the **k**th diagonal.

If we replace references to `triu` in the previous example with references to `tril`, we have

```
A = [1:2:7; 3:3:12; 4:-1:1; 1:4];
B = tril(A);
C = tril(A,-1);
D = tril(A,3);
```

The resulting matrices are

$$A = \begin{bmatrix} 1 & 3 & 5 & 7 \\ 3 & 6 & 9 & 12 \\ 4 & 3 & 2 & 1 \\ 1 & 2 & 3 & 4 \end{bmatrix} \quad B = \begin{bmatrix} 1 & 0 & 0 & 0 \\ 3 & 6 & 0 & 0 \\ 4 & 3 & 2 & 0 \\ 1 & 2 & 3 & 4 \end{bmatrix}$$

$$C = \begin{bmatrix} 0 & 0 & 0 & 0 \\ 3 & 0 & 0 & 0 \\ 4 & 3 & 0 & 0 \\ 1 & 2 & 3 & 0 \end{bmatrix} \quad D = \begin{bmatrix} 1 & 3 & 5 & 7 \\ 3 & 6 & 9 & 12 \\ 4 & 3 & 2 & 1 \\ 1 & 2 & 3 & 4 \end{bmatrix}$$

Practice!

Determine the matrices generated by the following function references. Then check your answers using MATLAB.

Assume that **a** and **b** are the following matrices:

$$A = \begin{bmatrix} 0 & -1 & 0 & 3 \\ 4 & 3 & 5 & 0 \\ 1 & 2 & 3 & 0 \end{bmatrix} \quad B = \begin{bmatrix} 1 & 3 & 5 & 0 \\ 3 & 6 & 9 & 12 \\ 4 & 3 & 2 & 1 \\ 1 & 2 & 3 & 4 \end{bmatrix}$$

1.	`rot90(B)`	2.	`rot90(A,3)`
3.	`fliplr(A)`	4.	`flipud(fliplr(B))`
5.	`reshape(A,4,3)`	6.	`reshape(A,6,2)`
7.	`reshape(A,2,6)`	8.	`reshape(flipud(B),8,2)`
9.	`triu(B)`	10.	`triu(B,-1)`
11.	`tril(A,2)`	12.	`diag(rot90(B))`

3.8   Loops

Loop

A **loop** is a structure that allows you to repeat a set of statements. In general, you should avoid loops in MATLAB because they can significantly increase the execution time of a program. However, there are occasions when loops are needed, so we give a brief introduction to **for** loops and **while** loops.

for LOOP

In an example in a previous section, we used the **find** function to find distance values greater than 30 feet and distance values less than or equal to 30 feet. We then computed the corresponding velocities using the appropriate equations, as repeated here:

```
lower = find(d < 30);
velocity(lower) = 0.425 + 0.00175*d(lower).^2;
upper = find(d >= 30);
velocity(upper) = 0.625 + 0.12*d(upper)...
                  - 0.00025*d(upper).^2;
```

Another way to perform these steps uses a **for** loop. In the following statements, the value of **k** is set to 1, and the statements inside the loop are executed. The value of **k** is incremented to 2, and the statements inside the loop are executed again. This continues until the value of **k** is greater than the length of the **d** vector.

```
for k=1:length(d)
   if d(k) < 30
      velocity(k) = 0.425 - 0.00175*d(k)^2;
   else
      velocity(k) = 0.625 + 0.12*d(k)...
                    - 0.00025*d(k)^2;
   end
end
```

Although these statements perform the same operations as the previous steps using the **find** function, the solution without a loop will execute much faster.

A **for** loop has the following general structure:

```
for  index=expression
       statements
end
```

The expression is a matrix (which could be a scalar or a vector), and the statements are repeated as many times as there are columns in the expression matrix. Each time through the loop, the index has the value of one of the elements in the expression matrix. The rules for writing and using a **for** loop are the following:

1.   The index of a **for** loop must be a variable.
2.   If the expression matrix is the empty matrix, a loop will not be executed. Control will pass to the statement following the **end** statement.

3. If the expression matrix is a scalar, a loop will be executed one time, with the index containing the value of the scalar.

4. If the expression matrix is a row vector, then each time through a loop, the index will contain the next value in the vector.

5. If the expression matrix is a matrix, then each time through a loop, the index will contain the next column in the matrix.

6. Upon completion of a **for** loop, the index contains the last value used.

7. The colon operator can be used to define the expression matrix using the following format:

```
for k = initial:increment:limit
```

Practice!

Determine the number of times that the **for** loops defined by the following statements will be executed. To check your answer, use the **length** function, which returns the number of values in a vector. Thus, the number of times that the **for** loop in problem 1 is executed is **length(3:20)**.

1. ```for k = 3:20```
2. ```for count = -2:14```
3. ```for k = -2:-1:-10```
4. ```for time =10:-1:0```
5. ```for time = 10:5```
6. ```for index = 2:3:12```

while LOOP

The **while** loop is a structure for repeating a set of statements as long as a specified condition is true. The general format for this control structure is

```
while expression
    statements
end
```

If the expression is true, the statements are executed. After these statements are executed, the condition is retested. If the condition is still true, the group of statements is executed again. When the condition is false, control skips to the statement following the **end** statement. The variables modified within the loop should include the variables in the expression, or the value of the expression will never change. If the expression is always true (or is a value that is nonzero), the loop becomes an **infinite loop**.

Infinite loop

Style

Loops are necessary structures in most high-level languages. However, the power of the matrix element-by-element operations generally can be used to avoid the use of loops in our MATLAB programs. *Before using a loop in a MATLAB program, you should carefully look at alternative ways to perform the desired computations without loops; this will allow your program to execute faster and, in general, will make your program more readable because it is shorter.*

CHAPTER SUMMARY

In this chapter, we explored the various MATLAB functions for creating matrices and for calculating new matrices from existing matrices. These functions included mathematical functions, trigonometric functions, data analysis functions, random number functions, and logical functions; we also illustrated the steps in developing a user-written function. In addition, we presented selection statements and functions so that we can analyze or modify selected portions of matrices. Finally, we included a brief discussion of loops because they are occasionally needed in MATLAB solutions.

KEY TERMS

0–1 matrix	normal random number
argument	parameter
complex number	polar notation
conjugate	polynomial
degree	random number
Euler's formula	rectangular notation
function	relational operator
Gaussian random number	root
histogram	seed value
logical operator	standard deviation
mean	uniform random number
median	utterance
metric	variance

MATLAB SUMMARY

This MATLAB summary lists all the special symbols, commands, and functions that were defined in this chapter. A brief description is also included for each one.

SPECIAL CHARACTERS

<	less than
<=	less than or equal
>	greater than
>=	greater than or equal
==	equal
~=	not equal
&	and
|	or
~	not

COMMANDS AND FUNCTIONS

abs	computes absolute value or magnitude
acos	computes arccosine
all	determines if all values are true
any	determines if any values are true
asin	computes arcsine
atan	computes 2-quadrant arctangent
atan2	computes 4-quadrant arctangent
ceil	rounds towards ∞
cos	computes cosine of angle
cumprod	determines cumulative products
cumsum	determines cumulative sums
else	optional clause in **if** statement
elseif	optional clause in **if** statement
end	defines end of a control structure
exp	computes value with base *e*
find	locates nonzero values
finite	determines if values are finite
fix	rounds toward zero

floor	rounds toward $-\infty$
for	generates loop structure
function	generates user-defined function
hist	plots histogram
if	tests logical expression
isempty	determines if matrix is empty
isnan	determines if values are NaN
length	determines number of values in a vector
log	computes natural logarithm
log10	computes common logarithm
max	determines maximum value
mean	determines mean value
median	determines median value
min	determines minimum value
polyval	evaluates a polynomial
prod	determines product of values
rand	generates a uniform random number
randn	generates a Gaussian random number
rem	computes remainder from division
round	rounds to nearest integer
sign	generates -1, or 0 or 1, based on sign
sin	computes sine of angle
sort	sorts values
sqrt	computes square root
std	computes standard deviation
sum	determines sum of values
tan	computes tangent of angle
what	lists files
while	generates a loop structure

Style NOTES

1. Indent the statements within an if structure for readability.
2. Avoid using loops because they can significantly increase the execution time of a program.

DEBUGGING NOTES

1. Be sure to enclose the arguments of each function in parentheses.
2. Do not use the variable name `i` or `j` for other variables in a program that also uses complex numbers.
3. When using relational and logical operators, be sure that the steps being performed are the ones that you intend.

PROBLEMS

Rocket Trajectory. A small rocket is being designed to make wind-shear measurements in the vicinity of thunderstorms. Before testing begins, the designers are developing a simulation of the rocket's trajectory. They have derived the following equation that they believe will predict the performance of the test rocket, where t is the elapsed time in seconds:

$$\text{height} = 60 + 2.13t^2 - 0.0013t^4 + 0.000034t^{4.751}$$

The equation gives the height above ground level at time t. The first term (60) is the height in feet above ground level of the nose of the rocket.

1. Give the commands to compute and print the time and height of the rocket from $t = 0$ to the time that it hits the ground, in increments of 2 seconds. If the rocket has not hit the ground within 100 seconds, print values only up through 100 seconds.
2. Modify the steps in problem 1 so that instead of a table, the program prints the time at which the rocket begins falling back to the ground and the time at which the rocket impacts.

Suture Packaging. Sutures are strands or fibers used to sew living tissue together after an injury or an operation. Packages of sutures must be sealed carefully before they are shipped to hospitals so that contaminants cannot enter the packages. The object that seals the package is referred to as a **sealing die**. Generally, sealing dies are heated with an electric heater. For the sealing process to be a success, the sealing die is maintained at an established temperature and must contact the package with a predetermined pressure for an established time period. The time period in which the sealing die contacts the package is called the dwell time. Assume that the acceptable range of parameters for an acceptable seal are the following:

Temperature: 150–170° C
Pressure: 60–70 psi
Dwell Time: 2–2.5 s

3. A data file named **suture.dat** contains information on batches of sutures that have been rejected during a one-week period. Each line in the data file contains the batch number, the temperature, the pressure, and the dwell time for a rejected batch. A quality control engineer would like to analyze this information to determine the percent of the batches rejected due to temperature, the percent rejected due to pressure, and the percent rejected due to dwell time. If a specific batch is rejected for more than one reason, it should be counted in all applicable totals. Give the MATLAB statements to compute and print these three percentages. Use the following data:

Batch Number	Temperature	Pressure	Dwell Time
24551	145.5	62.3	2.23
24582	153.7	63.2	2.52
26553	160.3	58.9	2.51
26623	159.5	58.9	2.01
26642	160.3	61.2	1.98

4. Modify the solution developed in problem 3 so that it also prints the number of batches in each rejection category and the total number of batches rejected. (Remember that a rejected batch should appear only once in the total, but could appear in more than one rejection category.)

5. Write a program to read the data file **suture.dat** and make sure that the information relates only to batches that should have been rejected. If any batch should not be in the data file, print an appropriate message with the batch information.

Timber Regrowth. A problem in timber management is to determine how much of an area to leave uncut so that the harvested area is reforested in a certain period of time. It is assumed that reforestation takes place at a known rate per year, depending on climate and soil conditions. A reforestation equation expresses this growth as a function of the amount of timber standing and the reforestation rate. For example, if 100 acres are left standing after harvesting and the reforestation rate is 0.05, then 100 + 0.05 × 100, or 105 acres, are forested at the end of the first year. At the end of the second year, the number of acres forested is 105 + 0.05 × 105, or 110.25 acres.

6. Assume that there are 14,000 acres total with 2500 acres uncut and that the reforestation rate is 0.02. Print a table showing the number of acres reforested at the end of each year, for a total of 20 years.

7. Modify the program developed in problem 6 so that the user can enter the number of years to be used for the table.

8. Modify the program developed in problem 6 so that the user can enter a

number of acres, and the program will determine how many years are required for the number of acres to be forested.

Sensor Data. Suppose that a data file named **sensor.dat** contains information collected from a set of sensors. Each row contains a set of sensor readings, with the first row containing values collected at 0.0 seconds, the second row containing values collected at 1.0 seconds, and so on.

9. Write a program to read the data file and print the number of sensors and the number of seconds of data contained in the file.

10. Write a program to preprocess the sensor data so that all values that are greater than 10.0 are set to 10.0, and all values less than −10.0 are set to −10.0.

11. Write a program to print the subscripts of sensor data values with absolute values greater than 20.0.

12. Write a program to print the percentage of sensor data values that are 0.

Power Plant Output. The power output in megawatts from a power plant over a period of eight weeks has been stored in a data file named **plant.dat**. Each line in the data file represents data for one week, and contains the output for day 1, day 2, . . . , day 7.

13. Write a program that uses the power plant output data and prints a report that lists the number of days with greater-than-average power output. The report should give the week number and the day number for each of these days, in addition to printing the average power output for the plant during the eight-week period.

14. Write a program that uses the power plant output data and prints the day and week during which the maximum and minimum power output occurred. If the maximum or minimum occurred on more than one day, print all the days involved.

15. Write a program that uses the power plant output data and prints the average power output for each week. Also print the average power output for day 1, for day 2, and so on.

4

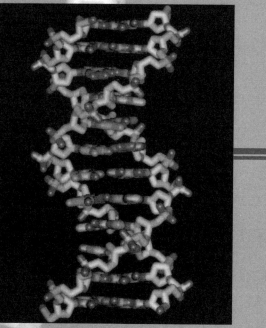

Courtesy of Photo Researchers, Inc.

GRAND CHALLENGE:
Mapping the Human Genome

The deciphering of the human genetic code involves locating, identifying, and determining the function of each of the 50,000 to 100,000 genes that are contained in human DNA. Each gene is a double-helix strand composed of base pairs of adenine bonded with thymine, or cytosine bonded with guanine, that are arranged in a step-like manner with phosphate groups along the side. Because DNA directs the production of proteins, the proteins produced by a cell provide a key to the sequence of base pairs in the DNA. Instrumentation developed for genetic engineering is extremely useful in this detective work. A protein sequencer developed in 1969 can identify the sequence of amino acids in a protein molecule. Once the amino acid order is known, biologists can begin to identify the gene that made the protein. A DNA synthesizer, developed in 1982, can build small genes or gene fragments out of DNA. This research, and its associated instrumentation, are key components in beginning to address the mapping of the human genome.

Linear Algebra and Matrices

OBJECTIVES

A matrix is a convenient way to represent engineering data. In previous chapters, we discussed mathematical computations and functions that could be applied element-by-element to values in matrices. In this chapter, we present a set of matrix operations and functions that apply to the matrix as a unit, as opposed to individual elements in the matrix. We first consider a set of mathematical computations that compute new values from a matrix (or matrices).

4.1   Matrix Operations

Many engineering computations use a matrix as a convenient way to represent a set of data. In this chapter, we are generally concerned with matrices that have more than one row and more than one column. Recall that scalar multiplication and matrix addition and subtraction are performed element-by-element and were covered in Chapter 2 in the discussion of array operations. Matrix multiplication is covered in this chapter; matrix division, presented in Chapter 5, is used to compute the solution to a set of simultaneous linear equations.

TRANSPOSE

Transpose

The **transpose** of a matrix is a new matrix in which the rows of the original matrix are the columns of the new matrix. We use a superscript T after a matrix name to refer to the transpose. For example, consider the following matrix and its transpose:

$$A = \begin{bmatrix} 2 & 5 & 1 \\ 7 & 3 & 8 \\ 4 & 5 & 21 \\ 16 & 13 & 0 \end{bmatrix} \qquad A^T = \begin{bmatrix} 2 & 7 & 4 & 16 \\ 5 & 3 & 5 & 13 \\ 1 & 8 & 21 & 0 \end{bmatrix}$$

If we consider a couple of the elements, we see that the value in position (3,1) of A has now moved to position (1,3) of A^T, and the value in position (4,2) of A has now moved to position (2,4) of A^T. In general, the row and column subscripts are interchanged to form the transpose; hence, the value in position (i,j) is moved to position (j,i).

In MATLAB, the transpose of the matrix **A** is denoted by **A'**. Observe that the transpose will have a different size than the original matrix if the original matrix is not square. We frequently use the transpose operation to convert a row vector to a column vector or a column vector to a row vector.

DOT PRODUCT

Dot product

The **dot product** is a scalar computed from two vectors of the same size. This scalar is the sum of the products of the values in corresponding positions in the vectors, as shown in the summation equation, which assumes that there are N elements in the vectors A and B:

$$\text{dot product} = A \cdot B = \sum_{i=1}^{N} a_i b_i$$

To illustrate, assume that A and B are the following vectors:

$$A = \begin{bmatrix} 4 & -1 & 3 \end{bmatrix} \qquad B = \begin{bmatrix} -2 & 5 & 2 \end{bmatrix}$$

The dot product is then

$$A \cdot B = 4 \cdot (-2) + (-1) \cdot 5 + 3 \cdot 2$$
$$= (-8) + (-5) + 6$$
$$= -7$$

In MATLAB, we can compute the dot product with the **dot** function:

dot(A,B)   Computes the dot product of **A** and **B**. If **A** and **B** are matrices, the dot product is a row vector containing the dot products for the corresponding columns of **A** and **B**.

Thus, we could use these statements to compute the value of $A \cdot B$ from the previous example:

```
A = [4,-1,3];
B = [-2,5,2];
C = dot(A,B);
```

Note that the dot product could also be computed with this statement:

```
C = sum(A.*B);
```

MATRIX MULTIPLICATION

Matrix
multiplication

Matrix multiplication is not computed by multiplying corresponding elements of the matrices. In **matrix multiplication**, the value in position $c_{i,j}$ of the product C of two matrices, A and B, is the dot product of row i of the first matrix and column j of the second matrix, as shown in the summation equation:

$$c_{i,j} = \sum_{k=1}^{N} a_{i,k} b_{k,j}$$

Because the dot product requires that the vectors have the same number of elements, the first matrix (A) must have the same number of elements (N) in each row as there are in the columns of the second matrix (B). Thus, if A and B both have five rows and five columns, their product has five rows and five columns. Furthermore, for these matrices, we can compute both AB and BA, but, in general, they will not be equal.

If A has two rows and three columns, and B has three rows and three columns, the product AB will have two rows and three columns. To illustrate, consider the following matrices:

$$A = \begin{bmatrix} 2 & 5 & 1 \\ 0 & 3 & -1 \end{bmatrix} \quad B = \begin{bmatrix} 1 & 0 & 2 \\ -1 & 4 & -2 \\ 5 & 2 & 1 \end{bmatrix}$$

The first element in the product C = AB is

$$c_{1,1} = \sum_{k=1}^{3} a_{1,k}b_{k,1}$$

$$= a_{1,1}b_{1,1} + a_{1,2}b_{2,1} + a_{1,3}b_{3,1}$$

$$= 2 \cdot 1 + 5 \cdot (-1) + 1 \cdot 5$$

$$= 2$$

Similarly, we can compute the rest of the elements in the product of A and B:

$$AB = C = \begin{bmatrix} 2 & 22 & -5 \\ -8 & 10 & -7 \end{bmatrix}$$

In this example, we cannot compute BA because B does not have the same number of elements in each row as A has in each column.

An easy way to decide if a matrix product exists is to write the sizes of the two matrices side by side. If the two inside numbers are the same, the product exists, and the size of the product is determined by the two outside numbers. To illustrate, in the previous example, the size of A is 2×3 and the size of B is 3×3. Therefore, if we want to compute AB, we write the sizes side-by-side:

2 × 3, 3 × 3

The two inner numbers are both the value 3, so AB exists, and its size is determined by the two outer numbers, 2×3. If we want to compute BA, we again write the sizes side-by-side:

3 × 3, 2 × 3

The two inner numbers are not the same, so BA does not exist.

In MATLAB, matrix multiplication is denoted by an asterisk. Thus, the commands to generate the matrices in our previous example and to compute the matrix product are

```
A = [2,5,1; 0,3,-1];
B = [1,0,2; -1,4,-2; 5,2,1];
C = A*B;
```

If we execute the MATLAB command `C = B*A`, we get a warning message that C does not exist. Use the `size` function to determine and check the sizes of matrices if you are not sure that the product exists.

Assume that I is a square identity matrix. (Recall from Chapter 2 that an identity matrix is a matrix with ones on the main diagonal and zeros elsewhere.) If A is a square matrix of the same size, then AI and IA are both equal to A. Use a small matrix A, and verify by hand that these matrix products are both equal to A.

MATRIX POWERS

Recall that if **a** is a matrix, then **a.^2** is the operation that squares each element in the matrix. If we want to square the matrix, that is, if we want to compute **A*A**, we can use the operation **A^2**. Then, **A^4** is equivalent to **A*A*A*A**. To perform a matrix multiplication between two matrices, the number of rows in the first matrix must be the same value as the number of columns in the second matrix; therefore, to raise a matrix to a power, the number of rows must equal the number of columns, and, hence, the matrix must be a square matrix.

MATRIX POLYNOMIALS

Recall that a polynomial is a function of x that can be expressed in the following general form

$$f(x) = a_0 x^N + a_1 x^{N-1} + a_2 x^{N-2} + \ldots + a_{N-2} x^2 + a_{N-1} x + a_N$$

where the variable is x and the polynomial coefficients are represented by the values of a_0, a_1, and so on. If x is a matrix, then the equation is a **matrix polynomial** and requires matrix multiplication to compute terms such as $a_0 x^N$. Consider the following polynomial:

$$f(x) = 3x^4 - 0.5x^3 + x - 5.2$$

If we want to evaluate this function for a matrix **x**, we can use matrix operations as shown in this command:

```
f = 3*x^4 - 0.5*x^3 + x - 5.2;
```

A matrix polynomial can also be evaluated using the **polyvalm** function:

polyvalm(a,x)   Evaluates a polynomial with coefficients **a** for the values in the square matrix **x**. The result is a matrix the same size as **x**.

Thus, the following commands can be used to evaluate the matrix polynomial discussed above:

```
a = [3,-0.5,0,1,-5.2];
f = polyvalm(a,x);
```

A scalar term in the polynomial (such as the term -5.2 in this example) will be evaluated by **polyvalm** as an identity matrix multiplied by the scalar value.

Practice!

Use MATLAB to define the following matrices. Then compute the specified matrices, if they exist.

$$A = \begin{bmatrix} 2 & 1 \\ 0 & -1 \\ 3 & 0 \end{bmatrix} \qquad B = \begin{bmatrix} 1 & 3 \\ -1 & 5 \end{bmatrix}$$

$$C = \begin{bmatrix} 3 & 2 \\ -1 & -2 \\ 0 & 2 \end{bmatrix} \qquad D = \begin{bmatrix} 1 & 2 \end{bmatrix}$$

1. DB^2 2. BC^T
3. $(CB)D^T$ 4. AC^T

4.2   Problem Solving Applied: Protein Molecular Weights

Amino acids

A **protein sequencer** is a sophisticated piece of equipment that plays a key role in genetic engineering. The sequencer can determine the order of **amino acids** that make up a chainlike protein molecule. This order of amino acids then aids genetic engineers in identifying the gene that made the protein. Enzymes are used to dissolve bonds to the neighboring genes, thus separating the valuable gene out of the DNA. This gene is then inserted into another organism, such as a bacterium, which will multiply itself along with the foreign gene.

Although there are only 20 different amino acids, protein molecules have hundreds of amino acids linked in a specific order. In this problem, we assume that the sequence of amino acids in a protein molecule has been identified and that we want to compute the molecular weight of the protein molecule. Table 4.1 contains an alphabetical listing of the amino acids, their three-letter reference, and their molecular weights.

The input to this problem is a data file that contains the number and type of amino acid molecules in each protein molecule. Assume that the data file is generated by the protein sequencer instrumentation. Each line in the data file corresponds to one protein, and each line contains 20 integers that correspond to the 20 amino acids in the alphabetical order shown in Table 4.1. Therefore, a line containing the following values would represent the protein LysGluMetAspSerGlu:

0 0 0 1 0 2 0 0 0 0 0 1 1 0 0 1 0 0 0 0

The data file is named **protein.dat**.

TABLE 4.1 Amino Acids

	Amino Acid	Reference	Molecular Weight
1.	Alanine	Ala	89
2.	Arginine	Arg	175
3.	Asparagine	Asn	132
4.	Aspartic	Asp	132
5.	Cysteine	Cys	121
6.	Glutamic	Glu	146
7.	Glutamine	Gln	146
8.	Glycine	Gly	75
9.	Histidine	His	156
10.	Isoleucine	Ile	131
11.	Leucine	Leu	131
12.	Lysine	Lys	147
13.	Methionine	Met	149
14.	Phenylalanine	Phe	165
15.	Proline	Pro	116
16.	Serine	Ser	105
17.	Threonine	Thr	119
18.	Tryptophan	Trp	203
19.	Tyrosine	Tyr	181
20.	Valine	Val	117

1.   PROBLEM STATEMENT

Compute the molecular weights for a group of protein molecules.

2.   INPUT/OUTPUT DESCRIPTION

The following I/O diagram indicates that the input is a file containing the amino acids identified in a group of protein molecules. The output of the program is the corresponding set of protein molecular weights.

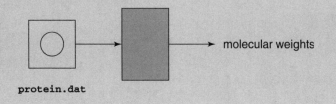

protein.dat   molecular weights

3.   HAND EXAMPLE

Suppose that the protein molecule is the following:

LysGluMetAspSerGlu

The corresponding molecular weights for the amino acids are

147, 146, 149, 132, 105, 146

Therefore, the protein molecular weight is 825. The data file would contain the following line for this protein:

0 0 0 1 0 2 0 0 0 0 0 1 1 0 0 1 0 0 0 0

The molecular weight for the protein is the sum of the product of the number of amino acids and the corresponding weights. This sum of products can be considered a dot product between the protein vector and the weight vector. If we compute the protein molecular weight for a group of proteins, the computations can be computed as a matrix product, as shown in the example below for two proteins:

$$\begin{bmatrix} 0 0 0 1 0 2 0 0 0 0 0 1 1 0 0 1 0 0 0 0 \\ 0 1 0 0 0 1 1 0 0 3 0 0 0 0 0 0 0 1 0 0 \end{bmatrix} \begin{bmatrix} 89 \\ 175 \\ 132 \\ 132 \\ 121 \\ 146 \\ 146 \\ 75 \\ 156 \\ 131 \\ 131 \\ 147 \\ 149 \\ 165 \\ 116 \\ 105 \\ 119 \\ 203 \\ 181 \\ 117 \end{bmatrix} = \begin{bmatrix} 825 \\ 1063 \end{bmatrix}$$

4.   MATLAB SOLUTION

By recognizing that this problem can be posed as a matrix multiplication, we have simplified the MATLAB solution. The amino acid information is read from the data file into a matrix **protein**, a column vector **mw** with the amino acid molecular weights is defined, and the protein molecular weights are then contained in the vector computed as the matrix product of **protein** and **mw**.

```
%    This program computes the molecular weights for
%    a group of protein molecules. A data file contains
%    the occurrence and number of amino acids in each
%    protein molecule
%
load protein.dat;
mw = [89 175 132 132 121 146 146 75 156 131 ...
      131 147 149 165 116 105 119 203 181 117];
%
weights = protein*mw';
%
[rows,cols] = size(protein);
for k=1:rows
    fprintf('protein %3.0f: molecular weight = %5.0f \n',...
            k, weights(k));
end;
```

5.   TESTING

Assume that the proteins that have been identified are the following:

```
GlyIleSerThrTrp
AspHisProGln
ThrTyrSerTrpLysMetHisMet
AlaValLeuValMet
LysGluMetAspSerGluLysGluGlyGlu
```

Then the corresponding data file is the following:

```
0 0 0 0 0 0 0 1 0 1 0 0 0 0 0 1 1 1 0 0
0 0 0 1 0 0 1 0 1 0 0 0 0 0 1 0 0 0 0 0
0 0 0 0 0 0 0 1 0 0 1 2 0 0 1 1 1 1 0
1 0 0 0 0 0 0 0 0 1 0 1 0 0 0 0 0 0 2
0 0 0 1 0 4 0 1 0 0 0 2 1 0 0 1 0 0 0 0
```

The output for this test file is the following:

```
protein     1: molecular weight =    633
protein     2: molecular weight =    550
protein     3: molecular weight =   1209
protein     4: molecular weight =    603
protein     5: molecular weight =   1339
```

The **for** loop in this example could easily be eliminated if we wanted to print only the molecular weights and did not want to alternate between a counter (or index) value and a molecular weight. To illustrate, suppose that the **for** loop was replaced by this statement:

```
fprintf('molecular weight = %5.0f \n', weights);
```

Then, the output would be

```
molecular weight =   633
molecular weight =   550
molecular weight =  1209
molecular weight =   603
molecular weight =  1339
```

Additional problems related to this application are included in the end-of-chapter problems.

4.3   Matrix Functions

A number of MATLAB functions relate to linear algebra uses of matrices. In this section, we present functions that relate to computing the inverse of a matrix and the determinant of a matrix. We also present functions to determine the eigenvectors and eigenvalues of a matrix and to decompose a matrix into a product of other matrices.

MATRIX INVERSE AND RANK

Inverse

By definition, the **inverse** of a square matrix A is the matrix A^{-1} for which the matrix products AA^{-1} and $A^{-1}A$ are both equal to the identity matrix. For example, consider the following two matrices, A and B:

$$A = \begin{bmatrix} 2 & 1 \\ 4 & 3 \end{bmatrix} \qquad B = \begin{bmatrix} 1.5 & -0.5 \\ -2 & 1 \end{bmatrix}$$

If we compute the products AB and BA, we obtain the following matrices. (Do the matrix multiplications by hand to be sure you follow the steps.)

$$AB = \begin{bmatrix} 1 & 0 \\ 0 & 1 \end{bmatrix} \qquad BA = \begin{bmatrix} 1 & 0 \\ 0 & 1 \end{bmatrix}$$

Therefore, A and B are inverses of each other, or $A = B^{-1}$ and $B = A^{-1}$.

The inverse for an **ill-conditioned** or **singular** matrix does not exist. A graphical interpretation of an ill-conditioned matrix is given in Chapter 5 and is related to a system of equations in which the equations are not independent of each other. The **rank** of a matrix is the number of independent equations represented by the rows of the matrix. Therefore, if the rank of a matrix is equal to the number of its rows, the matrix is **nonsingular** and its inverse exists.

Rank

Computing the rank of a matrix and the inverse of a matrix are tedious processes; fortunately, MATLAB contains functions to perform these computations for us:

rank(A)   Computes the rank of the matrix **A**. If the rank is equal to the number of rows of **A**, the matrix is nonsingular, and an inverse exists.

inv(A)   Computes the inverse of the matrix **A**, if it exists. If the inverse does not exist, an error message is printed.

Consider the following statements that use the matrix from the previous discussion:

```
A = [2,1; 4,3];
rank(A)
B = inv(A)
```

The value computed for the rank of **A** is 2, and the value of **B** is shown below:

$$\mathbf{B} = \begin{bmatrix} 1.5 & -0.5 \\ -2 & 1 \end{bmatrix}$$

The following statements determine the rank of a matrix **c** and then either compute the inverse of **c** or print a message indicating that the inverse of the matrix does not exist:

```
[nr,nc] = size(C);
if rank(C) == nr
    fprintf('Matrix Inverse: \n');
    inv(C)
else
    fprintf('Inverse does not exist. \n');
end
```

Style

As illustrated in this example, you should avoid performing computations that generate MATLAB error messages. *Instead, include your own error checks so that you can print more specific messages.*

DETERMINANTS

Determinant

A **determinant** is a scalar computed from the entries in a square matrix. Determinants have various applications in engineering, including computing inverses and solving systems of simultaneous equations. For a 2×2 matrix A, the determinant is

$$|A| = a_{1,1}a_{2,2} - a_{2,1}a_{1,2}$$

Therefore, the determinant of A, or $|A|$, is equal to 8 for the following matrix:

$$A = \begin{bmatrix} 1 & 3 \\ -1 & 5 \end{bmatrix}$$

For a 3×3 matrix A, the determinant is the following:

$$|A| = a_{1,1}a_{2,2}a_{3,3} + a_{1,2}a_{2,3}a_{3,1} + a_{1,3}a_{2,1}a_{3,2} - a_{3,1}a_{2,2}a_{1,3} - a_{3,2}a_{2,3}a_{1,1}$$
$$- a_{3,3}a_{2,1}a_{1,2}$$

If A is the following matrix,

$$A = \begin{bmatrix} 1 & 3 & 0 \\ -1 & 5 & 2 \\ 1 & 2 & 1 \end{bmatrix}$$

then $|A|$ is equal to $5 + 6 + 0 - 0 - 4 - (-3)$, or 10. A more involved process is necessary for computing determinants of matrices with more than three rows and columns.

MATLAB will compute the determinant of a matrix using the **det** function:

det(A)   Computes the determinant of a square matrix **A**.

Thus, the value of **det([1,3,0; -1,5,2; 1,2,1])** is 10.

Practice!

Use MATLAB to define the following matrices. Then compute the specified matrices and determinants if they exist.

$$A = \begin{bmatrix} 2 & 1 \\ 0 & -1 \\ 3 & 0 \end{bmatrix} \qquad B = \begin{bmatrix} 1 & 3 \\ -1 & 5 \end{bmatrix}$$

$$C = \begin{bmatrix} 3 & 2 \\ -1 & -2 \\ 0 & 2 \end{bmatrix} \qquad D = \begin{bmatrix} 1 & 2 \end{bmatrix}$$

1. $(AC^T)^{-1}$ 2. $|B|$
3. $|AC^T|$ 4. $(C^T A)^{-1}$

EIGENVECTORS AND EIGENVALUES

Assume that A is an $n \times n$ square matrix. Let X be a column vector with n rows, and let λ be a scalar. Consider the following equation:

$$AX = \lambda X \tag{4.1}$$

Both sides of this equation are equal to a column vector with n rows. If X is filled with zeros, this equation is true for any value of λ, but this is a trivial solution. The values of λ for which X are non-zero are called the **eigenvalues** of the matrix A, and the corresponding values of X are called the **eigenvectors** of the matrix A.

Eigenvalue
Eigenvector

Equation (4.1) can also be used to determine the following equation:

$$(A - \lambda I) X = 0 \tag{4.2}$$

where I is an $n \times n$ identity matrix. This equation represents a set of homogeneous equations, because the right side of the equation is zero. A set of homogeneous equations has nontrivial solutions if and only if the determinant is equal to zero:

$$|A - \lambda I| = 0 \tag{4.3}$$

Equation (4.2) represents an equation that is referred to as the **characteristic equation** of the matrix A. The solutions to the equation are also the eigenvalues of the matrix A.

In many applications, it is desirable to select eigenvectors so that $QQ^T = I$, where Q is the matrix whose columns are eigenvectors. This set of eigenvectors represents an orthonormal set, which means that they are both normalized and that they are mutually orthogonal. (A set of vectors is **orthonormal** if the dot product of a vector with itself is equal to unity and the dot product of a vector with another vector in the set is zero.)

To illustrate these relationships between a matrix A and its eigenvalues and eigenvectors, consider the following matrix A:

$$A = \begin{bmatrix} 0.50 & 0.25 \\ 0.25 & 0.50 \end{bmatrix}$$

The eigenvalues can be computed using the characteristic equation:

$$|A - \lambda I| = \begin{vmatrix} 0.50 - \lambda & 0.25 \\ 0.25 & 0.50 - \lambda \end{vmatrix}$$

$$= \lambda^2 - \lambda + 0.1875$$

$$= 0$$

This equation can be solved easily using the quadratic equation, yielding $\lambda_0 = 0.25$ and $\lambda_1 = 0.75$. (For a matrix A with more than two rows and two columns, determining the eigenvalues by hand can be a formidable task.) The eigenvectors can be determined using the eigenvalues and Equation 4.2, as shown here with the eigenvalue 0.25:

$$\begin{bmatrix} 0.50 - 0.25 & 0.25 \\ 0.25 & 0.50 - 0.25 \end{bmatrix} \begin{bmatrix} x_1 \\ x_2 \end{bmatrix} = \begin{bmatrix} 0 \\ 0 \end{bmatrix}$$

or

$$\begin{bmatrix} 0.25 & 0.25 \\ 0.25 & 0.25 \end{bmatrix} \begin{bmatrix} x_1 \\ x_2 \end{bmatrix} = \begin{bmatrix} 0 \\ 0 \end{bmatrix}$$

But this pair of equations yields the following equation:

$$x_1 = - x_2$$

Therefore, there are an infinite number of eigenvectors that are associated with the eigenvalue 0.25. Some of these eigenvectors are shown below:

$$\begin{bmatrix} 1 \\ -1 \end{bmatrix} \begin{bmatrix} 5 \\ -5 \end{bmatrix} \begin{bmatrix} 0.2 \\ -0.2 \end{bmatrix}$$

Similarly, it can be shown that the eigenvectors associated with the eigenvalue 0.75 have the following relationship:

$$x_1 = x_2$$

Again, an infinite number of eigenvectors are associated with this eigenvalue, such as

$$\begin{bmatrix} 1.5 \\ 1.5 \end{bmatrix} \begin{bmatrix} -5 \\ -5 \end{bmatrix} \begin{bmatrix} -0.2 \\ -0.2 \end{bmatrix}$$

To determine the orthonormal set of eigenvectors for the simple example that we have been using, recall that we want to select the eigenvectors so that $QQ^T = I$. Therefore, consider the following:

$$\begin{aligned} QQ^T &= \begin{bmatrix} c_1 & c_2 \\ -c_1 & c_2 \end{bmatrix} \begin{bmatrix} c_1 & -c_1 \\ c_2 & c_2 \end{bmatrix} \\ &= \begin{bmatrix} c_1^2 + c_2^2 & -c_1^2 + c_2^2 \\ -c_1^2 + c_2^2 & c_1^2 + c_2^2 \end{bmatrix} \\ &= \begin{bmatrix} 1 & 0 \\ 0 & 1 \end{bmatrix} \end{aligned}$$

Solving this set of equations gives

$$c_1^2 = c_2^2 = 0.5$$

Thus, c_1 can be either $1/(\sqrt{2})$ or $-1/(\sqrt{2})$; similarly, c_2 can be either $1/(\sqrt{2})$ or $1/(\sqrt{2})$. Thus, there are several variations of the same values that can be used to determine the set of orthonormal eigenvectors. We shall choose the following:

$$Q = \begin{bmatrix} \dfrac{1}{\sqrt{2}} & \dfrac{1}{\sqrt{2}} \\ -\dfrac{1}{\sqrt{2}} & \dfrac{1}{\sqrt{2}} \end{bmatrix}$$

The computations to obtain the eigenvectors and the associated set of orthonormal eigenvectors has been relatively simple for a matrix A with two rows and two columns. However, it should be evident that the computations become quite difficult as the size of the matrix A increases. Therefore, it is very convenient to be able to use MATLAB to determine both the eigenvectors and eigenvalues for a matrix A:

eig(A)   Computes a column vector containing the eigen-
                               values of **A**.

[Q,d] = eig(A)	Computes a square matrix Q containing the eigenvectors of A as columns and a square matrix d containing the eigenvalues (λ) of A on the diagonal. The values of Q and d are such that Q*Q' is the identity matrix and A*x equals λ times x.

We can illustrate the **eig** function with the example developed in this section as shown in the following statements:

```
A = [0.50, 0.25; 0.25, 0.50];
[Q,d] = eig(A);
```

The values of Q and d are the following:

$$Q = \begin{bmatrix} 0.7071 & 0.7071 \\ -0.7071 & 0.7071 \end{bmatrix}$$

$$d = \begin{bmatrix} 0.25 & 0.0 \\ 0.0 & 0.75 \end{bmatrix}$$

These values match the values that we computed by hand for this example, but remember that the solution is not unique; thus, hand computations could yield a different solution than the MATLAB function. Using matrix multiplication, we can easily verify that Q*Q' is the identity matrix and A*x equals λ times x.

Practice!

Let A be the following matrix:

$$\begin{bmatrix} 4 & 3 & 0 \\ 3 & 6 & 2 \\ 0 & 2 & 4 \end{bmatrix}$$

Use MATLAB to answer the following questions:

1. Determine λ_1, λ_2, λ_3, the three eigenvalues of A.
2. Determine a set of orthonormal eigenvectors, X_1, X_2, X_3 so that X_1 is associated with λ_1, and so on.
3. Compute $|A - \lambda I|$ and verify that it is equal to zero for each eigenvalue.
4. Show that $AQ = Qd$ where Q is the matrix containing the eigenvectors as columns and d is the matrix containing the corresponding eigenvalues on the main diagonal and zeros elsewhere.

DECOMPOSITIONS

In this section, we present three **decompositions** or **factorizations** of matrices that can be useful in solving problems containing matrices. Each of these techniques decomposes a matrix A into a product of other matrices. The use of the factored product reduces the number of calculations needed for many types of matrix computations; thus, many numerical techniques that use matrices convert the matrices into decomposed or factored forms.

Triangular Factorization. Triangular factorization expresses a square matrix as the product of two triangular matrices—a lower triangular matrix (or permuted lower triangular matrix) and an upper triangular matrix. This factorization is often called an **LU factorization** (for lower-upper). The LU factorization is not a unique factorization.

Triangular factorization is often used to simplify computations involving matrices. It is one of the steps often used in computing the determinant of a large matrix, computing the inverse of a matrix, and solving simultaneous linear equations.

The factorization can be performed by starting with the product IA where I is the same size as A. Row and column operations are performed on A to reduce it to an upper triangular form; the same operations are performed on the identity matrix. In the process of performing the row operations, we may find it necessary to interchange rows in order to produce the desired upper triangular form. These same row interchanges are performed on the identity matrix and will result in the identity matrix being transformed into a permuted lower triangular matrix instead of a strict lower triangular matrix. To illustrate, let A and B be the following matrices:

$$A = \begin{bmatrix} 1 & 2 & -1 \\ -2 & -5 & 3 \\ -1 & -3 & 0 \end{bmatrix} \quad B = \begin{bmatrix} 1 & 3 & 2 \\ -2 & -6 & 1 \\ 2 & 5 & 7 \end{bmatrix}$$

Using the process described above, it can be shown that A and B can be factored into the LU forms shown below:

$$A = \begin{bmatrix} 1 & 0 & 0 \\ -2 & 1 & 0 \\ -1 & 1 & 1 \end{bmatrix} \begin{bmatrix} 1 & 2 & -1 \\ 0 & -1 & 1 \\ 0 & 0 & -2 \end{bmatrix}$$

$$B = \begin{bmatrix} 1 & 0 & 0 \\ -2 & 0 & 1 \\ 2 & 1 & 0 \end{bmatrix} \begin{bmatrix} 1 & 3 & 2 \\ 0 & -1 & 3 \\ 0 & 0 & 5 \end{bmatrix}$$

Note that the factorization of B yields a permuted lower triangular form; if rows 2 and 3 are interchanged, the permuted lower triangular form becomes a strict lower triangular form.

The `lu` function in MATLAB computes the LU factorization:

`[L,U] = lu(A)`   Computes a permuted lower triangular factor in `L` and an upper triangular factor in `U` such that the product of `L` and `U` is equal to `A`.

To compute the LU factorization of the two matrices used in the example above, we use the following statements:

```
A = [1,2,-1; -2,-5,3; -1,-3,0];
[LA,UA] = lu(A);
B = [1,3,2; -2,-6,1; 2,5,7];
[LB,UB] = lu(B);
```

The LU factorization yields the following matrices:

$$\text{LA} = \begin{bmatrix} -0.5 & 1 & 0 \\ 1 & 0 & 0 \\ 0.5 & 1 & 1 \end{bmatrix} \quad \text{UA} = \begin{bmatrix} -2 & -5 & 3 \\ 0 & -0.5 & 0.5 \\ 0 & 0 & -2 \end{bmatrix}$$

$$\text{LB} = \begin{bmatrix} -0.5 & 0 & 1 \\ 1 & 0 & 0 \\ -1 & 1 & 0 \end{bmatrix} \quad \text{UB} = \begin{bmatrix} -2 & -6 & 1 \\ 0 & -1 & 8 \\ 0 & 0 & 2.5 \end{bmatrix}$$

It is easily verified that `A` is equal to `LA*UA`, and that `B` is equal to `LB*UB`. It is also interesting to observe that neither factorization matches the one generated by hand earlier in this section; this is not a concern, because it was pointed out that the LU factorization is not a unique factorization. Also, note that both factorizations include a permuted lower triangular factor.

QR Factorization. The QR factorization technique factors a matrix A into the product of an orthonormal matrix and an upper-triangular matrix. (Recall that a matrix Q is orthonormal if $QQ^T = I$.) It is not necessary that the matrix A be a square matrix in order to perform a QR factorization.

The QR factorization can be determined from performing the **Gram-Schmidt** process on the column vectors in A to obtain an orthonormal basis. The least-squares solution of an overdetermined system AX = B is the solution of the square system $RX = Q^TB$.

The `qr` function is used to perform the QR factorization in MATLAB:

`[Q,R] = qr(A)`   Computes the values of `Q` and `R` such that `A = QR`. `Q` will be an orthonormal matrix, and `R` will be an upper triangular matrix.

For a matrix `A` of size $m \times n$, the size of `Q` is $m \times m$, and the size of `R` is $m \times n$.

Singular Value Decomposition. The singular value decomposition (SVD) is another orthogonal matrix factorization. SVD is the most reliable decomposition, but it can require up to ten times as many arithmetic operations as the QR factorization. SVD decomposes a matrix A (of size $m \times n$) into a product of three matrix factors,

A = USV

where U and V are orthogonal matrices and S is a diagonal matrix. The size of U is $m \times m$, the size of V is $n \times n$, and the size of S is $m \times n$. The values on the diagonal matrix S are called singular values and, thus, give the decomposition technique its name. The number of nonzero singular values is equal to the rank of the matrix.

The SVD factorization can be be obtained using the **svd** function:

[U,S,V] = svd(A)	Computes the factorization of **A** into the product of three matrices, **USV**, where **U** and **V** are orthogonal matrices and **S** is a diagonal matrix.
svd(A)	Returns the diagonal elements of S, which are the singular values of **A**.

One of the main uses of the SVD factorization is in solving least squares problems. This application can also be extended to using the SVD for data compression.

CHAPTER SUMMARY

In this chapter, we defined the transpose, the inverse, the rank, and the determinant of a matrix. We also defined the computation of a dot product (between two vectors) and a matrix product (between two matrices). In addition, we presented MATLAB functions for computing the eigenvalues and eigenvectors of a matrix and for computing several different factorizations of a matrix.

KEY TERMS

determinant   rank
dot product   transpose
inverse

MATLAB SUMMARY

This MATLAB summary lists all the special symbols, commands, and functions that were defined in this chapter. A brief description is also included for each one.

SPECIAL CHARACTERS

'	Indicates a matrix transpose
*	Indicates matrix multiplication

COMMANDS AND FUNCTIONS

det	Computes the determinant of a matrix
dot	Computes the dot product of two vectors
eig	Computes the eigenvalues and eigenvectors of a matrix
inv	Computes the inverse of a matrix
lu	Computes the LU factorization of a matrix
qr	Computes the QR factorization of a matrix
rank	Computes the rank of a matrix
svd	Computes the SVD factorization of a matrix

Style NOTES

1. Include your own error checks so that you can print specific messages.

DEBUGGING NOTES

1. Use the **size** function to determine if the product of two matrices exists in order to avoid errors.

PROBLEMS

Amino Acids. The amino acids in proteins contain molecules of oxygen(O), carbon(C), nitrogen(N), sulfur(S), and hydrogen(H), as shown in Table 4.2. The molecular weights for oxygen, carbon, nitrogen, sulfur, and hydrogen are

Oxygen	15.9994
Carbon	12.011
Nitrogen	14.00674
Sulfur	32.066
Hydrogen	1.00794

TABLE 4.2 Amino Acid Molecules

Amino Acid	O	C	N	S	H
Alanine	2	3	1	0	7
Arginine	2	6	4	0	15
Asparagine	3	4	2	0	8
Aspartic	4	4	1	0	6
Cysteine	2	3	1	1	7
Glutamic	4	5	1	0	8
Glutamine	3	5	2	0	10
Glycine	2	2	1	0	5
Histidine	2	6	3	0	10
Isoleucine	2	6	1	0	13
Leucine	2	6	1	0	13
Lysine	2	6	2	0	15
Methionine	2	5	1	1	11
Phenylanlanine	2	9	1	0	11
Proline	2	5	1	0	10
Serine	3	3	1	0	7
Threonine	3	4	1	0	9
Tryptophan	2	11	2	0	11
Tyrosin	3	9	1	0	11
Valine	2	5	1	0	11

1. Write a program in which the user enters the number of oxygen atoms, carbon atoms, nitrogen atoms, sulfur atoms, and hydrogen atoms in an amino acid. Compute and print the corresponding molecular weight. Use a dot product to compute the molecular weight.

2. Write a program that computes the molecular weight of each amino acid in Table 4.2, assuming that the numeric information in this table is contained in a data file named **elements.dat**. Generate a new data file named **weights.dat** that contains the molecular weights of the amino acids. Use matrix multiplication to compute the molecular weights.

3. Modify the program developed in problem 2 so that it also computes and prints the average amino acid molecular weight.

4. Modify the program developed in problem 2 so that it also computes and prints the minimum and maximum molecular weights.

Determinants. The following problems define cofactors and minors of a square matrix and then use them to evaluate a determinant. The value computed is then compared to the determinant computed with the MATLAB function **det**.

5. The minor of an element $a_{i,j}$ of a matrix A is the determinant of the matrix obtained by removing the row and column to which the given element $a_{i,j}$ belongs. Thus, if the original matrix has four rows and columns, the minor is the determinant of a matrix with three rows and columns. Write a function named **minor** to compute the minor of a square matrix with four rows and four columns. The input arguments should be the matrix A and the values of i and j.

6. A cofactor $A_{i,j}$ of a matrix A is the product of the minor of $a_{i,j}$ and the factor $(-1)^{i+j}$. Write a function named **cofactor** to compute a cofactor of a square matrix with four rows and four columns. The arguments should be the matrix A and the values of i and j. You may want to reference the function in problem 5.

7. The determinant of a square matrix A can be computed in the following way:
   (a) Select any column.
   (b) Multiply each element in the column by its cofactor.
   (c) Add the products obtained in step (b).
   Write a function **determinant_r** to compute the determinant of a square matrix with four rows and four columns using this technique. You may want to reference the function developed in problem 6. Compare the value computed to the value computed by the **det** function.

8. The determinant of a square matrix A can be computed in the following way:
   (a) Select any row.
   (b) Multiply each element in the row by its cofactor.
   (c) Add the products obtained in step (b).
   Write a function **determinant_c** to compute the determinant of a square matrix with four rows and four columns using this technique. You may want to reference the function developed in problem 6. Compare the value computed to the value computed by the **det** function.

Factorizations. The following problems refer to the factorizations and decompositions of matrices discussed in this chapter.

9. Write a function **d_matrix** that receives a matrix. If the matrix is a diagonal matrix, the function should return the value 1; otherwise, the function should return the value 0.

10. Write a function `ut_matrix` that receives a matrix. If the matrix is an upper triangular matrix, the function should return the value 1; otherwise, the function should return the value 0.

11. Write a function `lt_matrix` that receives a matrix. If the matrix is a lower triangular matrix, the function should return the value 1; otherwise, the function should return the value 0. (Try to think of how you could use the function from problem 10 in this function.)

12. Write a function `p_ut_matrix` that receives a matrix. If the matrix is a permuted upper triangular matrix, the function should return the value 1; otherwise, the function should return the value 0. You may want to reference the function in problem 10 in your solution.

13. Write a function `p_lt_matrix` that receives a matrix. If the matrix is a permuted lower triangular matrix, the function should return the value 1; otherwise, the function should return the value 0. You may want to reference the function in problem 11 in your solution.

14. Write a function `attributes` that receives a matrix. The function should print any of the following terms that apply to the matrix: diagonal, upper triangular, lower triangular, permuted upper triangular, permuted lower triangular. Use the functions developed in problems 9 through 13.

15. Write a function `disparity` that receives a matrix. The function should return the difference between the largest eigenvalue and the smallest eigenvalue of the matrix.

PART II

Numerical Techniques

The chapters in Part II contain MATLAB operators and functions for performing the most commonly-used numerical techniques. Chapter 5 presents a graphical understanding of the solution to a set of equations, and then presents two techniques in MATLAB to solve a system of linear equations. Chapter 6 discusses interpolation of values between points using linear interpolation and cubic spline interpolation. Then, polynomial regression is used to find the "best fit" polynomial equation for modeling a set of data. In Chapter 7, we review the definitions of integrals and derivatives, and then develop techniques to estimate an integral as the area under a curve using the trapezoidal and Simpson's rule. The estimate of a derivative is performed using slope approximations with a backward difference, forward difference, or central difference. Finally, first-order ordinary differential equations (ODEs) are solved using Runge-Kutta techniques in Chapter 8.

5

Courtesy of General Motors Media Archives.

GRAND CHALLENGE:
Vehicle Performance

The car in this photograph is General Motor's new electric vehicle EV1, which will be distributed and marketed by Saturn Corporation. This car is a zero-emissions vehicle that accelerates from 0 to 60 miles per hour in eight seconds. It has a practical range of 80 miles per charge. (The average daily driving range in the United States is 30 miles a day.) The recharge time is approximately three hours on a 220-volt circuit. Recharging generally would be done overnight to spread the demand for electricity and reduce the burden on power plants. The battery pack consists of 26 12-volt valve regulated lead acid modules. Research within the next decade is expected to help give electric vehicles both performance and operating costs that are competitive with today's gasoline-powered cars.

Solutions to Systems of Linear Equations

OBJECTIVES

We begin this chapter with a graphical description of the solution to a set of simultaneous equations. Figures are used to illustrate the different possible situations that can occur in solving sets of equations with two and three variables. Solutions to sets of equations with more than three variables are discussed in terms of hyperplanes. We then present two different techniques for solving a system of simultaneous equations using matrix operations. Finally, we present an example from electrical circuit analysis that uses a set of simultaneous equations to determine the mesh currents in a circuit.

5.1   Graphical Interpretation

Simultaneous
equations

The need to solve a system of **simultaneous equations** occurs frequently in engineering problems. A number of methods exist for solving a system of equations, but they all involve tedious operations with a number of opportunities to make errors. Therefore, solving a system of equations is an operation that we would like the computer to perform for us. However, we must understand the process so that we can correctly evaluate and interpret the computer's results. To understand the process, we start with a graphical interpretation of the solution to a set of equations.

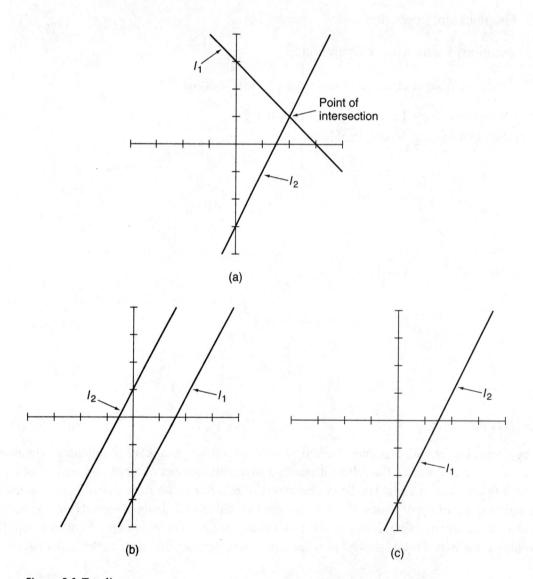

Figure 5.1 *Two lines.*

A linear equation with two variables, such as $2x - y = 3$, defines a straight line and is often written in the form $y = mx + b$, where m represents the slope of the line and b represents the y-intercept. Thus, $2x - y = 3$ can also be written as $y = 2x - 3$. If we have two linear equations, they can represent two different lines that intersect in a single point, or they can represent two parallel lines that never intersect, or they can represent the same line; these possibilities are shown in Figure 5.1. Equations that represent two intersecting lines can be identified easily because they will have different slopes, as in $y = 2x - 3$ and $y = -x + 3$. Equations that represent two parallel lines will have the same slope but different y-intercepts, as in $y = 2x - 3$ and $y = 2x + 1$. Equations that represent the same line have the same slope and y-intercept, as in $y = 2x - 3$ and $3y = 6x - 9$.

If a linear equation contains three variables, x, y, and z, it represents a plane in three-dimensional space. If we have two equations with three variables, they can represent two planes that intersect in a straight line, two parallel planes, or the same plane; these possibilities are shown in Figure 5.2. If we have three equations with three variables, the three planes can intersect in a single point, they can intersect in a line, they can have no common intersection point, or they can represent the same plane. Examples of the possibilities that exist if the three equations define three different planes are shown in Figure 5.3.

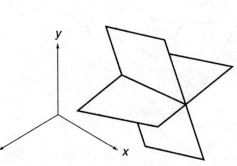

(a)

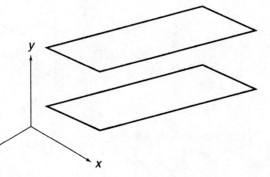

(b)

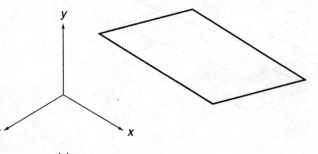

(c)

Figure 5.2 *Two planes.*

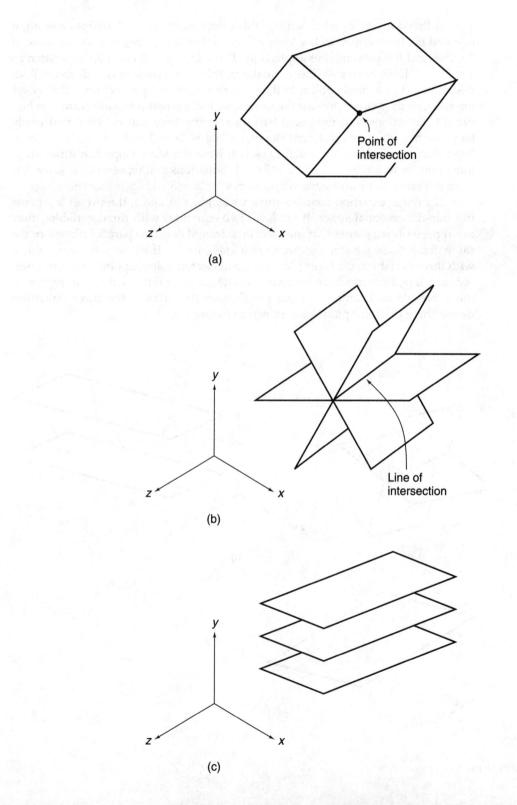

(a)

(b)

(c)

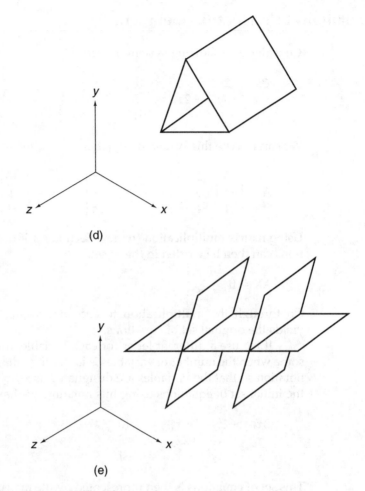

Figure 5.3 *Three distinct planes.*

These ideas can be extended to more than three variables, although it is harder to visualize the corresponding situations. We call the set of points defined by an equation with more than three variables a **hyperplane**. In general, we can consider a set of M linear equations that contain N unknowns, where each equation defines a unique hyperplane that is not identical to any other hyperplanes in the system. If $M < N$, the system is **underspecified**, and a unique solution does not exist. If $M = N$, a unique solution will exist if none of the equations represent parallel hyperplanes. If $M > N$, the system is **overspecified**, and a unique solution does not exist. The set of equations is also called a **system of equations**. A system with a unique solution is called a **nonsingular** system of equations, and a system with no unique solution is called a **singular** set of equations.

In many engineering problems, we are interested in determining if a solution exists to a system of equations. If a solution exists, we want to determine it. In the next section, we discuss two methods for solving a system of equations using MATLAB.

Hyperplane

5.2   Solutions Using Matrix Operations

Consider the following system of three equations with three unknowns:

$$
\begin{aligned}
3x &+2y &-z &= 10 \\
-x &+3y &+2z &= 5 \\
x &-y &-z &= -1
\end{aligned}
$$

We can rewrite this system of equations using the following matrices:

$$
A = \begin{bmatrix} 3 & 2 & -1 \\ -1 & 3 & 2 \\ 1 & -1 & -1 \end{bmatrix} \qquad X = \begin{bmatrix} x \\ y \\ z \end{bmatrix} \qquad B = \begin{bmatrix} 10 \\ 5 \\ -1 \end{bmatrix}
$$

Using matrix multiplication (review Section 4.1 if necessary), the system of equations can then be written in this form:

$$AX = B$$

Go through the multiplication to convince yourself that this matrix equation yields the original set of equations.

If we use a different letter for each variable, the notation becomes cumbersome when the number of variables is larger than three. Therefore, we modify our notation so that the variables are designated as x_1, x_2, x_3, and so on. If we rewrite the initial set of equations using this notation, we have:

$$
\begin{aligned}
3x_1 &+2x_2 &-x_3 &= 10 \\
-x_1 &+3x_2 &+2x_3 &= 5 \\
x_1 &-x_2 &-x_3 &= -1
\end{aligned}
$$

This set of equations is then represented by the matrix equation $AX = B$, where X is the column vector $[x_1, x_2, x_3]^T$.

The matrix equation $AX = B$ is generally used to express a system of equations; however, a system of equations can also be expressed using row vectors for B and X. For example, consider the set of equations used in the previous discussion. We can write the set of equations as $XA = B$ if X, A and B are defined as follows:

$$
X = \begin{bmatrix} x_1 & x_2 & x_3 \end{bmatrix} \qquad A = \begin{bmatrix} 3 & -1 & 1 \\ 2 & 3 & -1 \\ -1 & 2 & -1 \end{bmatrix} \qquad B = \begin{bmatrix} 10 & 5 & -1 \end{bmatrix}
$$

Again, go through the multiplication to convince yourself that the matrix equation generates the original set of equations. (Note that the matrix A in this equation is the transpose of the matrix A in the original matrix equation.)

Style

In order to keep the notation consistent, use matrices named A and B to represent the coefficients from the set of equations. Then, in a comment, be sure to indicate if the system is described by AX=B or XA=B.

A system of equations is nonsingular if the matrix A containing the coefficients of the equations is nonsingular. Recall from Section 4.3 that the **rank** of a matrix can be used to determine if it is nonsingular. Therefore, to avoid errors, evaluate the rank of A (using the `rank` function) to be sure that a system is nonsingular before attempting to compute the solution to it. We now present two methods for solving a nonsingular system.

MATRIX DIVISION

In MATLAB, a system of simultaneous equations can be solved using **matrix division**. The solution to the matrix equation $AX = B$ can be computed using matrix left division, as in `A\B`; the solution to the matrix equation $XA = B$ can be computed using matrix right division, as in `B/A`. (MATLAB uses a **Gauss elimination** numerical technique to perform both left and right matrix division.)

To illustrate, we can define and solve the system of equations in the previous example using the matrix equation $AX = B$ as shown in these statements:

```
A = [3,2,-1;-1,3,2;1,-1,-1];
B = [10,5,-1]';
x = A\B;
```

The vector **x** then contains the following values: $-2, 5, -6$. To confirm that the values of **x** do indeed solve each equation, we can multiply **A** by **x** using the expression **A*x**. The result is a column vector containing the values $10, 5, -1$.

We can also define and solve the same system of equations using the matrix equation $XA=B$ as shown in these statements:

```
A = [3,-1,1; 2,3,-1; -1,2,-1];
B = [10,5,-1];
X = B/A;
```

The vector **x** then contains the following values: $-2, 5, -6$. To confirm that the values of **x** do indeed solve each equation, we can multiply **x** by **A** using the expression **x*A**. The result is a row vector containing the values $10, 5, -1$.

If a set of equations is singular, an error message is displayed; the solution vector may contain values of **NaN** or $+\infty$ or $-\infty$, depending on the values of the matrices **A** and **B**. A set of equations may also define a system that contains some equations describing hyperplanes that are very close to the same hyperplane or are very close to being parallel hyperplanes. These systems are called **ill-conditioned** systems. MATLAB will compute a solution, but a warning message is printed indicating that the results may be inaccurate.

MATRIX INVERSE

A system of equations can also be solved using the inverse of the matrix A, assuming that the inverse exists. For example, assume that A, X, and B are the matrices defined earlier:

$$A = \begin{bmatrix} 3 & 2 & -1 \\ -1 & 3 & 2 \\ 1 & -1 & -1 \end{bmatrix} \qquad X = \begin{bmatrix} x_1 \\ x_2 \\ x_3 \end{bmatrix} \qquad B = \begin{bmatrix} 10 \\ 5 \\ -1 \end{bmatrix}$$

Then, AX = B. Suppose that we premultiply both sides of this matrix equation by A^{-1}, as in

$$A^{-1}AX = A^{-1}B$$

Because $A^{-1}A$ is equal to the identity matrix I, we have

$$IX = A^{-1}B$$

or

$$X = A^{-1}B$$

In MATLAB, we can compute this solution using the following command:

```
X = inv(A)*B
```

This solution is computed using a different technique from the solution using matrix left division, but both solutions will be the same for a system that is not ill-conditioned.

This same system of equations can also be solved using the inverse of a matrix if the system is expressed in the form XA = B, where

$$X = \begin{bmatrix} x_1 & x_2 & x_3 \end{bmatrix} \qquad A = \begin{bmatrix} 3 & -1 & 1 \\ 2 & 3 & -1 \\ -1 & 2 & -1 \end{bmatrix} \qquad B = \begin{bmatrix} 10 & 5 & -1 \end{bmatrix}$$

If we post-multiply the right sides of the matrix equation by A^{-1}, we have

$$XAA^{-1} = BA^{-1}$$

Because AA^{-1} is equal to the identity matrix I, we have

$$XI = BA^{-1}$$

or

$$X = BA^{-1}$$

In MATLAB, we can compute this solution using the following command:

```
X = B*inv(A)
```

Be sure to note that B must be defined to be a row vector if this solution form is used.

Practice!

Solve the following systems of equations using matrix division and inverse matrices. Use MATLAB to verify that each solution solves the system of equations using matrix multiplication. For each system that contains equations with two variables, plot the equations on the same graph to either show the intersection or to show that the system is a singular system without a unique solution.

1. $\begin{aligned} -2x_1 + x_2 &= -3 \\ x_1 + x_2 &= 3 \end{aligned}$

2. $\begin{aligned} -2x_1 + x_2 &= -3 \\ -2x_1 + x_2 &= 1 \end{aligned}$

3. $\begin{aligned} -2x_1 + x_2 &= -3 \\ -6x_1 + 3x_2 &= -9 \end{aligned}$

4. $\begin{aligned} -2x_1 + x_2 &= -3 \\ -2x_1 + x_2 &= -3.00001 \end{aligned}$

5. $\begin{aligned} 3x_1 + 2x_2 - x_3 &= 10 \\ -x_1 + 3x_2 + 2x_3 &= 5 \\ x_1 - x_2 - x_3 &= -1 \end{aligned}$

6. $\begin{aligned} 3x_1 + 2x_2 - x_3 &= 1 \\ -x_1 + 3x_2 + 2x_3 &= 1 \\ x_1 - x_2 - x_3 &= 1 \end{aligned}$

7. $\begin{aligned} 10x_1 - 7x_2 + 0x_3 &= 7 \\ -3x_1 + 2x_2 + 6x_3 &= 4 \\ 5x_1 + x_2 + 5x_3 &= 6 \end{aligned}$

8. $\begin{aligned} x_1 + 4x_2 - x_3 + x_4 &= 2 \\ 2x_1 + 7x_2 + x_3 - 2x_4 &= 16 \\ x_1 + 4x_2 - x_3 + 2x_4 &= 1 \\ 3x_1 - 10x_2 - 2x_3 + 5x_4 &= -15 \end{aligned}$

5.3   Problem Solving Applied: Electrical Circuit Analysis

The analysis of an electrical circuit frequently involves finding the solution to a set of simultaneous equations. These equations are often derived using either current equations that describe the currents entering and leaving a node or voltage equations that describe the voltages around mesh loops in the circuit. For example, consider the circuit shown in Figure 5.4. The three equations that describe the voltages around the three loops are the following:

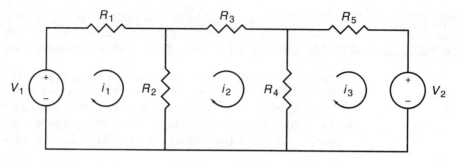

Figure 5.4 *Circuit with two voltage sources.*

$$
\begin{aligned}
-V_1 && +R_1 i_1 && +R_2(i_1 - i_2) && = 0 \\
R_2(i_2 - i_1) && +R_3 i_2 && +R_4(i_2 - i_3) && = 0 \\
R_4(i_3 - i_2) && +R_5 i_3 && +V_2 && = 0
\end{aligned}
$$

If we assume that the values of the resistors (R_1, R_2, R_3, R_4, R_5) and the voltage sources (V_1, V_2) are known, the unknowns in the system of equations are the mesh currents (i_1, i_2, i_3). We can then rearrange the system of equations to the following form:

$$
\begin{aligned}
(R_1 + R_2)\, i_1 && - R_2 i_2 && +0\, i_3 && = && V_1 \\
-R_2 i_1 && +(R_2 + R_3 + R_4) i_2 && -R_4 i_3 && = && 0 \\
0\, i_1 && -R_4 i_2 && +(R_4 + R_5) i_3 && = && -V_2
\end{aligned}
$$

Write a MATLAB program that allows the user to enter the values of the five resistors and the values of the two voltage sources. The program should then compute the three mesh currents.

1.   PROBLEM STATEMENT

Using input values for the resistors and voltage sources, compute the three mesh currents in the circuit shown in Figure 5.4.

2.   INPUT/OUTPUT DESCRIPTION

The following I/O diagram shows the five resistor value inputs and the two voltage source inputs to the program. The output consists of the three mesh currents.

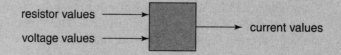

3.   HAND EXAMPLE

For a hand example, we use the following values:

$$R_1 = R_2 = R_3 = R_4 = R_5 = 1 \text{ ohm}$$
$$V_1 = V_2 = 5 \text{ volts}$$

The corresponding set of equations is then

$$
\begin{array}{rrrcr}
2i_1 & -i_2 & + 0i_3 & = & 5 \\
-i_1 & +3i_2 & -i_3 & = & 0 \\
0i_1 & -i_2 & +2i_3 & = & -5
\end{array}
$$

We can use MATLAB to compute the solution using either matrix division or the inverse of a matrix. For this example, we use the following steps:

```
A = [2,-1,0;-1,3,-1;0,-1,2];
B = [5,0,-5]';
X = A\B
ERR = sum(A*X-B)
```

The values in the solution vector are printed, along with the sum of the values of A*X-B, which should be 0 if the system is nonsingular. For this example, the output is the following:

```
X =
        2.5000
        0
       -2.5000
ERR =
        0
```

4.   MATLAB SOLUTION

In the MATLAB solution, we will ask the user to enter the circuit parameters. After solving the system of equations, we print the resulting mesh currents, which can then be used to compute the current or voltage at any point in the circuit. Although we used the variable i to match the equation notation, we need to be aware that we could not then use i for complex number computations.

```
%     This program reads resistor and voltage values
%     and then computes the corresponding mesh
%     currents for a specified electrical circuit.
%
R = input('Enter resistor values in ohms, [R1...R5] ');
V = input('Enter voltage values in volts, [V1 V2] ');
%
```

```
%     Initialize matrix A and vector B using AX = B form.
%
A = [ R(1)+R(2),              -R(2),               0 ;
           -R(2),   R(2)+R(3)+R(4),           -R(4) ;
               0,             -R(4),   R(4)+R(5) ];
B = [ V(1) ;
          0 ;
      -V(2) ];
%
if rank(A) == 3
   fprintf('Mesh Currents \n')
   i = A\B
else
   fprintf('No Unique Solution')
end
```

5. TESTING

The following program interaction verifies the data used in the hand example:

```
Enter resistor values in ohms, [R1...R5] [1 1 1 1 1]
Enter voltage values in volts, [V1 V2] [5 5]
Mesh Currents
i =
    2.5000
         0
   -2.5000
```

The next interaction computes the mesh currents using a different set of resistor values and voltage values.

```
Enter resistor values in ohms, [R1...R5] [2 8 6 6 4]
Enter voltage values in volts, [V1 V2] [40 20]
Mesh Currents
i =
    5.6000
    2.0000
   -0.8000
```

Verify this solution by multiplying the matrix **A** by the vector **i**.

CHAPTER SUMMARY

We began this chapter with a graphical interpretation of the solution of a set of simultaneous equations. We presented graphs illustrating the various cases that could occur with equations of two variables and with equations of three variables. We then extended the discussion to a discussion of N equations with N

unknowns, assuming that each equation represented a hyperplane. Two methods for solving a nonsingular system of equations using matrix operations were presented. One method uses matrix division; the other uses the inverse of a matrix to solve the system of equations. The techniques are illustrated with an example that solves a system of simultaneous equations to determine mesh currents.

KEY TERMS

hyperplane	rank
ill-conditioned	simultaneous equations
inverse	singular
nonsingular	system of equations
overspecified system	underspecified system

MATLAB SUMMARY

This MATLAB summary lists all the special symbols, commands, and functions that were defined in this chapter. A brief description is also included for each one.

SPECIAL CHARACTERS

\	matrix left division
/	matrix right division

Style NOTES

1. For documentation purposes, use the matrices **A** and **B** to store the coefficients of a system of equations. Then, in a comment, indicate if the form is AX = B or XA = B.

DEBUGGING NOTES

1. Use the **rank** function to be sure that a system of equations is nonsingular before attempting to compute the solution.

PROBLEMS

Problems 1–3 relate to the engineering applications presented in this chapter. Problems 4–8 relate to new engineering applications.

Electrical Circuit. These problems relate to the electrical circuit analysis problem given in Section 5.3.

1. Modify the program developed in Section 5.3 so that it accepts the resistor values in kilo-ohms. Be sure to modify the rest of the program accordingly.

2. Modify the program developed in Section 5.3 so that the two voltage sources are constrained to always be the same value.

3. Modify the program developed in Section 5.3 so that the voltage sources are each 5 volts. Then assume that the resistor values are all equal. Compute the mesh currents for resistor values of 100, 200, 300, . . ., 1000 ohms.

Single Voltage Source Electrical Circuit. These problems present a system of equations generated by an electrical circuit with a single voltage source and five resistors.

4. The following set of equations defines the mesh currents in the circuit shown in Figure 5.5. Write a MATLAB program to compute the mesh currents using resistor values and voltage source value entered by the program user.

$$-V_1 \quad +R_2(i_1 - i_2) \quad +R_4(i_1 - i_3) = 0$$
$$R_1 i_2 \quad +R_3(i_2 - i_3) \quad +R_2(i_2 - i_1) = 0$$
$$R_3(i_3 - i_2) \quad +R_5 i_3 \quad +R_4(i_3 - i_1) = 0$$

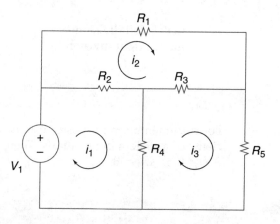

Figure 5.5. *Circuit with one voltage source.*

5. Modify the program in problem 4 so that it prints the coefficients and constants for the system of equations that is being solved.

Simultaneous Equations. Assume that a data file named **eqns.dat** contains the coefficients for a set of simultaneous equations. Each line in the file contains the coefficients and the constant for one equation; the data file contains data for N equations with N unknowns.

6. Write a program to read the data file **eqns.dat**. Determine if any of the equations represent parallel hyperplanes. (Recall that the equations for two parallel hyperplanes have the same linear coefficients or are multiples of the same coefficients, but with different constants.) Print the data for each group of lines that represents parallel hyperplanes.

7. Write a program to read the data file **eqns.dat**. Determine if any of the equations represent the same hyperplanes. (Recall that the equations for the same hyperplanes will be equal or multiples of each other.) Print the data for each group of lines that represents the same hyperplane.

8. Combine the steps in the previous two problems to generate a program that prints only the data for the equations from the data file that represent distinct and nonparallel hyperplanes. Also print the number of the equations that are left.

Inverse Matrix Solutions. Use the inverse matrix to determine the solutions to the following sets of linear equations. Describe each set using $AX = B$ notation and $XA = B$ notation; compare solutions using both notational forms. Use the transpose operator to convert the matrices from one form to the other.

9. $x + y + z + t = 4$
    $2x - y + t = 2$
    $3x + y - z - t = 2$
    $x - 2y - 3z + t = -3$

10. $2x + 3y + z + t = 1$
    $x - y - z + t = 1$
    $3x + y + z + 2t = 0$
    $-x + z - t = -2$

11. $x - 2y + z + t = 3$
    $x + z = t$
    $2y - z = t$
    $x + 4y + 2z - t = 1$

12. $x + 2y - w = 0$
    $3x + y + 4z + 2w = 3$
    $2x - 3y - z + 5w = 1$
    $x + 2z + 2w = -1$

Intersecting Hyperplanes. For each of the following points, generate two different sets of simultaneous equations that intersect uniquely in the given point. Then solve each set of equations to verify that the solution is the one expected.

13. $[3,-5,7]$

14. $[0,-2,1.5,5]$

15. $[1,2,3,-2,-1]$

Courtesy of NASA/Johnson Space Center.

GRAND CHALLENGE:
Vehicle Performance

The collection of data is an important part of developing new scientific principles and theories. In this photo, an astronaut sets up for a lengthy space suit thermal test in the cargo bay of the Endeavour. Also shown is the remote manipulator system that is used to move items into and out of the shuttle bay. Manipulator systems like this one and many others on various types of robots use an advanced control system to guide the manipulator arm to desired locations. One of the requirements of such a control system is that the arm must move from one location to another along a smooth path, avoiding sharp jerks that might cause objects to slip out of its grasp or damage the object or the arm itself.

Interpolation
and Curve Fitting

OBJECTIVES

In this chapter, we assume that we have a set of data that has been collected from an experiment or from observing a physical phenomenon. This data can generally be considered coordinates of points of a function $f(x)$. We would like to use these data points to determine estimates of the function $f(x)$ for values of x that were not part of the original set of data. For example, suppose that we have data points $(a, f(a))$ and $(c, f(c))$. If we want to estimate the value of $f(b)$, where $a < b < c$, we could assume that a straight line joins $f(a)$ and $f(c)$ and then use linear interpolation to obtain the value of $f(b)$. If we assume that the points $f(a)$ and $f(c)$ are joined by a cubic (third-degree) polynomial, we would use a cubic-spline interpolation method to obtain the value of $f(b)$. Most interpolation problems can be solved using one of these methods. A similar type of engineering problem requires computating an equation for a function that is a "good fit" to the data points. In this type of problem, it is not necessary that the function actually go through all the given points, but it should be a "best fit" in some sense. Least-squares methods provide a best fit in terms of minimizing the square of the distances between the given points and the function. We now provide further discussion and examples of interpolation and curve fitting.

6.1   Interpolation

In this section, we present two types of interpolation—linear interpolation and cubic-spline interpolation. In both techniques, we assume that we have a set of xy coordinates, for which y is a function of x; that is, $y = f(x)$. We further assume that we need to estimate a value $f(b)$ that is not one of the original data points, but for which b is between two of the x values from the original set of data points. In Figure 6.1, we show a set of six data points that have been connected with straight-line segments and with cubic (third-degree) polynomial segments. From this figure, we see that the values determined for the function between sample points depend on the type of interpolation that we select.

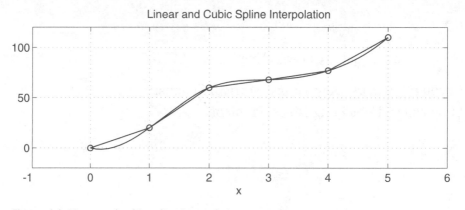

Figure 6.1 *Linear and cubic-spline interpolation.*

LINEAR INTERPOLATION

One of the most common techniques for estimating data between two given data points is **linear interpolation**. Figure 6.2 shows a graph with data points, $f(a)$ and $f(c)$. If we assume that the function between the two points can be estimated by a straight line, then we can compute the function value at any point between the two data values, using an equation derived from similar triangles. This general equation is

$$f(b) = f(a) + \frac{b - a}{c - a} \cdot (f(c) - f(a))$$

Given a set of data points, it is relatively straightforward to interpolate for a new point between two of the given points. However, the interpolation takes several steps, because we must first find the two values in our data between which the desired point falls. When we find these two values, we can use the interpolation equation. All these steps are performed by the MATLAB interpolation function `interp1`.

The `interp1` function performs interpolation using vectors of **x** and **y** values. Linear interpolation is the default interpolation technique, although it can also be

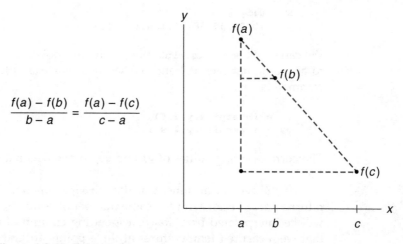

$$\frac{f(a) - f(b)}{b - a} = \frac{f(a) - f(c)}{c - a}$$

Figure 6.2 *Similar triangles.*

specified explicitly in the function. The function assumes that vectors **x** and **y** contain the original data values and that another vector **x_new** contains the new points for which we want to compute interpolated **y_new** values. The **x** values should be in ascending order, and the **x_new** values should be within the range of the **x** values in order for the function to work properly:

interp1(x,y,x_new)	Returns a vector of the size of **x_new**, which contains the interpolated **y** values that correspond to **x_new** using linear interpolation.
interp1(x,y,x_new,'linear')	Returns a vector of the size of **x_new**, which contains the interpolated **y** values that correspond to **x_new** using linear interpolation.

To illustrate the use of this function, we use the following set of temperature measurements taken from the cylinder head in a new engine that is being tested for possible use in a race car:

Time, s	Temperature, °F
0	0
1	20
2	60
3	68
4	77
5	110

We first store this information in vectors:

```
x = 0:5;
y = [0,20,60,68,77,110];
```

We can then use the **interp1** function to interpolate a temperature to correspond to any time between 0.0 and 5.0 seconds. For example, consider the following commands:

```
y1 = interp1(x,y,2.6);
y2 = interp1(x,y,4.9);
```

The corresponding values of **y1** and **y2**, to one decimal of accuracy, are 64.8 and 106.7.

If the second argument of the **interp1** function is a matrix, the function returns a row vector with the same number of columns, and each value returned will be interpolated from its corresponding column of data. Therefore, suppose that we measured temperatures at three points around the cylinder head in the engine, instead of at just one point, as in the previous example. The set of data is then the following:

Time, s	Temp1	Temp2	Temp3
0	0	0	0
1	20	25	52
2	60	62	90
3	68	67	91
4	77	82	93
5	110	103	96

We store this information in a matrix, with the time data in the first column:

```
x(:,1) = (0:5)';
y(:,1) = [0,20,60,68,77,110]';
y(:,2) = [0,25,62,67,82,103]';
y(:,3) = [0,52,90,91,93,96]';
```

To determine interpolated values of temperature at the three points in the engine at 2.6 seconds, we use the following command:

```
temps = interp1(x,y,2.6);
```

The value of **temps** is then [64.8, 65.0, 90.6].

CUBIC-SPLINE INTERPOLATION

Cubic spline   A **cubic spline** is a smooth curve constructed to go through a set of points. The curve between each pair of points is a third-degree polynomial, which is computed to provide a smooth curve between the two points and to provide a smooth transition from the third-degree polynomial between the previous two points.

Refer to the cubic spline shown in Figure 6.1 that connects six points; a total of five different cubic equations are used to generate this smooth function that joins all six points.

A cubic spline is computed in MATLAB with the **interp1** function using an argument that specifies cubic-spline interpolation as opposed to using the default linear interpolation. This function assumes that vectors **x** and **y** contain the original data values and that another vector **x_new** contains the new points for which we want to compute interpolated **y_new** values. The **x** values should be in ascending order, and the **x_new** values should be within the range of the **x** values:

interp1(x,y,x_new,'spline')   Returns a column vector which contains the interpolated **y** values that correspond to **x_new** using cubic-spline interpolation.

To illustrate, suppose that we want to use cubic-spline, instead of linear, interpolation to compute the temperature of the cylinder head at 2.6 seconds. We can use the following statements:

```
x = 0:5;
y = [0,20,60,68,77,110];
temp1 = interp1(x,y,2.6,'spline')
```

The value of **temp1** is 67.3. If we want to use cubic-spline interpolation to compute the temperatures at two different times, we can use this statement:

```
temp2 = interp1(x,y,[2.6,4.9],'spline')
```

The value of **temp2** is [67.3, 105.2]. (The values computed using linear interpolation were [64.8, 106.7].)

If we want to plot a cubic-spline curve over a range of values, we can generate a **new_x** vector with the desired resolution of the curve and then use the **new_x** vector as the third parameter in the **interp1** function. For example, the following statements generated the functions in Figure 6.1:

```
%    These statements compare linear interpolation
%    with cubic spline interpolation.
%
x = 0:5;
y = [0,20,60,68,77,110];
new_x = 0:0.1:5;
new_y1 = interp1(x,y,new_x,'linear');
new_y2 = interp1(x,y,new_x,'spline');
subplot(2,1,1),...
   plot(new_x,new_y1,new_x,new_y2,x,y,'o'),...
   title('Linear and Cubic Spline Interpolation'),...
   xlabel('x'),grid,...
   axis([-1,6,-20,120])
```

Practice!

Assume that we have the following set of data points:

Time, s	Temperature, °F
0.0	72.5
0.5	78.1
1.0	86.4
1.5	92.3
2.0	110.6
2.5	111.5
3.0	109.3
3.5	110.2
4.0	110.5
4.5	109.9
5.0	110.2

1. Generate a plot to compare connecting the temperature points with straight lines and with a cubic spline.
2. Compute temperature values at the following times using linear interpolation and cubic-spline interpolation.

   0.3, 1.25, 2.36, 4.48

3. Compare time values that correspond to these temperatures using linear interpolation and cubic-spline interpolation.

   81, 96, 100, 106

6.2   Problem Solving Applied: Robot Arm Manipulators

The introductory picture for this chapter shows the shuttle remote manipulator system grasping the Gamma Ray Observatory (GRO) as it begins to move the GRO out of the shuttle bay. Manipulator systems like this one and many others on various types of robots use an advanced control system to guide the manipulator arm to desired locations. One of the requirements of such a control system is that the arm must move from one location to another along a smooth path, avoiding sharp jerks that might cause objects to slip out of its grasp or damage the object or the arm itself. Therefore, the path for the arm is initially designed in terms of a number of points over which the arm is to move. Then, interpolation is used to design a smooth curve that will contain all the points. We will consider this problem assuming that the manipulator arm is moving in a plane, although a manipulator arm generally is moving in three-dimensional instead of two-dimensional space.

An important part of developing an algorithm or solution to a problem is to consider carefully whether or not there are any special cases that need to be considered. In this problem, we are assuming that the points over which the arm must pass are in a data file. We are assuming also that the points are in the necessary order for the arm to move to a location to grasp an object, to move to a location to release the object, and to move back to the original position. We will also assume that intermediate points are included in the path to guide the arm away from obstructions or to guide it over sensors that are collecting information. Therefore, each point will have three coordinates—the x and y coordinates relative to the home position of the manipulator arm and a third coordinate coded as follows:

Code	Interpretation
0	home position
1	intermediate positions
2	location of object to grasp
3	location to release object

We want to use a cubic spline to guide the manipulator arm to the object, then to the release point, and then back to the original position.

1.   **PROBLEM STATEMENT**

Design a smooth curve, using cubic-spline interpolation, that can be used to guide a manipulator arm to a location to grasp an object, to another location to release the object, and then back to the original position.

2.   **INPUT/OUTPUT DESCRIPTION**

The following diagram shows that the input is a file containing the xy coordinates of the points over which the manipulator arm must pass. The output of the program is the smooth curve covering these points.

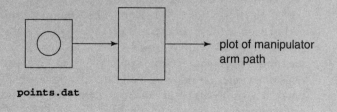

plot of manipulator arm path

points.dat

3.   HAND EXAMPLE

One of the functions of the hand example is to determine if there are any special cases that we must consider in developing the solution to the problem. Therefore, for a small example, we will consider a data file containing the following set of points for guiding the manipulator arm:

x	y	Code	Interpretation
0	0	0	home position
2	4	1	intermediate position
6	4	1	intermediate position
7	6	2	object-grasp position
12	7	1	intermediate position
15	1	3	object-release position
8	−1	1	intermediate position
4	−2	1	intermediate position
0	0	0	home position

These points are shown connected by straight lines in Figure 6.3.

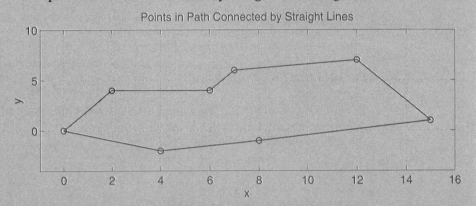

Figure 6.3 *Points in a path connected by straight lines.*

As we consider the steps in designing the cubic-spline path using MATLAB, we will break the path into three paths—from the home position to the object-grasp position, from the object-grasp position to the object-release position, and from the object-release position to the home position. These three paths are chosen for two reasons. First, the manipulator arm must stop at the end of each of these three paths, so they really are three separate paths. Second, because the cubic-spline function requires that the **x** coordinates be increasing, we cannot use a single cubic-spline reference to compute a path that essentially goes in a circle. The **x** coordinates in each path must be in ascending order, but we will assume that that has been checked by a preprocessing program, such as the ones discussed in the problems at the end of this chapter.

4.   MATLAB SOLUTION

The steps for separating the data file into the three separate paths is straight-forward. However, it is not as straightforward to determine the number of points to use in the cubic-spline interpolation. Because the coordinates could contain very large and very small values, we will determine the minimum x distance between points in the overall path. We then compute the x increment for the cubic spline to be equal to that minimum distance divided by 10. Hence, there will be at least ten points interpolated along the cubic spline between every pair of points, but there will be more points between most pairs of points.

```matlab
%    These statements read a data file containing the
%    points for a path for a manipulator arm to
%    go to a location to grasp an object, then
%    move to another location to release the
%    object, and then move back to the start position.
%
load points.dat;
x = points(:,1);
y = points(:,2);
code = points(:,3);
%
%    Generate the three separate paths.
%
grasp = find(code == 2);
release = find(code == 3);
lenx = length(x);
x1 = x(1:grasp);          y1 = y(1:grasp);
x2 = x(grasp:release);    y2 = y(grasp:release);
x3 = x(release:lenx);     y3 = y(release:lenx);
%
%    Compute time increment and corresponding time sequences.
%
incr = min(abs(x(2:lenx)-x(1:lenx-1)))/10;
t1 = x(1):incr*sign(x(grasp)-x(1)):x(grasp);
t2 = x(grasp):incr*sign(x(release)-x(grasp)):x(release);
t3 = x(release):incr*sign(x(lenx)-x(release)):x(lenx);
%
%    Compute splines.
%
s1 = interp1(x1,y1,t1,'spline');
s2 = interp1(x2,y2,t2,'spline');
s3 = interp1(x3,y3,t3,'spline');
%
%    Plot spline path.
%
subplot(2,1,1),...
   plot([t1 t2 t3],[s1' s2' s3'],[x1' x2' x3'],...
   [y1' y2' y3'],'o'),...
   title('Path for Manipulator Arm'),...
   xlabel('x'),ylabel('y'),grid,...
   axis([-1,16,-4,10])
```

5.   TESTING

If we test this solution using the data file from the hand example, we obtain the cubic spline path shown in Figure 6.4.

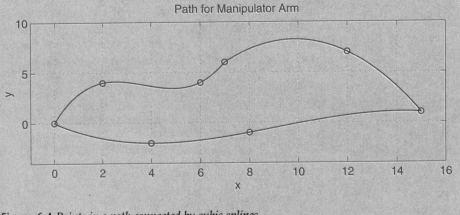

Figure 6.4 *Points in a path connected by cubic splines.*

6.3   Least-Squares Curve Fitting

Least-squares

Assume that we have a set of data points that were collected from an experiment. After plotting the data points, we find that they generally fall in a straight line. However, if we try to draw a straight line through points, probably only a couple of the points will fall on the line. A **least-squares** curve-fitting method could be used to find the straight line that was the closest to the points by minimizing the distance from each point to the straight line. Although this line can be considered a "best fit" to the data points, it is possible that none of the points will actually fall on the best fit line. (Note that this is very different from interpolation, because the curves used in linear interpolation and cubic-spline interpolation actually contain all the original data points.) In this section, we first present a discussion on fitting a straight line to a set of data points, and then we discuss fitting a polynomial to a set of data points.

Style

Because interpolation and curve fitting are such different processes, plot the original data and new data computed from one of these techniques on the same graph so that you can verify that the technique worked as desired. *Also, be sure that your program comments specify which technique is being used. For interpolation, also indicate whether it is linear interpolation or cubic-spline interpolation; for curve fitting, indicate the degree of the polynomial being used in the regression.*

LINEAR REGRESSION

Linear regression

Linear regression is the process that determines the linear equation that is the best fit to a set of data points in terms of minimizing the sum of the squared distances between the line and the data points. To understand this process, we first consider the set of temperature values presented in the previous section that were collected from the cylinder head of a new engine. If we plot these data points, it appears that a good estimate of a line through the points is y = 20 x, as shown in Figure 6.5. The following commands were used to generate this plot:

```
%     These statements compare a linear model
%     to a set of data points.
%
x = 0:5;
y = [0,20,60,68,77,110];
y1 = 20*x;
subplot(2,1,1),...
    plot(x,y1,x,y,'o'),title('Linear Estimate'),...
    xlabel('Time, s'),ylabel('Temperature, degrees F'),...
    grid,axis([-1,6,-20,120])
```

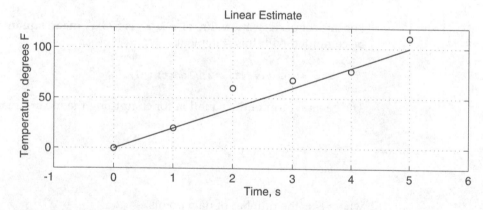

Figure 6.5 *A linear estimate.*

To measure the quality of the fit of this linear estimate to the data, we first determine the distance from each point to the linear estimate; these distances are shown in Figure 6.6. The first two points fall exactly on the line, so d_1 and d_2 are zero. The value of d_3 is equal to 60 − 40, or 20; the rest of the distances can be computed in a similar way. If we compute the sum of the distances, some of the positive and negative values would cancel each other and give a sum that is smaller than it should be. To avoid this problem, we could add absolute values or squared values; linear regression uses squared values. Therefore, the measure of the qual-

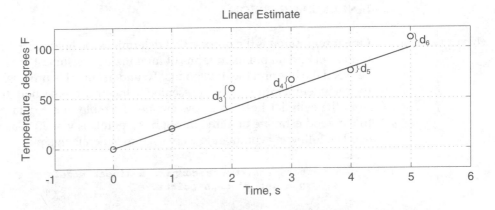

Figure 6.6 *Distances between points and linear estimates*

ity of the fit of this linear estimate is the sum of the **squared distances** between the *y* points and the linear estimates. This sum can be computed using MATLAB with the following commands, assuming that the previous statements, which defined **x, y**, and **y1**, have been executed.

```
sq_error = sum((y-y1).^2)
```

Mean squared error

For this set of data, the value of **sum_sq** is 573. A **mean squared error** of 95.5 can be computed with this statement:

```
mse = sum((y-y1).^2)/length(y);
```

The general form of the equation for computing the mean squared error is

$$mse = \frac{\sum_{k=1}^{N}(y_k - y1_k)^2}{N}$$

where N is the number of data points.

If we drew another line through the points, we could compute the sum of squares that corresponds to this new line. Of the two lines, the best fit is provided by the line with the smaller sum of squared distances. To find the line with the smallest sum of squared distances, we can write an equation that computes the distances using a general linear equation, $y = mx + b$. We then write an equation that represents the sum of the squared distances; this equation will have m and b as its variables. Using techniques from calculus, we can then compute the derivatives of the equation with respect to m and b and set the derivatives equal to zero. The values of m and b that are determined in this way represent the straight line with the minimum sum of squared distances. The MATLAB function for computing this best-fit linear equation is discussed in the next section. For the data presented in this section, the best fit is shown in Figure 6.7; the corresponding mean squared error is 59.4699.

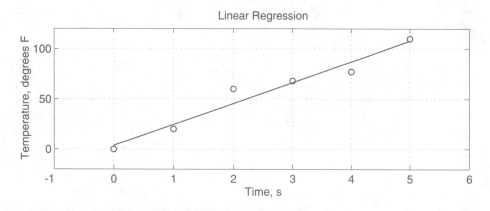

Figure 6.7 *Least-squares linear regression.*

POLYNOMIAL REGRESSION

In the previous discussion, we presented a technique for computing the linear equation that best fits a set of data. A similar technique can be developed using a single polynomial (not a set of polynomials as in a cubic spline) to fit the data by minimizing the distance of the polynomial from the data points. First, recall (from Section 3.1) that a polynomial with one variable can be written in the following general formula:

$$f(x) = a_0 x^N + a_1 x^{N-1} + a_2 x^{N-2} + \ldots + a_{N-1} x + a_N$$

Degree

The **degree** of a polynomial is equal to the largest value used as an exponent. Therefore, the general form for a cubic polynomial is

$$g(x) = a_0 x^3 + a_1 x^2 + a_2 x + a_3$$

Note that a linear equation is also a polynomial of degree one.

In Figure 6.8, we plot the original set of data points that we used in the linear regression example (and also in the linear interpolation and cubic-spline interpolation); we also plot the best fit for polynomials of degree 2 through degree 5. Note that as the degree of the polynomial increases, the number of points that fall on the curve also increases. If a set of $n+1$ points is used to determine an nth-degree polynomial, all $n+1$ points will fall on the polynomial curve. Regression analysis cannot determine a unique solution if the number of points is equal to or less than the degree of the polynomial model. Thus, it does not make sense to ask for a linear regression (degree 1) from one point or for a quadratic regression (degree 2) from one or two points.

`polyfit` FUNCTION

The MATLAB function for computing the best fit to a set of data with a polynomial with a specified degree is the **`polyfit`** function. This function has three arguments—the **x** and **y** coordinates of the data points and the degree **n** of the

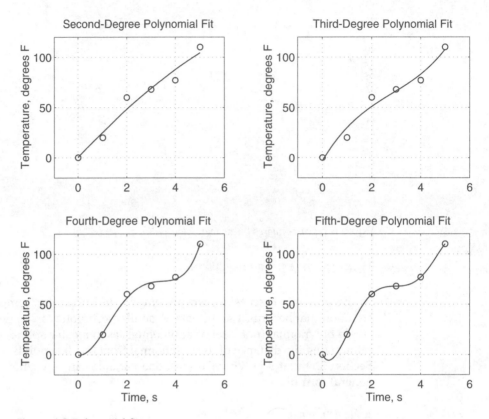

Figure 6.8 *Polynomial fits.*

polynomial. The function returns the coefficients, in descending powers of **x**, of the **n**th degree polynomial that fits the vectors **x** and **y**. (Note that there are **n+1** coefficients for an **n**th degree polynomial.) A summary of this function is as follows:

polyfit(x,y,n)   Returns a vector of **n+1** coefficients that represents the best-fit polynomial of degree **n** for the **x** and **y** coordinates. The coefficient order corresponds to decreasing powers of **x**.

The best linear fit for the cylinder head temperature data, plotted in Figure 6.7, has a mean squared error of 59.4699. The plot and the calculation of this error sum were performed by the following statements:

```
%    These statements compute a best-fit linear model
%    for a set of data points.
%
x = 0:5;
y = [0,20,60,68,77,110];
```

```
%
coef = polyfit(x,y,1);
m = coef(1);
b = coef(2);
ybest = m*x + b;
%
mse = sum((y - ybest).^2)/length(y)
subplot(2,1,1,),...
    plot(x,ybest,x,y,'o'),title('Linear Regression'),...
    xlabel('Time, s'),ylabel('Temperature, degrees F'),...
    grid,axis([-1,6,-20,120])
```

The `polyval` function (discussed in Section 3.1) is used to evaluate a polynomial at a set of data points. The first argument of the `polyval` function is a vector containing the coefficents of the polynomial (in an order corresponding to decreasing powers of `x`), and the second argument is the vector of `x` values for which we want polynomial values.

In the previous example, we computed the points of the linear regression using values from the coefficients; we could also have computed them using the `polyval` function as shown here:

```
ybest = polyval(coef,x);
```

Using the same data that was used for the linear regression, we can now illustrate the computation of the best-fit polynomials of degree 2 through degree 5 shown in Figure 6.8:

```
%    These statements compute polynomial models
%    for a set of data points.
%
x = 0:5;
y = [0,20,60,68,77,110];
newx = 0:0.05:5;
for n=1:4
    f(:,n) = polyval(polyfit(x,y,n+1),newx)';
end
```

Then, for example, to plot the second-degree polynomial, we could use this statement:

```
plot(newx,f(:,1),x,y,'o')
```

Additional statements are necessary to define the subplot, label each plot, and set the axis limits. From the discussion on polynomial fits earlier in this section, we would expect that the lower degree polynomials would not contain all data points, but that the fifth-degree polynomial would contain all six data points; the plots in Figure 6.8 verify these expectations.

CHAPTER SUMMARY

In this chapter, we explained the difference between interpolation and least-squares curve fitting. Two types of interpolation were presented—linear and cubic-spline. After presenting the MATLAB commands for performing these types of interpolations, we turned to least-squares curve fitting using polynomials. This discussion included determining the best fit to a set of data using a polynomial with a specified degree and then using the best-fit polynomial to generate new values of the function.

KEY TERMS

best fit   linear interpolation
cubic-spline interpolation   linear regression
curve fitting   mean squared error
interpolation   regression
least squares

MATLAB SUMMARY

This MATLAB summary lists all the special symbols, commands, and functions that were defined in this chapter. A brief description is also included for each one.

COMMANDS AND FUNCTIONS

`interp1`	computes one-dimensional interpolation
`polyfit`	computes a least-squares polynomial

Style NOTES

1. When using interpolation, be sure that your program comments indicate whether it is linear or cubic-spline interpolation. When using curve fitting, be sure that your program comments indicate the degree of the polynomial being used in the regression.

DEBUGGING NOTES

1. When using the **interp1** function, be sure that the values in the **x** vector are increasing and that the values in the **new_x** vector are within the range of the first and last values of the **x** vector.

2. When using an interpolation or a curve-fitting technique, always plot the original data on the same graph as the new interpolated data to verify that the technique worked as desired.

3. Regression analysis cannot determine a unique solution if the number of points is equal to or less than the degree of the polynomial model.

PROBLEMS

Problems 1–7 relate to the engineering applications presented in this chapter. Problems 8–11 relate to new engineering applications.

Robot Arm Manipulator. These problems relate to the robot arm manipulator problem given in Section 6.2. Example coordinate files are are available as indicated in the Preface and have names such as **msn1.dat, msn2.dat**, and so on, which stand for various missions assigned to the robot arm manipulator.

1. Write a program to perform the initial testing of the data values in a mission file to be sure that the x-coordinates in each of the three paths are strictly increasing or are strictly decreasing. If errors are detected, identify the path in which they occurred and list the values in that path.

2. Assume that the data file in a mission file can include more than three paths. For example, the paths might describe moving several objects to new places in the cargo bay. Write a program that will count the number of individual paths, in which a path ends with grasping an object, releasing an object, or returning to the home position.

3. Modify the program written to perform the cubic-spline interpolation so that it prints the interpolated data points for the complete set of paths to an output file named **paths.dat**. Remove any repeated points. Be sure to include the proper codes with the data points.

4. Write a program to read the file **paths.dat** described in problem 3. Plot the entire set of paths, and insert circles at points at which the robot arm stops. (The robot arm stops to grasp an object, release an object, or return to the home position.)

5. Modify the program written in problem 1 so that it assumes that the file might contain multiple paths as described in problem 2.

6. Instead of assuming that an error occurs if the **x** values are not strictly increasing or strictly decreasing within a path, assume instead that when this occurs, the path is to be separated into subpaths. For example, if the **x** coordinates from the home position to the grasping position are [0,1,3,6,3,7], then the subpaths would have **x** coordinates of [0,1,3,6], [6,3], and [3,7]. Write a program to read a mission file. Your program should generate a new file, **points.dat**, which will contain the coordinates and codes to accompany the new set of paths.

7. In problem 6, we were able to separate a path with x coordinates, such as [0,1,3,6,3,7], into subpaths. Suppose the path that we are considering has the following set of coordinates: (0,0), (3,2), (3,6), (6,9). The x coordinates have positions [0,3,3,6]. Breaking this path into subpaths, as in problem 3, does not solve the problem, because the path is moving in a vertical direction. To solve this problem, we need to insert new point between the points that are vertical with each other. Assume that the new point is to be midway between the points with an x coordinate that is 5% greater than the x coordinate of the vertical points. Write a program that reads a file **points.dat** and uses this method to convert it into subpaths where necessary to store the complete new set of paths in a file named **final.dat**.

Oil Well Production. Assume that we are trying to determine how the production of an operating oil well is related to temperature. Therefore, we have collected a set of data that contains the average oil-well production in barrels of oil per day along with the average temperature for the day. This set of data is stored in an ASCII file named **oil.dat**.

8. Because the data is not ordered by oil production or by temperature, it will need to be reordered. Write a program to read the data and generate two new data files. The file **oiltmp.dat** should contain the data with the oil in ascending order, with the corresponding temperatures. The file **tmpoil.dat** should contain the data with the temperatures in ascending order, with the corresponding oil productions. If there are points with the same first coordinates, the output file should contain only one point with the coordinate; the corresponding second coordinate should be the average of the second coordinates with the same first value.

9. Write a program to plot the data from the file **tmpoil.dat**, along with second-degree and third-degree polynomial approximations to the data. Print the polynomial models and the least-squares errors.

10. Write a program to plot the data from the file `oiltmp.dat`, along with second-degree and third-degree polynomial approximation to the data. Print the polynomial models and the least-squares errors.

11. Assume that a third-degree polynomial approximation is going to be used to model the oil-well production in terms of the temperature. Write a program that will allow the user to enter a temperature; the program will print the predicted production in barrels per day.

Courtesy of Alaska Division of Tourism.

7

GRAND CHALLENGE:
Enhanced Oil and Gas Recovery

The design and construction of the Alaska pipeline presented numerous engineering challenges. One of the most important problems was protecting the
permafrost (the perennially frozen subsoil in arctic or subarctic regions) from the
heat of the pipeline itself. The oil flowing in the pipeline is warmed by pumping
stations and by friction from the walls of the pipe, enough so that the supports
holding the pipeline have to be insulated or even cooled to keep them from
melting the permafrost at their bases. In addition, the components of the pipeline
had to be very reliable because of the inaccessibility of some locations. More
importantly, component failure could cause damage to human life, animal life,
and the environment around the pipeline.

Numerical Integration and Differentiation

7.1   Numerical Integration

7.2   *Problem Solving Applied: Pipeline Flow Analysis*

7.3   Numerical Differentiation

Chapter Summary, Key Terms, MATLAB Summary
Style Notes, Debugging Notes, Problems

OBJECTIVES

Integration and differentiation are the key concepts presented in calculus classes. These concepts are fundamental to solving a large number of engineering and science problems. Although many of these problems can be solved analytically using integration and differentiation, there are many that cannot be solved this way; these problems require numerical integration or numerical differentiation techniques. In this chapter, we discuss numerical solutions to integration and differentiation and then present MATLAB functions for computing these numerical solutions.

7.1   Numerical Integration

Integral

The **integral** of a function $f(x)$ over the interval $[a,b]$ is defined as the area under the curve of $f(x)$ between a and b, as shown in Figure 7.1. If the value of this integral is K, then the notation to represent it is

$$K = \int_a^b f(x)dx$$

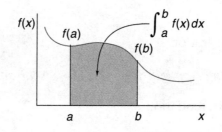

Figure 7.1 *Integral of f(x) from a to b.*

For many functions, this integral can be computed analytically. However, for a number of functions, this integral cannot easily be computed analytically, and thus requires a numerical technique to estimate its value. The numerical evalua-

Quadrature

tion of an integral is called **quadrature**, which comes from an ancient geometrical problem.

Numerical integration techniques estimate the function $f(x)$ by another function $g(x)$, where $g(x)$ is chosen so that we can easily compute the area under $g(x)$. Then, the better the estimate of $g(x)$ to $f(x)$, the better will be the estimate of the integral of $f(x)$. Two of the most common numerical integration techniques estimate $f(x)$ with a set of piecewise linear functions or with a set of piecewise parabolic functions. If we estimate the function with piecewise linear functions, we can compute the area of the trapezoids that compose the area under the piecewise linear functions; this technique is called the trapezoidal rule. If we estimate the function with piecewise quadratic functions, we can then compute and add the areas of these components; this technique is called Simpson's rule.

TRAPEZOIDAL RULE AND SIMPSON'S RULE

Trapezoidal rule

If the area under a curve is represented by trapezoids and if the interval $[a,b]$ is divided into n equal sections, then the area can be approximated by the following formula (**trapezoidal rule**),

$$K_T = \frac{b-a}{2n}\left(f(x_0) + 2f(x_1) + 2f(x_2) + \ldots + 2f(x_{n-1}) + f(x_n)\right)$$

where the x_i values represent the endpoints of the trapezoids and where $x_0 = a$ and $x_n = b$.

If the area under a curve is represented by areas under quadratic sections of a curve and if the interval [a,b] is divided into $2n$ equal sections, then the area can be approximated by the following formula (**Simpson's rule**),

Simpson's rule

$$K_S = \frac{h}{3} \left(f(x_0) + 4f(x_1) + 2f(x_2) + 4f(x_3) + \ldots + 2f(x_{2n-2}) \right.$$
$$\left. + 4f(x_{2n-1}) + f(x_{2n}) \right)$$

where the x_i values represent the endpoints of the sections and where $x_0 = a$ and $x_{2n} = b$, and $h = (b - a)/(2n)$.

If the piecewise components of the approximating function are higher-degree functions (trapezoidal rule uses linear functions and Simpson's rule uses quadratic functions), the integration techniques are referred to as Newton-Cotes integration techniques.

The estimate of an integral improves as we use more components (such as trapezoids) to approximate the area under a curve. If we attempt to integrate a function with a **singularity** (a point at which the function or its derivatives are infinity or are not defined), we may not be able to get a satisfactory answer with a numerical integration technique.

Singularity

QUADRATURE FUNCTIONS

MATLAB has two quadrature functions for performing numerical function integration. The **quad** function uses an adaptive form of Simpson's rule, and **quad8** uses an adaptive Newton Cotes 8-panel rule. The **quad8** function is better at handling functions with certain types of singularities, such as $\int_0^1 \sqrt{x}\, dx$. Both functions print a warning message if they detect a singularity, but an estimate of the integral is still returned.

The simplest forms of the **quad** and **quad8** functions require three arguments. The first argument is the name (in quote marks) of the MATLAB function that returns a vector of values of $f(x)$ when given a vector of input values. The function name can be the name of another MATLAB function, such as **sin**, or it can be the name of a user-written MATLAB function. The second and third arguments are the integral limits **a** and **b**. A summary of these functions follows:

`quad('function_name',a,b)`	Returns area of the function between **a** and **b** using a form of Simpson's rule.
`quad8('function_name',a,b)`	Returns area of the function between **a** and **b** using an adaptive Newton-Cotes 8-panel rule. This function is better than the **quad** function at handling some functions with singularities.

To illustrate these functions, assume that we want to determine the integral of the square-root function for nonnegative values of a and b:

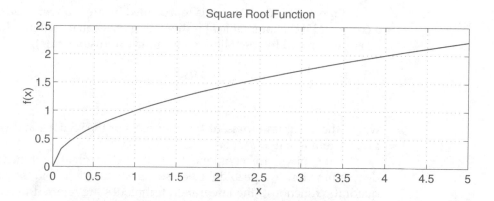

Figure 7.2 *Square root function.*

$$K = \int_a^b \sqrt{x}\, dx$$

The square root function $f(x) = \sqrt{x}$ is plotted in Figure 7.2 for the interval [0,5]; the function values are complex for $x < 0$. This function can be integrated analytically to yield the following for nonnegative values of a and b:

$$K = \frac{2}{3}\left(b^{3/2} - a^{3/2} \right)$$

To compare the results of the quadrature functions with the analytical results for a user-specified interval, we use the following program:

```
%    These statements compare the quadrature functions
%    with the analytical results for the integration
%    of the square root of x over an interval [a,b],
%    where a and b are nonnegative.
%
a = input('Enter left endpoint (nonnegative): ' );
b = input('Enter right endpoint (nonnegative): ' );
k = 2/3*(b^(1.5) - a^(1.5));
kq = quad('sqrt',a,b);
kq8 = quad8('sqrt',a,b);
fprintf('Analytical: %f \n Numerical: %f %f \n',k,kq,kq8)
```

This program was tested using several intervals, giving the following results:

Interval [0.5,0.6]

```
Analytical: 0.074136
 Numerical: 0.074136 0.074136
```

Interval [0,0.5]

```
Analytical: 0.235702
 Numerical: 0.235701 0.235702
```

Interval [0,1]

```
Analytical:  0.666667
Numerical:  0.666663 0.666667
```

The **quad** and **quad8** functions can also include a fourth argument, which represents a tolerance. The integration function continues to refine its estimate for the integration until the relative error is less than the tolerance:

$$\frac{\text{previous estimate} - \text{current estimate}}{\text{previous estimate}} < \text{tolerance}$$

If the tolerance is omitted, a default value of 0.001 is assumed. If an optional fifth argument is nonzero, a graph or trace is plotted, containing a point plot of the function values used in the integration computations.

These integration techniques can handle some singularities that occur at one or the other interval endpoints, but they cannot handle singularities that occur within the interval. For these cases, you should consider dividing the interval into subintervals and providing estimates of the singularities using other results, such as l'Hôpital's rule.

Practice!

Sketch the function $f(x) = |x|$, and indicate the areas specified by the following integrals. Then compute the integrals by hand, and compare your results to those generated by the **quad** function.

1. $\displaystyle\int_{0.5}^{0.6} |x|\ dx$ 2. $\displaystyle\int_{0}^{1} |x|\ dx$

3. $\displaystyle\int_{-1}^{-0.5} |x|\ dx$ 4. $\displaystyle\int_{-0.5}^{0.5} |x|\ dx$

7.2 Problem Solving Applied: Pipeline Flow Analysis

In this application, we address the flow of oil in a pipeline. However, the analysis of a liquid flow in a circular pipe applies to many different systems, including the veins and arteries in a body, the water system of a city, the irrigation system for a farm, the piping system that transports fluids in a factory, the hydraulic lines of an aircraft, and the ink jet of a computer's printer.

The friction in a circular pipeline causes a velocity profile to develop in the flowing oil. Oil that is in contact with the walls of the pipe is not moving at all, whereas the oil at the center of the flow is moving the fastest. The diagram in Figure 7.3 shows how the velocity of the oil varies across the diameter of the pipe and

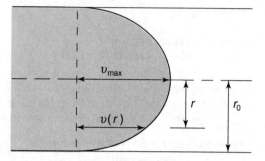

Figure 7.3 *Velocity profile in flowing oil.*

defines the variables used in this analysis. The following equation describes this velocity profile:

$$v(r) = v_{max}\left(1 - \frac{r}{r_0}\right)^{1/n}$$

The variable n is an integer between 5 and 10 that defines the shape of the forward flow of the oil. The average flow velocity of the pipe is the area integral of the velocity profile, which can be shown to be

$$v_{ave} = \frac{\displaystyle\int_0^{r_0} v(r)2\pi r\,dr}{\pi r_0^2}$$

$$= \frac{2v_{max}}{r_0^2}\int_0^{r_0} r\left(1 - \frac{r}{r_0}\right)^{1/n} dr$$

The values of v_{max} and n can be measured experimentally, and the value of r_0 is the radius of the pipe. Write a MATLAB program to integrate the velocity profile to determine the average flow velocity of the pipe.

1.   PROBLEM STATEMENT

Compute the average flow velocity for a pipeline.

2.   INPUT/OUTPUT DESCRIPTION

The following diagram shows that shows that the output of the program is the value of the average flow velocity of the pipeline. The values of the maximum velocity v_{max}, the radius of the pipe r_0, and the value of n are specified as constants in the program.

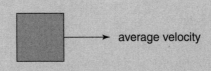

average velocity

3.   HAND EXAMPLE

If we assume that the value of r_0 is 0.5 m and that the value of n is 8, we can plot the function $r(1 - r/r_0)^{1/n}$, as shown in Figure 7.4. We can also compute an estimate to the integral of this function by summing the areas of the triangle and the rectangle shown in Figure 7.5. This estimate of the area is

$$\text{area} = 0.5(0.4)(0.35) + (0.1)(0.35)$$
$$= 0.105$$

This area is then multiplied by the factor $2v_{max}/r_0^2$ to give the average flow velocity of the pipe. If we assume that v_{max} is 1.5 m, the average flow velocity is approximately 1.260.

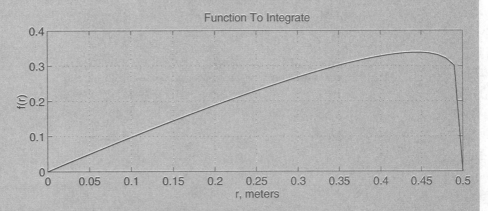

Figure 7.4 *Function related to average flow velocity.*

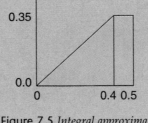

Figure 7.5 *Integral approximation.*

4.   MATLAB SOLUTION

In the MATLAB solution, we use the quad function to evaluate the integral. One of the quad function parameters is the name of the function that computes values of the function to be numerically integrated, so we must also write an M-file that computes values of the function inside the integral. We will specify the values of v_{max}, r_0, and n as constants in both the program and the function. In the following function, we print the value of the integral so we can compare it to the value determined in the hand calculation.

```
%    These statements compute the value of the
%    average flow velocity for a pipeline
%    using numerical integration.
%
vmax = 1.5;
r0 = 0.5;
%
integral = quad('velocity',0,0.5)
%
ave_velocity = (2*vmax/(r0^2))*integral
```

The M-file that defines the function to be integrated in order to compute the average velocity is the following:

```
function v = velocity(r)
%    VELOCITY   This function is related to the
%                average flow velocity of the pipe.
%
r0 = 0.5;
n = 8;
%
v = r.*(1-r/r0).^(1/n);
```

5.   TESTING

The output of the program is the following:

```
integral =
    0.1046
ave_velocity =
    1.2548
```

The value estimated in the hand example for the integral was 0.105, and the corresponding value estimated for the average velocity was 1.260.

7.3   Numerical Differentiation

Derivative

The **derivative** of a function $f(x)$ is defined as a function $f'(x)$, which is equal the rate of change of $f(x)$ with respect to x. The derivative can be expressed as a ratio, with the change in $f(x)$ indicated by $df(x)$ and the change in x indicated by dx, giving

$$f'(x) = \frac{df(x)}{dx}$$

There are many physical processes in which we want to measure the rate of change of a variable. For example, velocity is the rate of change of position (as in meters per second), and acceleration is the rate of change of velocity (as in meters per second squared). It can also be shown that the integral of acceleration is velocity and that the integral of velocity is position. Hence, integration and differentiation have a special relationship in that they can be considered inverses of each other—the integral of a derivative returns the original function, and the derivative of an integral returns the original function, to within a constant value.

The derivative $f'(x)$ can be described graphically as the slope of the function $f(x)$, where the slope of $f(x)$ is defined as the slope of the tangent line to the function at the specified point. Thus, the value of $f'(x)$ at the point a is $f'(a)$, and it is equal to the slope of the tangent line at the point a, as shown in Figure 7.6.

Because the derivative of a function at a point is the slope of the tangent line at the point, a value of zero for the derivative of a function at the point x_k indicates that the line is horizontal at that point. Points with derivatives of zero are called
Critical points
critical points and can represent either a horizontal region of the function or an **extrema point** (a local maximum or a local minimum of the function). The point may also be the global maximum or global minimum as shown in Figure 7.7, but more analysis of the entire function would be needed to determine this. If we evaluate the derivative of a function at several points in an interval and observe that the sign of the derivative changes, then a local maximum or a local minimum occurs in the interval. The second derivative (the derivative of $f'(x)$) can be used to determine whether or not the critical points represent local maxima or local minima. More specifically, if the second derivative at an extrema point is positive, then the function value at the extrema point is a local minimum; if the second derivative at an extrema point is negative, then the function value at the extrema point is a local maximum.

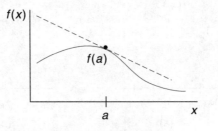

Figure 7.6 *Derivative of f(x) at x = a.*

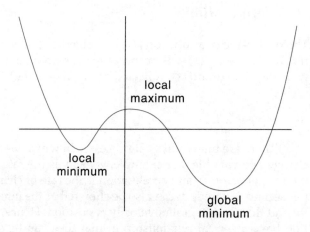

Figure 7.7 *Example of function with critical points.*

DIFFERENCE EXPRESSIONS

Numerical differentiation techniques estimate the derivative of a function at a point x_k by approximating the slope of the tangent line at x_k using values of the function at points near x_k. The approximation of the slope of the tangent line can be done in several ways, as shown in Figure 7.8. Figure 7.8(a) assumes that the derivative at x_k is estimated by computing the slope of the line between $f(x_{k-1})$ and $f(x_k)$, as in

$$f'(x_k) = \frac{f(x_k) - f(x_{k-1})}{x_k - x_{k-1}}$$

Backward
difference

This type of derivative approximation is called a **backward difference** approximation.

Figure 7.8(b) assumes that the derivative at x_k is estimated by computing the slope of the line between $f(x_k)$ and $f(x_k+1)$, as in

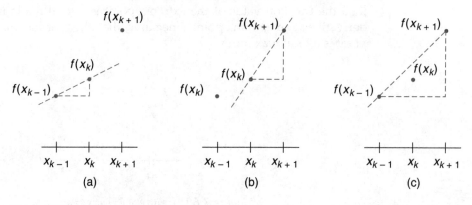

Figure 7.8 *Techniques for computing $f'(x_k)$.*

$$f'(x_k) = \frac{f(x_{k+1}) - f(x_k)}{x_{k+1} - x_k}$$

Forward difference

This type of derivative approximation is called a **forward difference** approximation.

Figure 7.8(c) assumes that the derivative at x_k is estimated by computing the slope of the line between $f(x_{k-1})$ and $f(x_{k+1})$, as in

$$f'(x_k) = \frac{f(x_{k+1}) - f(x_{k-1})}{x_{k+1} - x_{k-1}}$$

Central difference

This type of derivative approximation is called a **central difference** approximation. We usually assume that x_k is halfway between x_{k-1} and x_{k+1}.

The quality of all of these types of derivative computations depends on the distance between the points used to estimate the derivative; the estimate of the derivative improves as the distance between the two points decreases.

The second derivative of a function $f(x)$ is the derivative of the first derivative of the function:

$$f''(x) = \frac{df'(x)}{dx}$$

This function can be evaluated using slopes of the first derivative. Thus, if we use backward differences, we have

$$f''(x_k) = \frac{f'(x_k) - f'(x_{k-1})}{x_k - x_{k-1}}$$

Similar expressions can be derived for computing estimates of higher derivatives.

diff FUNCTION

The **diff** function computes differences between adjacent values in a vector, generating a new vector with one less value. If the **diff** function is applied to a matrix, it operates on the columns of the matrix as if each column were a vector. Thus, the matrix returned has the same number of columns, but one fewer rows. A summary of this function follows:

> **diff(x)**   Returns a new vector containing differences between adjacent values in the vector **x**. Returns a matrix containing differences between adjacent values in the columns if **x** is a matrix.

To illustrate, assume that the vector **x** contains the values [0,1,2,3,4,5] and the vector **y** contains the values [2,3,1,5,8,10]. Then the vector generated by **diff(x)** is [1,1,1,1,1], and the vector generated by **diff(y)** is [1,−2,4,3,2]. The derivative **dy** is computed with **diff(y)./diff(x)**. Note that these values of **dy** are correct for both the forward-difference equation and the backward-difference equation. The distinction between the two methods for computing the derivative is determined by the values of **xd** that correspond to the derivative **dy**. If the corresponding

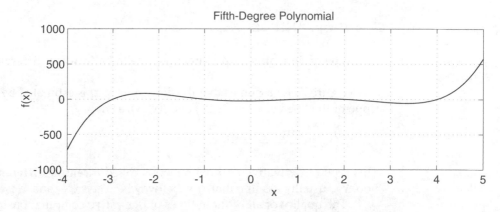

Figure 7.9 *Plot of a polynomial.*

values of **xd** are [1,2,3,4,5], then **dy** computes a backward difference; if the corresponding values of **xd** are [0,1,2,3,4], then **dy** computes a forward difference. *Be sure to specify the type of difference equation (forward, backward, central) in the comments in a program that computes a numerical derivative.*

Suppose that we have a function given by the following polynomial:

$$f(x) = x^5 - 3x^4 - 11x^3 + 27x^2 + 10x - 24$$

A plot of this function is shown in Figure 7.9. Assume that we want to compute the derivative of this function over the interval $[-4,5]$, using a backward-difference equation. We can perform this operation using the **diff** function as

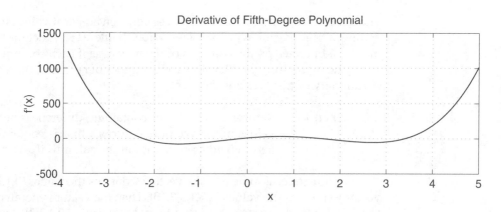

Figure 7.10 *Plot of the derivative of a polynomial.*

shown in these equations, where **df** represents $f'(x)$, and **xd** represents the **x** values corresponding to the derivative:

```
%    Evaluate f(x) and f'(x) using backward differences.
%
x = -4:0.1:5;
f = x.^5 - 3*x.^4 - 11*x.^3 + 27*x.^2 + 10*x - 24;
df = diff(f)./diff(x);
xd = x(2:length(x));
```

Figure 7.10 contains a plot of this derivative. Note that the zeros of the derivative include the points of local minima or local maxima of this function; this function does not have a global minimum or a global maximum because the function ranges from $-\infty$ to $+\infty$. We can print the locations of the critical points (which occur at -2.3, -0.2, 1.5, and 3.4, to one decimal of accuracy) for this function with the following statements:

```
%    Find locations of critical points of f'(x).
%
product = df(1:length(df)-1).*df(2:length(df));
critical = xd(find(product < 0))
```

The **find** function determines the indices of the locations in **product** that are negative because these points indicate a change in sign in the derivative. These indices are then used with the **xd** vector to print the approximation to the locations of the critical points.

To compute a central difference derivative using the **x** and **f** vectors, we could use the following statements:

```
%    Evaluate f'(x) using central differences.
%
numerator = f(3:length(f)) - f(1:length(f)-2);
denominator = x(3:length(x)) - x(1:length(x)-2);
dy = numerator./denominator;
xd = x(2:length(x)-1);
```

In the example discussed in this section, we assumed that we had the equation of the function to be differentiated; thus, we could generate points of the function. In many engineering problems, the data to be differentiated is collected from experiments. Thus, we cannot choose the points to be close together to get a more accurate measure of the derivative. In these cases, it might be a good solution to use the techniques from Chapter 6 that allow us to determine an equation that fits a set of data and then compute points from the equation to use in computing values of the derivative.

Practice!

For each of the following, plot the function, its first derivative, and its second derivative over the interval $[-10,10]$. Then use MATLAB commands to print the locations of the local minima, followed on a separate line by the locations of the local maxima.

1. $g_1(x) = x^3 - 5x^2 + 2x + 8$
2. $g_2(x) = x^2 + 4x + 4$
3. $g_3(x) = x^2 - 2x + 2$
4. $g_4(x) = 10x - 24$
5. $g_5(x) = x^5 - 4x^4 - 9x^3 + 32x^2 + 28x - 48$

CHAPTER SUMMARY

Techniques for numerical integration and differentiation were presented in this chapter. Numerical integration techniques approximate the area under a curve, and numerical differentiation techniques approximate the slope of a curve. The MATLAB functions for integration are **quad** and **quad8**, which perform an iterative form of Simpson's rule and an iterative Newton-Cotes technique, respectively. Both functions require that the function to be integrated be a MATLAB function, either standard or user-written. The MATLAB function that can be used to compute the derivative of a function is **diff**, which computes differences between adjacent elements of a vector. To compute the derivative of a function f with respect to x, two references to the **diff** function are required, as in **diff(f)./diff(x)**.

KEY TERMS

backward difference
central difference
critical point
extrema point
forward difference
numerical differentiation

numerical integration
quadrature
Simpson's rule
singularity
trapezoidal rule

MATLAB SUMMARY

This MATLAB summary lists all the commands and functions that were defined in this chapter. A brief description is also included for each one.

COMMANDS AND FUNCTIONS

diff	computes the differences between adjacent values
quad	computes the integral under a curve (Simpson)
quad8	computes the integral under a curve (Newton-Cote)

Style NOTES

1. Be sure to specify the type of difference equation (forward, backward, central) in the comments in a program that computes a numerical derivative.

DEBUGGING NOTES

1. If a function contains a singularity in the interval of interest, divide it into subintervals so that the singularity is on the endpoints. Evaluate the singularity using other techniques, such as L'Hopital's rule.

PROBLEMS

Problems 1–4 relate to the engineering application presented in this chapter. Problems 5–11 relate to new applications.

Pipeline Flow Analysis. These problems relate to the pipeline flow analysis problem given in Section 7.2.

1. Modify the **velocity** function so that r_0 and n are also function arguments.
2. Generate a table showing the average flow velocity for a pipeline using the integer values of n from 5 to 10. Use the function from Problem 1.
3. Generate a table showing the average flow velocity for pipelines with radii of 0.5, 1.0, 1.5, and 2.0 m. Assume that the other parameters are not changed from the values specified in this original problem. Use the function from Problem 1.
4. Modify the program developed in Section 7.2 so that the user can enter the value of v_{max}.

Sounding Rocket Trajectory. The following data represents time and altitude values for a sounding rocket that is performing high-altitude atmospheric research on the ionosphere.

Time, s	Altitude, m
0	60
10	2,926
20	10,170
30	21,486
40	33,835
50	45,251
60	55,634
70	65,038
80	73,461
90	80,905
100	87,368
110	92,852
120	97,355
130	100,878
140	103,422
150	104,986
160	106,193
170	110,246
180	119,626
190	136,106
200	162,095
210	199,506
220	238,775
230	277,065
240	314,375
250	350,704

5. The velocity function is the derivative of the altitude function. Using numerical differentiation, compute the velocity values from this data, using a backward difference. Plot the altitude data and velocity data on two separate plots. (Note that this is a two-stage rocket.)

6. The acceleration function is the derivative of the velocity function. Using the velocity data determined from problem 5, compute the acceleration data, using a backward difference. Plot the velocity data and the acceleration data on two different plots.

7. Plot the velocity data on the same plot using all three difference equations.

8. Start with the acceleration data for this rocket that was computed in problem 6. Integrate the data to obtain velocity values. (You won't be able to use the **quad** functions because you have only data points. Use either the trapezoidal

rule or Simpson's rule.) Plot the velocity data computed from problem 5 and the velocity data computed in this problem on the same graph.

9. Start with the velocity data for this rocket that was computed in problem 5. Integrate the data to obtain altitude values. (You won't be able to use the **quad** functions because you have only data points. Use either the trapezoidal rule or Simpson's rule.) Plot the altitude data given with this set of problems and the altitude data computed in this problem on the same graph.

Function Analysis. The following problems relate to numerical integration and numerical differentiation.

10. Let the function f be defined by the following equation:

$$f(x) = 4e^{-x}$$

Plot the function over the interval [0,1]. Use numerical integration techniques to estimate the integral of $f(x)$ over the intervals [0,0.5] and [0,1].

11. Write a program to identify inflection points of a function in a given interval. (An inflection point is a critical point that is not an extrema point.)

8

Courtesy of NASA Lewis Research Center.

GRAND CHALLENGE:
Vehicle Performance

One of the promising new propulsion technologies being developed for future transport aircraft is an advanced turboprop engine called the Unducted Fan (UDF). The UDF engine employs significant advancements in propeller technology. New materials, blade shapes, and higher rotation speeds enable UDF-powered aircraft to fly almost as fast as fanjets, and with greater fuel efficiency. The UDF uses sets of blades that rotate in opposite directions, as shown in this photo. Notice how the shape of the UDF blades differs from more traditional propeller blades.

Ordinary Differential Equations

OBJECTIVES

In this section, we present a group of first-order differential equations and their analytical solutions. After describing the Runge-Kutta methods for integrating first-order differential equations, we compare the numerical solutions for the group of first-order differential equations to the analytical solutions. An application problem that requires the solution of a differential equation is then discussed and solved, using the MATLAB function that implements second- and third-order Runge-Kutta methods. The chapter closes with a discussion of converting higher-order differential equations to first-order differential equations in order to solve them using the techniques discussed in this chapter.

8.1   First-Order Ordinary Differential Equations

A **first-order ordinary differential equation** (ODE) is an equation that can be written in the following form,

$$y' = \frac{dy}{dx} = g(x,y)$$

where x is the independent variable and y is a function of x. The following equations are examples of first-order ODEs:

Equation 1: $y' = g_1(x,y) = 3x^2$
Equation 2: $y' = g_2(x,y) = -0.131y$
Equation 3: $y' = g_3(x,y) = 3.4444E\text{-}05 - 0.0015y$
Equation 4: $y' = g_4(x,y) = 2 \cdot x \cdot \cos^2(y)$
Equation 5: $y' = g_5(x,y) = 3y + e^{2x}$

Observe that y' is given as a function of x in Equation 1; y' is a function of y in Equations 2 and 3; y' is a function of both x and y in Equations 4 and 5.

A solution to a first-order ODE is a function $y = f(x)$, such that $f'(x) = g(x,y)$. Computing the solution to a differential equation involves integration in order to obtain y from y'; thus, the techniques for solving differential equations are often referred to as techniques for integrating differential equations. The solution to a differential equation is generally a family of functions. An **initial condition** or **boundary condition** is usually needed in order to specify a unique solution. The analytical solutions to the ODEs presented at the beginning of this section were determined using certain initial conditions, and are listed below:

Initial condition

Equation 1 Solution: $y = x^3 - 7.5$
Equation 2 Solution: $y = 4e^{-0.131x}$
Equation 3 Solution: $y = 0.022963 - 0.020763e^{-0.0015x}$
Equation 4 Solution: $y = \tan^{-1}(x^2 + 1)$
Equation 5 Solution: $y = 4e^{3x} - e^{2x}$

The details for computing these analytical solutions are beyond the scope of this text, but can be found in a differential equation text.

Although an analytical solution to a differential equation is preferred, many differential equations have complicated analytical solutions or no analytical solutions at all. For these cases, a numerical technique is needed to solve the differential equation. The most common numerical techniques for solving ordinary differential equations are Euler's method and the Runge-Kutta methods.

Both Euler's method and the Runge-Kutta methods approximate a function using its Taylor series expansion. Recall that a **Taylor series** is an expansion that can be used to approximate a function whose derivatives exist on an interval containing a and b. The Taylor's series expansion for $f(b)$ is

Taylor series

$$f(b) = f(a) + (b - a)f'(a) + \frac{(b-a)^2}{2!}f''(a) + \ldots + \frac{(b-a)^n}{n!}f^{(n)}(a) + \ldots$$

A **first-order Taylor's series approximation** uses the terms involving the function and its first derivative:

$$f(b) \approx f(a) + (b - a) f'(a)$$

A **second-order approximation** uses the terms involving the function, its first derivative, and its second derivative:

$$f(b) \approx f(a) + (b - a) f'(a) + \frac{(b - a)^2}{2!} f''(a)$$

The more terms of the Taylor series that are used to approximate a function, the more accurate is the approximation. The two MATLAB functions discussed in the next section use approximations of orders 2, 3, 4, and 5 to approximate the function value $f(b)$.

8.2   Runge-Kutta Methods

Runge-Kutta
method

The most popular methods for integrating a first-order differential equation are **Runge-Kutta methods**. These methods are based on approximating a function using its Taylor series expansion; thus, a first-order Runge-Kutta method uses a first-order Taylor series expansion, a second-order Runge-Kutta method uses a second-order Taylor series expansion, and so on. (**Euler's method** is equivalent to a first-order Runge-Kutta method.) The MATLAB functions presented later in this section use approximations of orders 2, 3, 4, and 5 to approximate values of an unknown function f using a differential equation.

The Taylor series for evaluating $f(b)$ is given by the following expansion:

$$f(b) = f(a) + (b - a) f'(a) + \frac{(b - a)^2}{2!} f''(a) + \ldots + \frac{(b - a)^n}{n!} f^{(n)}(a) + \ldots$$

If we assume that the term $(b - a)$ represents a step size h, we can then rewrite the Taylor's series in this form:

$$f(b) = f(a) + h f'(a) + \frac{h^2}{2!} f''(a) + \ldots + \frac{h^n}{n!} f^{(n)}(a) + \ldots$$

Because $y = f(x)$, we can simplify the notation further if we assume that $y_b = f(b)$, $y_a = f(a)$, $y_a' = f'(a)$, and so on:

$$y_b = y_a + h y_a' + \frac{h^2}{2!} y_a'' + \ldots + \frac{h^n}{n!} y_a^{(n)} + \ldots$$

FIRST-ORDER APPROXIMATION (EULER'S METHOD)

A first-order Runge-Kutta integration equation is the following:

$$y_b = y_a + h y_a'$$

This equation estimates the function value y_b using a straight line that is tangent to the function at y_a, as shown in Figure 8.1. To compute the value of y_b (which is assumed to be on the tangent line), we use the step size h (which is equal to $b - a$) and a starting point y_a; the differential equation is used to compute the value of

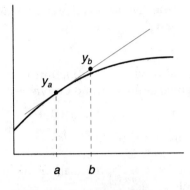

Figure 8.1 *Computation of y_b using first-order Runge-Kutta.*

y_a'. Once we have determined the value of y_b, we can estimate the next value of the function $f(c)$ using the following:

$$y_c = y_b + hy_b'$$

This equation uses the tangent line at y_b to estimate y_c, as shown in Figure 8.2. Because an initial value or boundary value is needed to start the process of estimating other points of the function $f(x)$, the Runge-Kutta methods (and Euler's method) are also called **initial-value solutions** or **boundary-value solutions**.

The first-order Runge-Kutta integration equation is simple to apply, but because it approximates the function with a series of short straight-line segments, it may not be very accurate if the step size is large or if the slope of the function changes rapidly. Therefore, higher-order Runge-Kutta integration equations are often used to approximate the unknown function. These higher-order techniques average several tangent-line approximations to the function, and thus obtain more accurate results. For example, a fourth-order Runge-Kutta integration equation uses terms in the Taylor's series expansion that include the first, second, third, and fourth derivatives, and computes the function estimate using four tangent-line estimates.

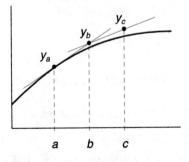

Figure 8.2 *Computation of y_c using first-order Runge-Kutta.*

ode Functions

MATLAB contains two functions for computing numerical solutions to ordinary differential equations—**ode23** and **ode45**. The arguments are described below, and a number of examples are then presented.

[x,y] = ode23('function_name',a,b,initial)

> Returns a set of **x** and **y** coordinates that represent the function $y = f(x)$ and are computed using second-order and third-order Runge-Kutta methods. The **'function_name'** defines a function f that returns values of the differential equation $y' = g(x,y)$ when it receives values for x and y. The values of **a** and **b** specify the endpoints of the interval over which we want to evaluate the function $y = f(x)$. The value of **initial** specifies the function value at the left endpoint of the interval **[a,b]**.

[x,y] = ode45('function_name',a,b,initial)

> Returns a set of **x** and **y** coordinates that represent the function $y = f(x)$ and are computed using fourth-order and fifth-order Runge-Kutta methods. The **'function_name'** defines a function f that returns values of the differential equation $y' = g(x,y)$ when it receives values for x and y. The values of **a** and **b** specify the endpoints of the interval over which we want to evaluate the function $y = f(x)$. The value of **initial** specifies the function value at the left endpoint of the interval **[a,b]**.

The **ode23** and **ode45** functions can also be used with two additional parameters. A fifth parameter can be used to specify a **tolerance** that is related to the step size; the default tolerances are 0.001 for **ode23** and 0.000001 for **ode45**. A sixth parameter can be used to request that the function print intermediate results (called a **trace**); the default value of 0 specifies no trace of the results. *When using numerical techniques with optional arguments, be sure to include program comments that define the optional arguments and their purpose when they are used.*

Style

To illustrate the **ode23** function, we present the steps to compute the numerical solutions to the differential equations given in Section 8.1. Because we know the analytical solutions to these ODEs, we also compute and plot the analytical solution as a series of points, whereas the numerical solution is plotted as a line graph. The MATLAB statements below define the functions required to evaluate the differential equations, assuming scalar inputs for **x** and **y**:

```
function dy = g1(x,y)
%   G1   This function evaluates a
%        first-order ODE.
%
dy = 3*x.^2;
```

```
function dy = g2(x,y)
%   G2   This function evaluates a
%        first-order ODE.
%
dy = -0.131*y;

function dy = g3(x,y)
%   G3   This function evaluates a
%        first-order ODE.
%
dy = 3.4444E-05 - 0.0015*y;

function dy = g4(x,y)
%   G4   This function evaluates a
%        first-order ODE.
%
dy = 2*x.*cos(y).^2;

function dy = g5(x,y)
%   G5   This function evaluates a
%        first-order ODE.
%
dy = 3*y + exp(2*x);
```

We now present the commands to compute the numerical solutions to the differential equations using given initial conditions. The numerical solution (**x,num_y**) is plotted along with points from the analytical solution (**x,y**) to demonstrate the accuracy of the numerical solutions.

Equation 1. The following statements solve $g_1(x,y)$ over the interval [2,4], assuming that the initial condition $y = f(2)$ is equal to 0.5.

```
%    Determine solution to ODE 1.
%
[x,num_y] = ode23('g1',2,4,0.5);
y = x.^3 - 7.5;
subplot(2,1,1),plot(x,num_y,x,y,'o'),...
    title('Solution to Equation 1'),...
    xlabel('x'),ylabel('y=f(x)'),grid
```

Figure 8.3 contains the comparison of the numerical solution to the analytical solution over the interval [2,4].

Equation 2. The following statements solve $g_2(x,y)$ over the interval [0,5], assuming that the initial condition $y=f(0)$ is equal to 4.

```
%    Determine solution to ODE 2.
%
[x,num_y] = ode23('g2',0,5,4);
y = 4*exp(-0.131*x);
subplot(2,1,1),plot(x,num_y,x,y,'o'),...
    title('Solution to Equation 2'),...
    xlabel('x'),ylabel('y=f(x)'),grid
```

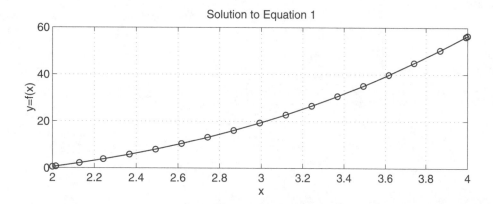

Figure 8.3 *Numerical and analytical solutions to Equation 1.*

Figure 8.4 contains the comparison of the numerical solution to the analytical solution over the interval [0,5].

Equation 3. The following statements solve $g_3(x,y)$ over the interval [0,120], assuming that the initial condition $y=f(0)$ is equal to 0.0022.

```
%    Determine solution to ODE 3.
%
[x,num_y] = ode23('g3',0,120,0.0022);
y = 0.022963 - 0.020763*exp(-0.0015*x);
subplot(2,1,1),plot(x,num_y,x,y,'o'),...
    title('Solution to Equation 3'),...
    xlabel('x'),ylabel('y=f(x)'),grid
```

Figure 8.5 contains the comparison of the numerical solution to the analytical solution over the interval [0,120].

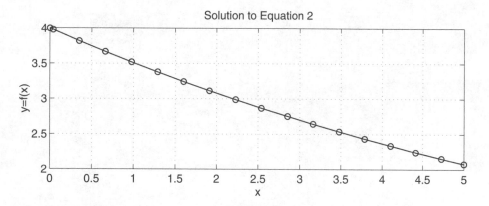

Figure 8.4 *Numerical and analytical solutions to Equation 2.*

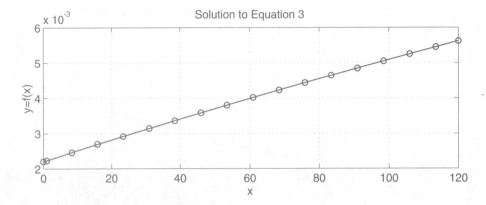

Figure 8.5 *Numerical and analytical solutions to Equation 3.*

Equation 4. The following statements solve $g_4(x,y)$ over the interval [0,2], assuming that the initial condition $y=f(0)$ is equal to $\pi/4$.

```
%    Determine solution to ODE 4.
%
[x,num_y] = ode23('g4',0,2,pi/4);
y = atan(x.*x+1);
subplot(2,1,1),plot(x,num_y,x,y,'o'),...
   title('Solution to Equation 4'),...
   xlabel('x'),ylabel('y=f(x)'),grid
```

Figure 8.6 contains the comparison of the numerical solution to the analytical solution over the interval [0,2].

Equation 5. The following statements solve $g_5(x,y)$ over the interval [0,3], assuming that the initial condition $y=f(0)$ is equal to 3.

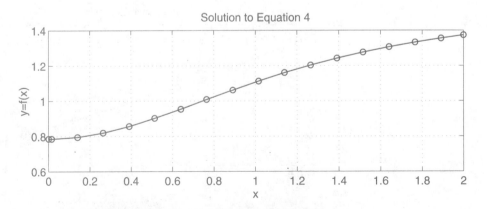

Figure 8.6 *Numerical and analytical solutions to Equation 4.*

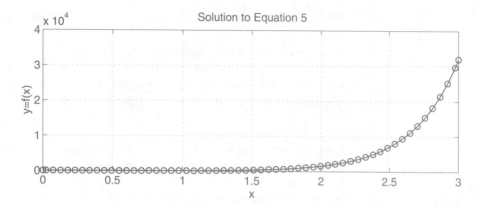

Figure 8.7 *Numerical and analytical solutions to Equation 5.*

```
%    Determine solution to ODE 5.
%
[x,num_y] = ode23('g5',0,3,3);
y = 4*exp(3*x) - exp(2*x);
subplot(2,1,1),plot(x,num_y,x,y,'o'),...
   title('Solution to Equation 5'),...
   xlabel('x'),ylabel('y=f(x)'),grid
```

Figure 8.7 contains the comparison of the numerical solution to the analytical solution over the interval [0,3].

The number of points computed for the function $y=f(x)$ by the **ode23** and **ode45** functions is determined by the MATLAB functions and is not an input parameter. To compute more points of the function $f(x)$, an interpolation method can be used with the points returned by **ode23** and **ode45**. For example, the cubic-spline interpolation technique presented in Chapter 6 would be a good candidate for an interpolation method to give a smoother plot of the function $f(x)$.

It is an interesting exercise to rerun the five examples presented using the **ode45** function along with the **ode23** function and plotting the y values returned by the two functions to compare them. Generally, the **ode23** function gives very good results, but the **ode45** function should be used in problems that need as much accuracy as possible.

Practice!

Two ordinary differential equations are listed below:

$$y' = g_a(x,y) = -y$$

$$y' = g_b(x,y) = \frac{-x - e^x}{3y^2}$$

1. Write MATLAB functions to evaluate these differential equations, given values for x and y.

2. Assume that an initial condition of $f(0) = -3.0$ is given for the first differential equation. Use MATLAB to solve this differential equation over the interval [0,2]. Plot the corresponding values of y.

3. The analytical solution to the first differential equation is

    $$y = -3e^{-x}$$

    Replot your solution in problem 2, and add points represented by this analytical solution in order to compare the numerical solution to the analytical solution.

4. Assume that an initial condition of $f(0) = 3.0$ is given for the second differential equation. Use MATLAB to solve this differential equation over the interval [0,2]. Plot the corresponding values of y.

5. The analytical solution to the second differential equation is

    $$y = \sqrt[3]{28 - 0.5x^2 - e^x}$$

    Replot your solution in problem 4, and add points represented by this analytical solution in order to compare the numerical solution to the analytical solution.

8.3   Problem Solving Applied: Acceleration of UDF-Powered Aircraft

An advanced turboprop engine called an **unducted fan** (UDF) is one of the promising new propulsion technologies being developed for future transport aircraft. Turboprop engines, which have been in use for decades, combine the power and reliability of jet engines with the efficiency of propellers. They are a significant improvement over earlier piston-powered propeller engines. Their application has been limited to smaller commuter-type aircraft, however, because they are not as fast or powerful as the fanjet engines used on larger airliners. The UDF engine employs significant advancements in propeller technology that narrow the performance gap between turboprops and fanjets. New materials, blade shapes, and higher rotation speeds enable UDF-powered aircraft to fly almost as fast as fanjets, and with greater fuel efficiency. The UDF is also significantly quieter than the conventional turboprop.

During a test flight of a UDF-powered aircraft, the test pilot has set the engine power level at 40,000 Newtons, which causes the 20,000 kg aircraft to attain a cruise speed of 180 m/s (meters per second). The engine throttles are then set to a power level of 60,000 Newtons, and the aircraft begins to accelerate. As the speed of the plane increases, the aerodynamic drag increases in proportion to the square of the airspeed. Eventually, the aircraft reaches a new cruise speed at which the thrust from the UDF engines is just offset by the drag. The differential equation that determines the acceleration of the aircraft is

$$a = \frac{T}{m} - 0.000062v^2$$

where

$$a = \frac{dv}{dt}$$

T = thrust level in Newtons
m = mass in kg
v = velocity in m/s

Write a MATLAB program to determine the new cruise speed after the change in power level of the engines by plotting the solution to the differential equation.

1.   PROBLEM STATEMENT

Compute the new cruise speed of the aircraft after a change in power level.

2.   INPUT/OUTPUT DESCRIPTION

The following I/O diagram shows that the output of the program is a plot from which the new cruise speed can be obtained.

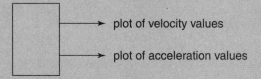

plot of velocity values

plot of acceleration values

3.   HAND EXAMPLE

The differential equation that is being solved is the following:

$$\frac{dv}{dt} = g(t,v) = \frac{T}{m} - 0.000062v^2$$

Thus, for the specified plane mass and the specified thrust, the differential equation is

$$v' = 3.0 - 0.000062v^2$$

where $v = f(t)$. The velocity at the time that the higher thrust was applied was 180 m/s; this velocity represents the initial condition $v=f(0)$. We can use the ode23 function to determine the velocity over a specified period of time, which begins with the application of the higher thrust. We expect the velocity to increase initially and then level off to a new higher cruise speed. Because the acceleration is equal to v', we can use the velocity values computed by the **ode23** function to determine the acceleration over the specified period of time. We would expect that the acceleration should decrease after the initial new thrust and return to a value of zero as the velocity (cruise speed) becomes constant.

4.   MATLAB SOLUTION

In the MATLAB solution, we use the **ode23** function to evaluate the differential equation. The solution to the differential equation will give us values of velocity, which can be used to determine values of acceleration. We will then plot both the velocity and the acceleration over an interval of 4 minutes to observe their changes. The velocity should increase and then stabilize at a new cruise speed; the acceleration should decrease to zero.

```
%    These statements compute the velocity and acceleration
%    of an aircraft after a new thrust is applied.
%
initial_vel = 180;
seconds = 240;
%
[t,num_v] = ode23('g',0,seconds,initial_vel);
acc = 3 - 0.000062*num_v.^2;
%
subplot(2,1,1),plot(t,num_v),title('Velocity'),...
   ylabel('m/s'),grid,...
subplot(2,1,2),plot(t,acc),title('Acceleration'),...
   xlabel('Time,s'),ylabel('m/s^2'),grid
```

The M-file that defines the function used to compute values of the differential equation is the following:

```
function dv = g(t,v)
%   G  This function computes values
%      given velocity values.
%
dv = 3 - 0.000062*v.^2;
```

5.   TESTING

The plots generated by this program are shown in Figure 8.8. The new cruise speed of the aircraft is approximately 220 m/s. As expected, the acceleration approaches zero as the new cruise speed is reached.

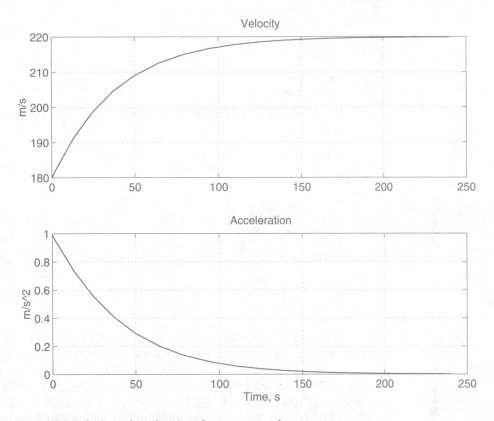

Figure 8.8 *Velocity and acceleration after new power thrust.*

8.4   Higher-Order Differential Equations

A higher-order differential equation can be written as a system of coupled first-order differential equations using a change of variables. For example, consider the following nth order differential equation:

$$y(n) = g(x,y,y',y'',\ldots,y^{(n-1)})$$

First, define n new unknown functions with these equations:

$$
\begin{aligned}
u_1(x) &= y^{(n-1)} \\
u_2(x) &= y^{(n-2)} \\
&\cdots \\
u_{n-2}(x) &= y'' \\
u_{n-1}(x) &= y' \\
u_n(x) &= y
\end{aligned}
$$

Then, the following system of n first-order equations is equivalent to the nth order differential equation given above:

$$u_1' \quad = y^{(n)} \qquad = g(x, u_n, u_{n-1}, \ldots, u_1)$$
$$u_2' \quad = u_1$$
$$\ldots$$
$$u_{n-2}' = u_{n-3}$$
$$u_{n-1}' = u_{n-2}$$

To demonstrate this process, consider this second-order linear differential equation:

$$y'' = g(x, y, y') = y'(1 - y^2) - y$$

We first define two new functions:

$$u_1(x) = y'$$

$$u_2(x) = y$$

We then obtain this system of coupled first-order differential equations:

$$u_1' = y'' = g(x, u_2, u_1) = u_1(1 - u_2^2) - u_2$$
$$u_2' = u_1$$

A system of coupled first-order differential equations can be solved using MATLAB's **ode** functions for solving first-order differential equations. However, the function that is used to evaluate the differential equation must compute the values of the coupled first-order differential equations in a vector. The initial condition must also be a vector that contains an initial condition for $y^{(n-1)}$, $y^{(n-2)}$, ..., y', y. MATLAB's **ode** functions return solutions for each of the first-order differential equations, which, in turn, represent $y^{(n-1)}$, $y^{(n-2)}$, ..., y', y.

To solve the set of two coupled equations developed in the previous example, we first define a function to compute values of the first-order differential equations:

```
function u_prime = eqns2(x,u)
%    EQNS2   This function computes values
%            for two coupled equations.
%
u_prime(1) = u(1)*(1-u(2)^2)-u(2);
u-prime(2) = u(1);
```

Then, to solve the system of first-order differential equations over the interval [0,20] using initial conditions of $y'(0) = 0.0$ and $y(0) = 0.25$, we use these MATLAB statements:

```
%    These statements solve a 2nd order ODE.
%
initial = [0 0.25];
[x,num_y] = ode23('eqns2',0,20,initial);
%
```

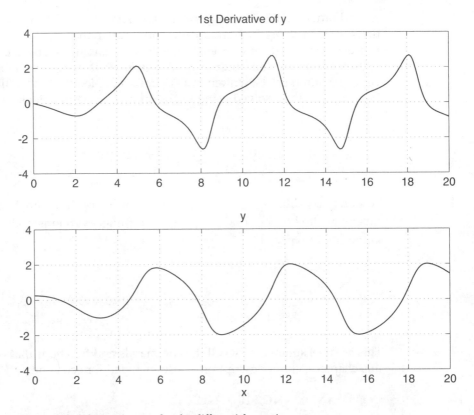

Figure 8.9 *Solution to second-order differential equation.*

```
subplot(2,1,1),plot(x,num_y(:,1)),...
    title('1st Derivative of y'),grid,...
subplot(2,1,2),plot(x,num_y(:,2)),...
    title('y'),xlabel('x'),grid
```

The plots generated by these statements are shown in Figure 8.9.

CHAPTER SUMMARY

This chapter described the Runge-Kutta methods for integrating first-order differential equations. The Runge-Kutta methods approximate the desired function using its Taylor series expansion: A first-order Runge-Kutta method uses a first-order Taylor series approximation, a second-order Runge-Kutta method uses a second-order Taylor series approximation, and so on. MATLAB contains two functions for integrating first-order differential equations. The function **ode23** implements second- and third-order Runge-Kutta techniques, and the function **ode45** implements fourth- and fifth-order Runge-Kutta techniques. Higher-order differential equations can be written as a system of coupled first-order differential equations which can be solved using the **ode23** and **ode45** functions.

KEY TERMS

boundary condition	ordinary differential equation
Euler's method	Runge-Kutta methods
initial condition	

MATLAB SUMMARY

This MATLAB summary lists all the commands and functions that were defined in this chapter. A brief description is also included for each one.

COMMANDS AND FUNCTIONS

ode23	second and third order Runge-Kutta solution
ode45	fourth and fifth order Runge-Kutta solution

Style NOTES

1. When using numerical techniques with optional arguments, be sure to include program comments that define the optional arguments and their purposes when they are used.

DEBUGGING NOTES

1. Use the **ode45** function in problem solutions that need as much accuracy as possible.

PROBLEMS

Problems 1–4 relate to the engineering application presented in this chapter. Problems 5–17 relate to new applications.

Acceleration of UDF-Powered Aircraft. These problems relate to the aircraft acceleration problem given in Section 8.3.

1. Modify the program to print the new cruise velocity. Assume that the new cruise velocity is achieved when three velocity values in a row are essentially the same values.
2. Modify the program in problem 1 to also print the time (relative to the power thrust) at which the new cruise velocity was achieved.
3. Modify the program in problem 1 to assume that the new cruise velocity is achieved when three acceleration values in a row are essentially zero.
4. Modify the program such that the plots use units of miles/hour and ft/s^2.

Mixture Problems. The following problems use differential equations that are determined from considering the inflow and outflow of materials into a known solution.

5. The following differential equation describes the relationships between the volume of pollutants $x(t)$ in a lake and the time t (in years), using equal rates of inflow and outflow, and assuming an initial pollutant concentration:

    $x' = 0.0175 - 0.3821x$

    Using an initial pollution volume at $t=0.0$ of 0.2290, determine and plot the volume of pollutants over a period of five years.
6. Use data obtained from problem 5 to determine when the pollution volume in the lake will be reduced to 0.1.
7. The analytical solution to the differential equation presented in problem 5 is

    $x(t) = 0.0458 + 0.1832e^{-0.3821t}$

    Compare the analytical solution to the numerical solution determined in problem 5 by plotting both solutions on the same graph.
8. Using the analytical solution presented in problem 7, determine an analytical value for the answer to problem 6.
9. A 120-gallon tank contains 90 pounds of salt dissolved in 90 gallons of water. Brine containing 2 pounds of salt per gallon is flowing into the tank at a rate of 4 gallons per minute. The mixture flows out of the tank at the rate of 3

gallons per minute. The differential equation that specifies the amount of salt $x(t)$ in pounds in the tank at time t in minutes is

$$x' = 8 - \frac{3}{90 + t}$$

The tank is full after 30 minutes. Determine and plot the amount of salt in the tank from time = 0 until the tank is full.

10. Using the data from problem 9, determine the amount of time required for the tank to contain 150 pounds of salt.

11. The analytical solution to the differential equation given in problem 9 is

$$x(t) = 2(90 + t) - \frac{90^4}{(90 + t)^3}$$

Compare the numerical solution to the analytical solution by plotting both solutions on the same graph.

12. Use the analytical solution given in problem 9 to compute the amount of time required for the tank to contain 150 pounds of salt. Compare this answer to the answer determined in problem 10.

Bungee Jump. A bungee jumper is preparing to make a high-altitude jump from a hot air balloon using a 150-meter bungee line. He wants to estimate his peak acceleration, velocity, and drop distance so that he can be sure that the arresting force of the bungee is not too great and that the balloon is high enough so that he will not hit the ground. The equation that he uses for his analysis is Newton's Second Law,

$$F = ma$$

where F is the sum of the gravitational, aerodynamic drag, and bungee forces acting on him, m is his mass (which is 70 kg), and a is his acceleration. He begins by defining the distance he falls as the variable x (which is a function of time, $x(t)$). His velocity and acceleration are then represented as x' and x'', respectively. He then rearranges Newton's equation to solve for the acceleration:

$$x'' = F/m$$

Next, he determines the forces making up F. The gravitational force will be his weight, which is

$$\begin{aligned} W &= m \cdot g \\ &= (70 \ kg) \cdot (9.8 \ m/s^2) \\ &= 686 \ N \end{aligned}$$

He knows that the aerodynamic drag, D, will be proportional to the square of his velocity, $D = c(x')^2$, but he does not know c, the constant of proportionality. However, he does know from his experience as a skydiver that his terminal velocity in a free-fall is about 55 m/s. At that speed, the aerodynamic drag is equal to his weight, so he determines c using

$$c = D/(x')^2$$
$$= (686\ N)/(55\ m/s)^2$$
$$= 0.227\ kg/m$$

Finally, after he has fallen 150 m, the slack in the bungee will be eliminated, and it will begin to exert an arresting force, B, of 10 N for every meter that it is stretched beyond 150 m. Thus, there will be two regions for computing the acceleration. The first will be used when the distance x is less than or equal to 150 m:

$$x'' = F/m$$
$$= (W - D)/m$$
$$= (686 - 0.227(x')^2)/70 \tag{8.1}$$
$$= 9.8 - 0.00324(x')^2\ m/s^2$$

A second equation will be used when x is greater than 150 m:

$$x'' = F/m$$
$$= (W - D - B)/m$$
$$= (686 - 0.227(x')^2 - 10(x - 150))/70 \tag{8.2}$$
$$= 31.23 - 0.00324(x')^2 - 0.143x\ m/s^2$$

The following set of problems refers to this bungee jump problem.

13. Integrate (8.1) for the interval beginning at 0 seconds to find the acceleration, velocity, and distance as a function of time from the beginning of the jump (which is assumed to occur at $t = 0.0$). From the results, determine the velocity and the time when $\mathbf{x} = 150$. (This is the point at which the slack in the bungee is eliminated.) You may need to experiment with the time interval in order to choose one that will give you the velocity and time desired.

14. Integrate (8.2) over a time interval that starts with the time that $x = 150$ to find the acceleration, velocity, and distance after the bungee becomes taut. (The results obtained in problem 13 at $x = 150$ are the initial conditions for this region.) What are the peak values of acceleration, velocity, and distance? The bungee jumper does not want the maximum acceleration to exceed 2 g's $(1\ g = 9.8\ m/sec^2)$. Is the estimate of the peak acceleration higher or lower? How close does he come to reaching the estimated terminal velocity of 55 m/sec? How far does he fall before he starts back up? How many seconds does he fall? How high should the balloon be to ensure a safety factor of 4?

15. Assume that the bungee also has a viscous friction force, R, once it begins to stretch, which is given by

$$R = -1.5x'$$

Modify the equation used for Problem 14 to include this force and determine the new results. How many seconds does it take for the bungee jumper to almost come to rest (or for the oscillations to almost stop)? What is the final stretched length of the bungee? Does this make sense?

16. For Problem 15, determine the length of the bungee that will cause the peak upward acceleration to be close to 2 g's.

17. For Problem 15, determine the arresting force per meter that will cause a peak acceleration of approximately 1.5 g's.

18. From his experience as a skydiver, the bungee jumper knows that if he dives straight down so that he is streamlined into the wind, he could reach a speed of about 120 m/s. Determine the new value for the aerodynamic drag constant of proportionality c that corresponds to this situation, and recompute the results of problem 15. Next, assume that the bungee is 300 meters long, and determine the jumper's peak velocity, the maximum g level, and how far below the balloon the jumper falls if he dives so that he is streamlined into the wind. Does he reach the 2 g limit? Plot the net force acting on the bungee jumper as a function of time. Can you explain the appearance of the graph?

Special Topics

The chapters in Part III contain MATLAB functions for solving special types of problems. In Chapter 9, MATLAB's functions for symbolic mathematics are introduced. These functions allow you to perform symbolic operations and to develop closed form expressions for solutions to equations (including ordinary differential equations) and systems of equations. Symbolic mathematics can also be used to determine analytical expressions for the derivative and integral of an expression. In Chapter 10, we introduce a number of MATLAB functions that are used in signal processing. These functions include an FFT function that is used to analyze the frequency content of a signal and functions for analyzing, designing, and implementing digital filters which are used to extract specific information from a digital signal. Chapter 11 presents a number of functions for converting a system model in one standard form to another standard form. In addition, a number of functions are presented for generating plots such as Bode plots, Nyquist plots, and root locus plots so that the characteristics of a system can be viewed graphically.

9

Courtesy of National Center for Atmospheric Research.

GRAND CHALLENGE:
Weather Prediction

Weather balloons collect data from the upper atmosphere for use in developing weather models. These balloons are filled with helium and rise to an equilibrium point, where the difference between the densities of the helium inside the balloon and the air outside the balloon is just enough to support the weight of the balloon. During the day, the sun warms the balloon, causing it to rise to a new equilibrium point; in the evening, the balloon cools, and it descends to a lower altitude. The balloon can be used to measure the temperature, pressure, humidity, chemical concentrations, or other properties of the air. A weather balloon may stay aloft for only a few hours or as long as several years collecting environmental data. The balloon falls back to earth as the helium leaks out or is released.

Symbolic Mathematics

OBJECTIVES

The previous chapters have demonstrated MATLAB's capabilities for numerical computations. In this chapter, we present some of its capabilities for symbolic manipulations. After showing you how to define a symbolic expression, we discuss the functions for simplifying mathematical expressions and for performing operations on mathematical expressions. In addition, we present sections on solving equations using symbolic mathematics and on performing differentiation and integration using symbolic expressions.

9.1 Symbolic Algebra

In the previous chapters, we used MATLAB to compute using numbers; in this chapter, we use MATLAB to compute using symbols. This capability to manipulate mathematical expressions without using numbers can be very useful in solving certain types of engineering problems. The symbolic functions in MATLAB are based on the **Maple V software package**, which comes from Waterloo Maple Software, Inc., in Canada. A complete set of these symbolic functions is available in the **Symbolic Math Toolbox**, which is available for the Professional Version of MATLAB; a subset of the symbolic functions is included with the Student Edition of MATLAB, Version 4.

Symbolic Math Toolbox

In this chapter, we focus on **symbolic algebra**, which is used to factor and simplify mathematical expressions, to determine solutions to equations, and to perform integration and differentiation of mathematical expressions. Additional capabilities that we do not discuss in this chapter include linear algebra symbolic functions for computing inverses, determinants, eigenvalues, and canonical forms of symbolic matrices; variable precision arithmetic for numerically evaluating mathematical expressions to a specified accuracy; and special mathematical functions that evaluate functions such as Fourier transforms. For details on these additional symbolic capabilities, refer to the Symbolic Math Toolbox Documentation.

Style

Because symbolic mathematics is not commonly available in computer languages and software tools, extra comments are needed to document its use.

SYMBOLIC EXPRESSIONS

A symbolic expression is stored in MATLAB as a **character string**. Thus, single quote marks are used to define symbolic expressions, as illustrated by the following examples:

```
'tan(y/x)'              'x^3 - 2*x^2 + 3'
'1/(cos(angle) + 2)'    '3*a*b - 6'
```

Independent variable

In expressions with more than one variable, it is often important to know, or to specify, the **independent variable**. In many functions, the independent variable can be specified as an additional function argument. When an independent variable is not specified, MATLAB will select one. If there are several variables, MATLAB selects the one that is a single lowercase letter, other than **i** and **j**, that is closest to **x** alphabetically; if there is a tie, the letter later in the alphabet is chosen. If there is no such character, then **x** is chosen as the independent variable.

The function **symvar** will return the independent variable:

symvar(s)   Returns the independent variable for the symbolic expression **s**.

The following examples illustrate the use of these rules in determining the independent variable in symbolic expressions:

expression S	symvar (S)
`'tan(y/x)'`	x
`'x^3 - 2*x^2 + 3'`	x
`'1/(cos(angle) + 2)'`	x
`'3*a*b - 6'`	b

MATLAB includes a function named **ezplot**, which generates a plot of a symbolic expression of one variable. The independent variable generally ranges over the interval $[-2\pi, 2\pi]$, unless this interval contains a **singularity** (a point at which the expression is not defined). A summary of the forms of this function follows:

`ezplot(S)`	Generates a plot of **s**, where **s** is assumed to be a function of one variable; the independent variable typically ranges from -2π to 2π.
`ezplot(S,[xmin,xmax])`	Generates a plot of **s**, where **s** is assumed to be a function of one variable; the independent variable ranges from **xmin** to **xmax**.

SIMPLIFICATION OF MATHEMATICAL EXPRESSIONS

A number of functions are available to simplify mathematical expressions by collecting coefficients, expanding terms, factoring expressions, or just simplifying the expression. A summary of these functions follows:

`collect(S)`	Collects coefficients of **s**.
`collect(S,'v')`	Collects coefficients of **s** with respect to the independent variable `'v'`.
`expand(S)`	Performs an expansion of **s**.
`factor(S)`	Returns the factorization of **s**.
`simple(S)`	Simplifies the form of **s** to a shorter form, if possible.
`simplify(S)`	Simplifies **s** using Maple's simplification rules.

To illustrate these functions, assume that the following symbolic expressions have been defined:

```
S1 = 'x^3-1';
S2 = '(x-3)^2+(y-4)^2';
S3 = 'sqrt(a^4*b^7)';
S4 = '14*x^2/(22*x*y)';
```

The following list shows function references and their corresponding values:

reference	function value
`factor(S1)`	`(x-1)*(x^2+x+1)`
`expand(S2)`	`x^2-6*x+25+y^2-8*y`
`collect(S2)`	`x^2-6*x+9+(y-4)^2`

reference	function value
collect(S2,'y')	y^2-8*y+(x-3)^2+16
simplify(S3)	a^2*b^(7/2)
simple(S4)	7/11*x/y

OPERATIONS ON SYMBOLIC EXPRESSIONS

The standard arithmetic operations can be applied to symbolic expressions using symbolic functions. Additional symbolic functions can be used to convert a symbolic expression from one form to another. These functions are summarized below:

horner(S)	Transposes s into its **Horner**, or nested, representation.
numden(S)	Returns two symbolic expressions that represent, respectively, the numerator expression and the denominator expression for the rational representation of s.
numeric(S)	Converts s to a numeric form. (s must not contain any symbolic variables.)
poly2sym(c)	Converts a polynomial coefficient vector c to a symbolic polynomial.
pretty(S)	Prints s in an output form that resembles typeset mathematics.
sym2poly(S)	Converts s to a polynomial coefficient vector.[*]
symadd(A,B)	Performs a symbolic addition, A+B.
symdiv(A,B)	Performs a symbolic division, A/B.
symmul(A,B)	Performs a symbolic multiplication, A*B.
sympow(S,p)	Performs a symbolic power, S^p.
symsub(A,B)	Performs a symbolic subtraction, A-B.

To illustrate the use of some of these functions, assume that the following symbolic expressions have been defined:

```
p1 = '1/(y-3)';
p2 = '3*y/(y+2)';
p3 = '(y+4)*(y-3)*y';
```

The following list shows function references and their corresponding values:

[*]Some early versions of the Student Edition contained an error in the M-file for this function. To correct the error, a change needs to be made in the last line of **sym2poly.m** in the symbolic toolbox: insert **ans := ** between the first quote and the second square bracket.

reference	function value
`symmul(p1,p3)`	`(y+4)*y`
`sympow(p2,3)`	`27*y^3/(y+2)^3`
`symadd(p1,p2)`	`1/(y-3)+3*y/(y+2)`
`[num,den]=numden(symadd(p1,p2))`	`[-8*y+2+3*y^2,(y-3)*(y+2)]`
`horner(symadd(p3,'1'))`	`1+(-12+(1+y)*y)*y`

Practice!

Use MATLAB to perform the following symbolic operations. Assume the following symbolic expressions have been defined:

```
S1 = '1/(x+4)';
S2 = 'x^2+8*x+16';
S3 = '(x+4)*(x-2)';
```

1. `S1/S2`
2. `S2/(S1²)`
3. `(S3)(S1)/S2`
4. `S2²`

9.2   Equation Solving

Symbolic math functions can be used to solve a single equation, a system of equations, and differential equations. The first discussion addresses the solution to a single equation or a system of equations; the second discussion addresses the solution to an ordinary differential equation.

SOLUTIONS TO EQUATIONS

A brief description of the functions for solving a single equation or a system of equations follows:

`solve(f)`	Solves a symbolic equation `f` for its symbolic variable. If `f` is a symbolic expression, this function solves the equation `f=0` for its symbolic variable.
`solve(f1,...fn)`	Solves the system of equations represented by `f1, . . ., fn`.

To illustrate the use of the `solve` function, assume that the following equations have been defined:

```
eq1 = 'x-3=4';
eq2 = 'x^2-x-6=0';
eq3 = 'x^2+2*x+4=0';
eq4 = '3*x+2*y-z=10';
eq5 = '-x+3*y+2*z=5';
eq6 = 'x-y-z=-1';
```

The following list shows the resulting values from the **solve** function:

reference	function value
solve(eq1)	7
solve(eq2)	[[3],[-2]]'
solve(eq3)	[[-1+i*3^(1/2)],[-1-i*3^(1/2)]]'
solve(eq4,eq5,eq6)	x = -2, y = 5, z = -6

Practice!

Solve the following systems of equations using symbolic mathematics. Compare your answers to those computed using the matrix methods from Chapter 4. (Remember to use single letter variables.)

1. $\begin{aligned} -2x_1 + x_2 &= -3 \\ x_1 + x_2 &= 3 \end{aligned}$

2. $\begin{aligned} -2x_1 + x_2 &= -3 \\ -2x_1 + x_2 &= 1 \end{aligned}$

3. $\begin{aligned} -2x_1 + x_2 &= -3 \\ -6x_1 + 3x_2 &= -9 \end{aligned}$

4. $\begin{aligned} -2x_1 + x_2 &= -3 \\ -2x_1 + x_2 &= -3.00001 \end{aligned}$

5. $\begin{aligned} 3x_1 + 2x_2 - x_3 &= 10 \\ -x_1 + 3x_2 + 2x_3 &= 5 \\ x_1 - x_2 - x_3 &= -1 \end{aligned}$

6. $\begin{aligned} 3x_1 + 2x_2 - x_3 &= 1 \\ -x_1 + 3x_2 + 2x_3 &= 1 \\ x_1 - x_2 - x_3 &= 1 \end{aligned}$

7. $\begin{aligned} 10x_1 - 7x_2 + 0x_3 &= 7 \\ -3x_1 + 2x_2 + 6x_3 &= 4 \\ 5x_1 + x_2 + 5x_3 &= 6 \end{aligned}$

8. $\begin{aligned} x_1 + 4x_2 - x_3 + x_4 &= 2 \\ 2x_1 + 7x_2 + x_3 - 2x_4 &= 16 \\ x_1 + 4x_2 - x_3 + 2x_4 &= 1 \\ 3x_1 - 10x_2 - 2x_3 + 5x_4 &= -15 \end{aligned}$

SOLUTIONS TO DIFFERENTIAL EQUATIONS

First-order
ordinary
differential
equation

A **first-order ordinary differential equation** (ODE) is an equation that can be written in the following form:

$$y' = \frac{dy}{dx} = g(x,y)$$

where x is the independent variable and y is a function of x. A solution to a first-order ODE is a function $y = f(x)$ such that $f'(x) = g(x,y)$. Computing the solution of a differential equation involves integration in order to obtain y from y'; thus, the techniques for solving differential equations are often referred to as techniques for integrating differential equations. The solution to a differential equation is generally a family of functions. An **initial condition** or **boundary condition** is usually needed in order to specify a unique solution.

In Chapter 8, we presented MATLAB's functions for computing the numerical solution to a differential equation. However, when it exists, an analytical solution to a differential equation is usually the preferred solution. The symbolic function for solving ordinary differential equations is **dsolve**:

> **dsolve('equation','condition')**   Symbolically solves the ordinary differential equation specified by **'equation'**. The optional argument **'condition'** specifies a boundary or initial condition.

The symbolic equation uses the letter **D** to denote differentiation with respect to the independent variable. A **D** followed by a digit denotes repeated differentiation. Thus, **Dy** represents dy/dx, and **D2y** represents d^2y/dx^2.

To illustrate the use of the **dsolve** function, we use three ODEs that were also used in Chapter 8 as examples for determining numerical solutions to ordinary differential equations:

Example 1:
    ode: $y' = 3x^2$
    initial condition: $y(2) = 0.5$
Example 2:
    ode: $y' = 2 \cdot x \cdot cos^2(y)$
    initial condition: $y(0) = \pi/4$
Example 3:
    ode: $y' = 3y + e^{2x}$
    initial condition: $y(0) = 3$

The MATLAB statements that determine symbolic solutions for these differential equations are the following:

```
soln_1 = dsolve('Dy = 3*x^2','y(2) = 0.5')
soln_2 = dsolve('Dy = 2*x*cos(y)^2','y(0) = pi/4')
soln_3 = dsolve('Dy = 3*y + exp(2*x)','y(0) = 3')
```

After executing these statements, the following output is generated:

```
soln_1 =
x^3-7.500000000000000
soln_2 =
atan(x^2+1)
soln_3 =
-exp(2*x)+4*exp(3*x)
```

These solutions match the analytical solutions presented in Chapter 8. To plot the first solution, we could use the **ezplot** function over the interval [2,4]:

```
ezplot(soln_1,[2,4])
```

9.3   Differentiation and Integration

The operations of differentiation and integration are used extensively in solving engineering problems. In Chapter 7, we discussed techniques for performing numerical differentiation and numerical integration using data values; in this section, we discuss the differentiation and integration of symbolic expressions;

DIFFERENTIATION

The **diff** function is used to determine the symbolic derivative of a symbolic expression. There are four forms in which the **diff** function can be used to perform symbolic differentiation:

diff(f)	Returns the derivative of the expression **f** with respect to the default independent variable.
diff(f,'t')	Returns the derivative of the expression **f** with respect to the variable **t**.
diff(f,n)	Returns the **n**th derivative of the expression **f** with respect to the default independent variable.
diff(f,'t',n)	Returns the **n**th derivative of the expression **f** with respect to the variable **t**.

Because the **diff** function is also used for numeric differentiation, you might wonder how the function knows whether it is to compute numeric differences or perform symbolic differentiation. The function can determine which is desired by analyzing the input arguments: If the argument is a vector, it computes numeric differences; if the argument is a symbolic expression, it performs symbolic differentiation.

We now present several examples using the **diff** function for symbolic differentiation. Assume that the following expressions have been defined:

```
S1 = '6*x^3-4*x^2+b*x-5';
S2 = 'sin(a)';
S3 = '(1 - t^3)/(1 + t^4)';
```

The following list shows function references and their corresponding values:

reference	function value
diff(S1)	18*x^2-8*x+b
diff(S1,2)	36*x-8
diff(S1,'b')	x
diff(S2)	cos(a)
diff(S3)	-3*t^2/(1+t^4)-4*(1-t^3)/(1+t^4)^2*t^3
simplify(diff(S3))	t^2*(-3+t^4-4*t)/(1+t^4)^2

Practice!

Determine the first and second derivatives of the following functions using MATLAB's symbolic functions.

1. $g_1(x) = x^3 - 5x^2 + 2x + 8$
2. $g_2(x) = (x^2 + 4x + 4)*(x - 1)$
3. $g_3(x) = (3x - 1)/x$
4. $g_4(x) = (x^5 - 4x^4 - 9x^3 + 32)^2$

INTEGRATION

The **int** function is used to integrate a symbolic expression **f**. This function attempts to find the symbolic expression **F** such that **diff(F)** = **f**. It is possible that the integral (or **antiderivative**) may not exist in closed form or that MATLAB cannot find the integral. In these cases, the function will return the expression unevaluated. The **int** function can be used in the following forms:

int(f)	Returns the integral of the expression **f** with respect to the default independent variable.
int(f,'t')	Returns the integral of the expression **f** with respect to the variable **t**.
int(f,a,b)	Returns the integral of the expression **f** with respect to the default independent variable evaluated over the interval [**a,b**], where **a** and **b** are numeric expressions.
int(f,'t',a,b)	Returns the integral of the expression **f** with respect to the variable **t** evaluated over the interval [**a,b**], where **a** and **b** are numeric expressions.
int(f,'m','n')	Returns the integral of the expression **f** with respect to the default independent variable evaluated over the interval [**m,n**], where **m** and **n** are symbolic expressions.

To avoid potential problems, it is a good idea to specify the independent variable in symbolic differentiation and symbolic integration.

We now present several examples using the **int** function for symbolic integration. Assume that the following expressions have been defined:

```
S1 = '6*x^3-4*x^2+b*x-5';
S2 = 'sin(a)';
S3 = 'sqrt(x)';
```

The following list shows function references and their corresponding values:

reference	function value
int(S1)	3/2*x^4-4/3*x^3+1/2*b*x^2-5*x
int(S2)	-cos(a)
int(S3)	2/3*x^(3/2)
int(S3,'a','b')	2/3*b^(3/2) - 2/3*a^(3/2)
int(S3,0.5,0.6)	2/25*15^(1/2)-1/6*2^(1/2)
numeric(int(S3,0.5,0.6))	0.0741

Practice!

Use MATLAB's symbolic functions to determine the values of the following integrals. Compare your answers to those computed by numerical integration in Chapter 7 on page 187.

1. $\displaystyle\int_{0.5}^{0.6} |x|\, dx$ 2. $\displaystyle\int_{0}^{1} |x|\, dx$

3. $\displaystyle\int_{-1}^{-0.5} |x|\, dx$ 4. $\displaystyle\int_{-0.5}^{0.5} |x|\, dx$

9.4   Problem Solving Applied: Weather Balloons

Weather balloons are used to gather temperature and pressure data at various altitudes in the atmosphere. The balloon rises because the density of the helium in the balloon is less than the density of the surrounding air outside the balloon. As the balloon rises, the surrounding air becomes less dense, and the balloon's ascent slows until it reaches a point of equilibrium. During the day, sunlight warms the helium trapped inside the balloon, the helium expands and becomes less dense, and the balloon rises higher. During the night, however, the helium in the balloon cools and becomes more dense, and the balloon descends to a lower altitude. The next day, the sun heats the air again, and the balloon rises. This process generates a set of altitude measurements over time that can be approximated with a polynomial equation.

Assume that the following polynomial represents the altitude in meters during the first 48 hours following the launch of a weather balloon:

$$h(t) = -0.12t^4 + 12t^3 - 380t^2 + 4100t + 220$$

where the units of t are hours. Generate plots of the altitude, velocity, and acceleration for this weather balloon using units of meters and meters/sec. Also, determine and print the peak altitude and its corresponding time.

1.   PROBLEM STATEMENT

Using the polynomial given, determine the velocity and acceleration that correspond to the altitude information. Plot the altitude, velocity, and acceleration. Also find the maximum altitude and its corresponding time.

2.   INPUT/OUTPUT DESCRIPTION

The following I/O diagram shows that there is no external input to the program. The output consists of the plots and the maximum altitude and corresponding time.

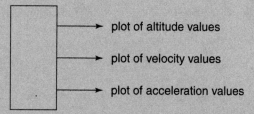

3.   HAND EXAMPLE

A hand example is not needed, because the program will use symbolic mathematics to determine the equations for the velocity and acceleration. The data will then be plotted, and the maximum value determined. However, it is important to note that because the units of the x axis are in hours, we will need to convert meters per hour to meters per second by replacing the time in hours with the time in seconds.

4.   MATLAB SOLUTION

In the MATLAB solution, we use the `polyval` function to generate the data values to plot. The `max` function is then used to determine the maximum altitude and its corresponding position.

```
%     These statements generate velocity and acceleration
%     plots using a polynomial model for the altitude
%     of a weather balloon.
%
altitude = '-0.12*t^4 + 12*t^3 - 380*t^2 + 4100*t + 220';
velocity = diff(altitude,'t');
acceleration = diff(velocity,'t');
%
t = 0:0.1:48;
alt_coef = sym2poly(altitude);
vel_coef = sym2poly(velocity);
acc_coef = sym2poly(acceleration);
%
subplot(2,1,1),plot(t,polyval(alt_coef,t)),...
   title('Balloon Altitude'),...
   xlabel('t, hours'),ylabel('meters'),grid,pause
subplot(2,1,1),plot(t,polyval(vel_coef,t)/3600),...
   title('Balloon Velocity'),...
   ylabel('meters/sec'),grid,...
subplot(2,1,2),plot(t,polyval(acc_coef,t)/(3600*60)),...
   title('Balloon Acceleration'),xlabel('t, hours'),...
   ylabel('meters/sec^2'),grid,pause
%
[max_alt,k] = max(polyval(alt_coef,t));
max_time = t(k);
fprintf('Maximum altitude: %8.2f Time: %6.2f \n',...
   max_alt(1), max_time(1))
```

5.   TESTING

The plots of the altitude, velocity, and acceleration and the output from the program are:

```
Maximum altitude: 17778.57 Time:   42.40
```

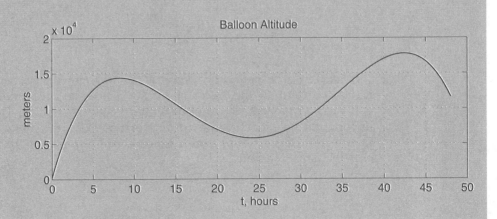

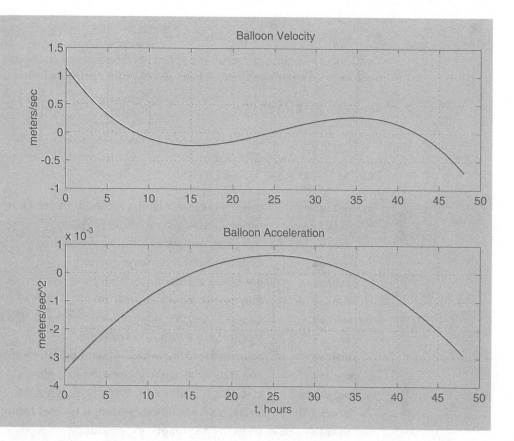

9

CHAPTER SUMMARY

In this chapter, we presented MATLAB's functions for performing symbolic mathematics. We gave examples to illustrate simplification of expressions, operations with symbolic expressions, and deriving symbolic solutions to equations. In addition, we presented the MATLAB functions for determining the symbolic derivatives and integrals of expressions.

KEY TERMS

character string   symbolic algebra
independent variable   symbolic expression
symbol

MATLAB SUMMARY

This MATLAB summary lists all the special symbols, commands, and functions that were defined in this chapter. A brief description is also included for each one.

SPECIAL CHARACTERS

'   used to enclose a symbolic expression.

COMMANDS AND FUNCTIONS

collect	collects coefficients of a symbolic expression
diff	differentiates a symbolic expression
dsolve	solves an ordinary differential equation
expand	expands a symbolic expression
ezplot	generates a plot of a symbolic expression
factor	factors a symbolic expression
horner	converts a symbolic expression into a nested form
int	integrates a symbolic expression
numden	returns the numerator and denominator expressions
numeric	converts a symbolic expression to a number
poly2sym	converts a vector to a symbolic polynomial
pretty	prints a symbolic expression in typeset form
simple	shortens a symbolic expression
simplify	simplifies a symbolic expression
solve	solves an equation or system of equations
sym2poly	converts a symbolic expression to a coefficient vector
symadd	adds two symbolic expressions
symdiv	divides two symbolic expressions
symmul	multiplies two symbolic expressions
sympow	raises a symbolic expression to a power
symsub	subtracts two symbolic expressions
symvar	returns independent variable

Style NOTES

1.   Because symbolic mathematics is not commonly available in computer languages and software tools, extra comments are needed to document its use.

DEBUGGING NOTES

1. To avoid potential problems, it is a good idea to specify the independent variable in symbolic differentiation and symbolic integration.

PROBLEMS

Water Flow. Assume that water is pumped into an initially empty tank. It is known that the rate of flow of water into the tank at time t (in seconds) is $50 - t$ liters per second. The amount of water Q that flows into the tank during the first x seconds can be shown to be equal to the integral of the expression $50 - t$ evaluated from 0 to x seconds.

1. Determine a symbolic equation that represents the amount of water in the tank after **x** seconds.
2. Determine the amount of water in the tank after 30 seconds.
3. Determine the amount of water that flowed into the tank between 10 seconds and 15 seconds after the flow was initiated.

Elastic Spring. Consider a spring with the left end held fixed and the right end free to move along the x-axis. We assume that the right end of the spring is at the origin $x =$ **0** when the spring is at rest. When the spring is stretched, the right end of the spring is at some new value of x that is greater than 0; when the spring is compressed, the right end of the spring is at some value of x that is less than 0. Assume that a spring has a natural length of 1 ft and that a force of 10 lbs is required to compress the spring to a length of 0.5 ft. It can then be shown that the work (in ft/lb) done to stretch this spring from its natural length to a total length of n ft is equal to the integral of $20x$ over the interval from 0 to $n - 1$.

4. Use MATLAB to determine a symbolic expression that represents the amount of work necessary to stretch the spring to a total length of n ft.
5. What is the amount of work done to stretch this spring to a total of 2 feet.
6. If the amount of work exerted is 25 ft/lb, what is the length of the stretched spring?

9

10

Courtesy of Texas Instruments.

GRAND CHALLENGE:
Computerized Speech Understanding

Computer algorithms for word recognition are complicated algorithms that work best when the speech signals are "clean." However, when speech signals are collected by microphones, the background noise is also collected. Therefore, preprocessing steps are often used to remove some of the background noise before attempting to identify the words in the speech signals. These preprocessing steps may require a number of operations that fall into the area of signal processing, such as analyzing the characteristics of a signal, decomposing a signal into sums of other signals, coding a signal in a form that is easy to transmit across a communication channel, and extracting information from a signal. Signal processing can be performed using computers such as those that you use at work or at school; it is also often performed using special microprocessor chips called digital signal processors, or DSP chips. The microprocessor shown in this photograph is Texas Instrument's TMS320C80 digital signal processor.

Signal Processing

Chapter Summary, Key Terms, MATLAB Summary
Style Notes, Debugging Notes, Problems

OBJECTIVES

The Student Edition of MATLAB contains a number of functions that have been selected from the Signal Processing Toolbox and the Control Systems Toolbox, which are option toolboxes that can be purchased with the professional version of MATLAB. These selected functions have been combined in a Signals and Systems Toolbox. This chapter discusses a number of these functions that are related to signal processing; the next chapter discusses a number of the remaining functions that are related to control systems. The functions discussed in this chapter have been divided into four categories: frequency domain analysis, filter analysis, filter implementation, and filter design. In these sections, we assume that the reader is already familiar with the signal processing concepts of time domain, frequency domain, transfer functions, and filters. Because the notation varies among the signal-processing literature, we define the notation that is used in the discussions on the signal processing functions.

10.1   Frequency Domain Analysis

Digital signal
processing

Although this chapter discusses both analog signal processing and digital signal processing, the focus is on **digital signal processing**, or DSP. An **analog signal** is a continuous function (usually of time, as in $f(t)$) that represents information, such as a speech signal, a blood pressure signal, or a seismic signal. In order to process this information with the computer, an analog signal can be sampled every T seconds, thus generating a **digital signal** that is a sequence of values from the original analog signal. We represent a digital signal that has been sampled from a continuous signal $x(t)$ using the following notation:

$$x_k = x(kT)$$

The digital signal is the sequence of samples x_k.

The time that we begin collecting the digital signal is usually assumed to be 0; thus, the first sample of a digital signal is usually referred to as x_0. Hence, if a signal is sampled at 10 Hz (10 cycles per second, or equivalently, 10 times per second), the first three values of the digital signal correspond to the following analog signal values:

$$x_0 = x(0T) = x(0.0)$$
$$x_1 = x(1T) = x(0.1)$$
$$x_2 = x(2T) = x(0.2)$$

Figure 10.1 compares an analog signal to its corresponding digital signal. In this figure, we show the digital signal as a sequence of points or samples, but, in general, we plot a digital signal with the points connected with line segments. The y-axis will be labeled as $x(k)$ or $x(kT)$ to indicate that it is a digital signal.

Recall that the subscripts of a MATLAB vector always start with 1, as in **x(1)**, **x(2)**, and so on. The subscripts of a signal usually start with 0, as in g_0, g_1, and so on. However, the subscripts of a signal might start with any value, even a negative value, as in h_{-2}, h_{-1}, h_0, and so on. Because many of the equations that relate to signal processing contain these various possible subscripts, we would like to be able to use the equations without rewriting them to adjust the subscripts. This can often be accomplished by associating two vectors with a signal. One vector contains the values of the signal, and the other vector contains the subscripts that are associated with those values. Thus, if the signals g and h mentioned earlier in this paragraph contain 10 values, the corresponding vectors **g** and **h** also contain 10 values. We can then use two additional vectors, such as **kg** and **kh**, to represent the subscripts that correspond to the 10 values in **g** and **h**. Thus, the vector **kg** would contain the values 0 to 9; the vector **kh** would contain the values -2 to 7. Although the advantages of using this extra vector to represent subscripts will become more clear as we present examples using MATLAB and signals, the main advantage will be that we can use equations from signal processing without having to adjust the subscripts—which can introduce errors.

In signal processing, a signal is often analyzed in two domains: the time domain and the frequency domain. The **time domain** signal is represented by the data values x_k; the **frequency domain** signal can be represented by a set of complex values X_k, which represent the sinusoids that can be used to represent the sig-

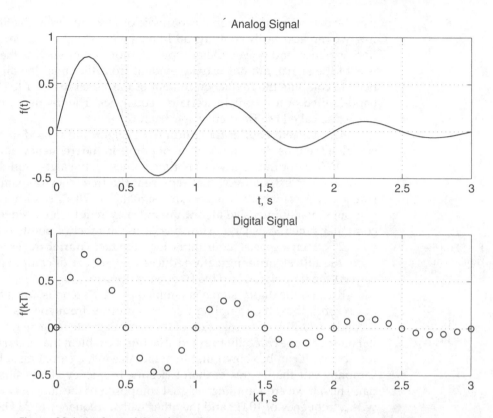

Figure 10.1 *Analog and digital signals.*

Sinusoid

nal. A **sinusoid** is cosine function with an **amplitude** A, a **frequency** ω, and a **phase shift** ϕ:

$$x(t) = A \cos(\omega t + \phi)$$
$$x_k = A \cos(\omega kT + \phi)$$

Note that a sine or a cosine function is a function of angle (in radians), but a sinusoid is a function of time. The index k of the complex value X_k can be used to determine the frequency of the sinusoid, the magnitude of X_k represents a scaled version of the amplitude of the sinusoid, and the phase of X_k specifies the phase shift of the sinusoid. Because the angular frequency ω has units of radians per second, we can also write the sinusoid using an angular frequency f, which has units

Hertz

of **cycles per second**, or **Hertz** (Hz), in this form:

$$x(t) = A \cos(2\pi f t + \phi)$$
$$x_k = A \cos(2\pi f kT + \phi)$$

Use MATLAB to generate and plot sinusoids. Experiment with different frequencies, amplitudes, and phase shifts; make sure that the plots have the characteristics that you expected.

Some types of information are most evident from the time-domain representation of a signal. For example, by looking at a time-domain plot, we can usually determine if the signal is periodic or random. From the time-domain values, we can also easily compute additional values such as mean, standard deviation, variance, and power. Other types of information, such as the frequency content of the signal, are not usually evident from the time domain; thus, we may need to compute the frequency content of the signal in order to determine if it is band-limited or if it contains certain frequencies. The frequency content of a signal is also called the **frequency spectrum**.

Frequency
spectrum

The **discrete Fourier transform** (DFT) algorithm is used to convert a digital signal in the time domain into a set of points in the frequency domain. The input to the DFT algorithm is a set of N time values x_k; the algorithm then computes a set of N complex values X_k that represent the frequency-domain information or sinusoidal decomposition of the time signal. The DFT algorithm is, in general, a computationally intensive algorithm and may require a considerable amount of computer time if N is large. However, if the number of points is a power of two ($N = 2^M$), then a special algorithm called the **fast Fourier transform** (FFT) can be used; the FFT algorithm greatly reduces the number of computations needed to convert the time signal into the frequency domain.

Fast Fourier
transform

Because the digital signal is sampled every T seconds, there are $1/T$ samples per second; thus, the sampling rate or **sampling frequency** is $1/T$ samples per second, or $1/T$ Hz. The selection of the sampling rate for generating a digital signal must be done carefully to avoid **aliasing**, a problem that is caused by sampling too slowly. It can be shown that to avoid aliasing, a signal must be sampled at a sampling rate that is greater than twice the frequency of any sinusoid in the signal. Thus, if we are sampling a signal composed of the sum of two sinusoids, one with a frequency of 10 Hz and the other with a frequency of 35 Hz, we must sample the signal with a sampling frequency greater than 70 Hz to avoid aliasing. The **Nyquist frequency** is equal to half the sampling frequency and represents the upper limit of the frequencies that should be contained in the digital signal.

Sampling
frequency

Nyquist
frequency

The MATLAB function for computing the frequency content of a signal is the `fft` function:

`fft(x)`	Computes the frequency content of the signal **x** and returns the values in a vector the same size as **x**.
`fft(x,N)`	Computes the frequency content of the signal **x** and returns the values in a vector with **N** values.

If the number of values in **x** is a power of 2, or if **N** is a power of 2, this function uses an FFT algorithm to compute the output values; otherwise, the function uses a DFT algorithm to compute the output values. If two input arguments are used and the number of values in **x** is less than **N**, zeros will be appended to the end of the time signal before the frequency domain values are computed. If the number of values is greater than **N**, then the first **N** values of the time signal will be used to compute the corresponding frequency-domain values.

The frequency-domain values computed by the **fft** function correspond to frequencies separated by $1/(NT)$ Hz. Thus, the kth output from the FFT corresponds to a frequency of $k/(NT)$ Hz. To illustrate with a specific case, if we have 32 samples of a time signal that was sampled at 1000 Hz, the frequency values computed by the **fft** algorithm correspond to 0 Hz, 1/0.032 Hz, 2/0.032 Hz, and so on. These values are also equal to 0 Hz, 31.25 Hz, 62.5 Hz, and so on. The Nyquist frequency is equal to $1/(2T)$, and will correspond to F_{16}. *We usually do not print the information that corresponds to values at the Nyquist frequency and above because these values are due to the periodicity of the DFT and the FFT, and not to higher frequency components in the signal.*

Consider the following set of MATLAB statements that generate a time signal containing 64 samples:

```
%    Generate a 20 Hz sinusoid sampled at 128 Hz.
N = 64;
T = 1/128;
k = 0:N-1;
x = sin(2*pi*20*k*T);
```

The signal x represents values of a 20-Hz sinusoid sampled every 1/128 seconds, which is equivalent to a sampling rate of 128 Hz. (The sinusoid has a frequency of 20 Hz, so it should be sampled at a rate higher than 40 Hz. The specified sampling rate is 128 Hz, so we are assured that aliasing does not occur.) Figure 10.2 contains a plot of the digital signal **x**. (Note that the vector **k** gives the subscript values that correspond to the signal **x**.)

Because the signal **x** is a single sinusoid, we expect that the frequency content should be 0 everywhere except at the point in the frequency domain that corresponds to 20 Hz. To determine the X_k that corresponds to 20 Hz, we need to compute the increment in Hz between points in the frequency domain, which is

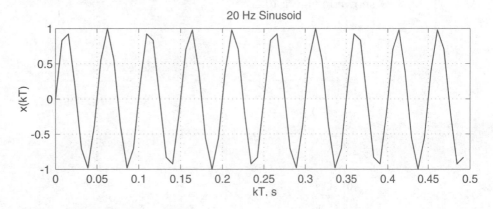

Figure 10.2 *Sinusoidal digital signal, x_k.*

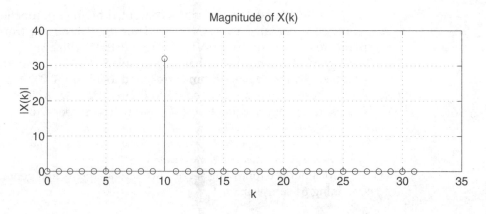

Figure 10.3 *Magnitude of X_k.*

$1/NT$, or 2 Hz. Therefore, a 20-Hz component should appear as $\mathbf{x_{10}}$, as we can see in Figure 10.3, which was generated with these additional statements:

```
%    Compute and plot the frequency content.
X = fft(x);
magX = abs(X);
subplot(2,1,1),stem(k(1:N/2),magX(1:N/2)),...
    title('Magnitude of X(k)'),...
    xlabel('k'),ylabel('|X(k)|'),grid
```

Note the use of a new plot function called **stem** which generates a point plot with lines, or stems, connecting the points to the x-axis. In this plot, you see that the 20-Hz component shows up as $\mathbf{x_{10}}$, as expected. It is often desirable to plot the magnitude of X_k using an x-axis scale in Hz instead of the index k. The preferred plot of the magnitude of X_k is thus computed by the following statements and shown in Figure 10.4.

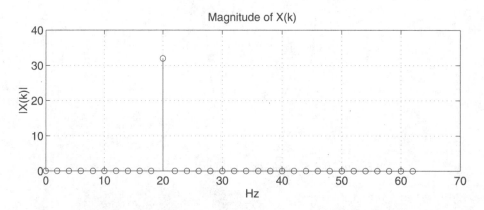

Figure 10.4 *Magnitude of X_k in Hz.*

```
%    Plot the frequency content as a function of Hz.
hertz = k*(1/(N*T));
subplot(2,1,1),stem(hertz(1:N/2),magX(1:N/2)),...
   title('Magnitude of X(k)'),...
   xlabel('Hz'),ylabel('|X(k)|'),grid
```

Suppose that the frequency of the sinusoid used in this example had been 19 Hz instead of 20 Hz. Because the increment in Hz between values of X_k for this example is 2 Hz, this sinusoid should appear at X_k where $k = 9.5$. However, the values of k are integers, so there is no value $X_{9.5}$. In this situation, the sinusoid appears at values of X nearest to the computed index. For this example, the sinusoid appears at values X_9 and X_{10} which correspond to 18 and 20 Hz, as shown in Figure 10.5, which was generated with the following statements:

```
%    Generate time signal and plot spectrum.
N = 64;
T = 1/128;
k = 0:N-1;
x = sin(2*pi*19*k*T);
%
magX = abs(fft(x));
hertz = k*(1/(N*T));
subplot(2,1,1),stem(hertz(1:N/2),magX(1:N/2)),...
   title('Magnitude of X(k)'),...
   xlabel('Hz'),ylabel('|X(k)|'),grid
```

Leakage

Figures 10.4 and 10.5 both contain the frequency spectrum of a single sinusoid, but one sinusoid falls exactly on a point corresponding to an output point of the FFT algorithm, and the other does not. This is an example of **leakage**, which occurs when a sinusoidal component does not fall exactly on one of the points in the FFT output.

The **ifft** function uses an **inverse Fourier transform** to compute the time domain signal x_k from the complex frequency domain values X_k:

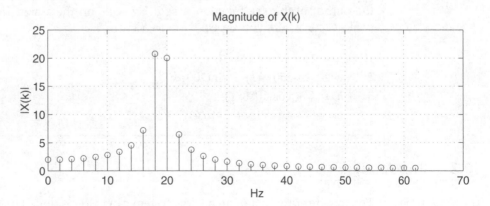

Figure 10.5 *Magnitude of signal with leakage.*

`ifft(X)`	Computes the time signal **x** from its frequency values **x** and returns the values in a vector the same size as **x**.
`ifft(X,N)`	Computes the time signal **x** from its frequency values **x** and returns the values in a vector with **N** values.

A fast algorithm is used if the number of points in the computations is a power of 2. If two input arguments are used and the number of values in **x** is less than **N**, then zeros will be appended to the end of the frequency signal before the time-domain values are computed. If the number of values is greater than **N**, then the first **N** values of the frequency signal will be used to compute the corresponding time-domain values.

The following example computes the values of X_k and then uses the `ifft` to compute the values of x_k from X_k. The final computation determines the sum of the differences between the original signal and the signal computed by the `ifft` function:

```
%    Compute the difference between x and ifft(fft(x)).
N = 64;
T = 1/128;
k = 0:N-1;
x = sin(2*pi*19*k*T);
sum(x - ifft(fft(x)))
```

The value printed was $-5.5511\mathrm{e}{-017}$, or essentially 0.

The FFT algorithm is an extremely powerful analysis tool for working with digital signals. Our discussion has focused on the magnitude of the value F_k, but very important information is also obtained from the phase of F_k.

Practice!

Generate and plot 128 points of the following signals using a sampling rate of 1 kHz. Then, using the FFT algorithm, generate and plot the first 64 points of the output of the `fft` function. Use a Hz scale on the x-axis. Verify that the peaks occur where you expect them to occur.

1. $f_k = 2 \sin (2\pi 50kT)$
2. $g_k = \cos(250\pi kT) - \sin(200\pi kT)$
3. $h_k = 5 - \cos(1000kT)$
4. $m_k = 4 \sin (250\pi kT - \pi/4)$

10.2 Filter Analysis

Transfer function

The **transfer function** of an analog system can be represented by a complex function $H(s)$, and the transfer function of a digital system is represented by a complex function $H(z)$. These transfer functions describe the effect of the system on an input signal and also describe the filtering effect of the system. Both $H(s)$ and $H(z)$ are continuous function of frequency, where $s = j\omega$ and $z = e^{j\omega T}$. (Recall that ω represents frequency in radians per second.) Thus, for a given frequency ω_0, assume that the transfer function magnitude is B and that the transfer function phase is ϕ. Then, if the input to the filter contains a sinusoid with frequency ω_0, the magnitude of the sinusoid will be multiplied by B, and the phase will be incremented by ϕ. The effects of these changes are shown for both analog filters and digital filters in Figure 10.6.

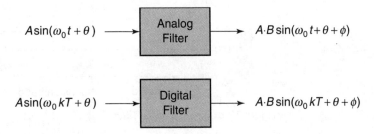

Figure 10.6 *Effect of filters on sinusoids.*

Although the transfer function of a filter defines the effect of the filter in terms of frequencies, it can often be described in terms of the band of frequencies that it passes. For example, a **lowpass** filter will pass frequencies below a cutoff frequency and remove those above the cutoff frequency. A **highpass** filter will pass frequencies above a cutoff frequency and remove those below. A **bandpass** filter will pass frequencies within a specified band and remove all others. A **bandstop** filter will remove frequencies within a specified band and pass all others. Figure 10.7 contains example transfer functions for these four general types of filters.

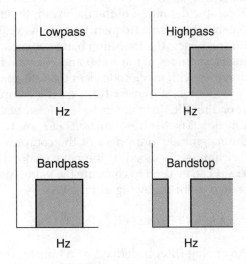

Figure 10.7 *Ideal transfer functions.*

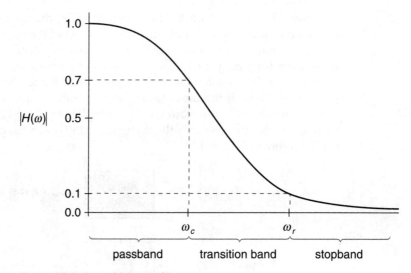

Figure 10.8 *Typical lowpass filter.*

The transfer functions in Figure 10.7 are ideal filters, with a frequency either passed or removed. We will see that it is not possible to design filters with exactly the same characteristics as these ideal filters.

Figure 10.8 contains an example of the magnitude of a typical lowpass filter that illustrates the types of characteristics of most lowpass filters. Instead of each frequency being passed or rejected, there are three regions: a **passband**, a **transition band**, and a **stopband**. These regions are defined by a **cutoff frequency** ω_c and a **rejection frequency** ω_r. Unless otherwise indicated, we will assume that the frequency that corresponds to a magnitude of 0.7 is the cutoff frequency and the frequency that corresponds to a magnitude of 0.1 is the rejection frequency. With these definitions of the cutoff and rejection frequencies, we can be more specific about the definition of the passband, the transition band, and the stopband. The passband contains frequencies with magnitudes above the magnitude of the cutoff frequency; the transition band contains frequencies with magnitudes between the magnitudes of the cutoff and rejection frequencies; the stopband contains frequencies with magnitudes less than the magnitude of the rejection frequency.

Because a transfer function is a complex function, the analysis of the corresponding filter usually includes plots of the magnitude and phase of the transfer function. The MATLAB functions **abs, angle,** and **unwrap** can be used to determine the magnitude and phase of the complex functions $H(s)$ and $H(z)$. (The **unwrap** function is discussed in the next section.) In addition, the functions **freqs** and **freqz** can be used to compute the values of the functions $H(s)$ and $H(z)$, as will be shown in the following discussion.

ANALOG TRANSFER FUNCTIONS

Analog filter   An **analog filter** is defined by a transfer function $H(s)$, where $s = j\omega$. The general form of the transfer function $H(s)$ is the following:

$$H(s) = \frac{B(s)}{A(s)}$$

$$= \frac{b_0 s^n + b_1 s^{n-1} + b_2 s^{n-2} + \ldots + b_n}{a_0 s^n + a_1 s^{n-1} + a_2 s^{n-2} + \ldots + a_n} \tag{10.1}$$

This transfer function corresponds to an nth order analog filter. Some examples of specific transfer functions are the following:

$$H_1(s) = \frac{0.5279}{s^2 + 1.0275s + 0.5279}$$

$$H_2(s) = \frac{s^2}{s^2 + 0.1117s + 0.0062}$$

$$H_3(s) = \frac{1.05s}{s^2 + 1.05s + 0.447}$$

$$H_4(s) = \frac{s^2 + 2.2359}{s^2 + 2.3511s + 2.2359}$$

In order to determine the characteristics of the systems with the transfer functions that are given above, we need to plot the magnitude and phase of the transfer functions. The MATLAB function **freqs** computes values of the complex function $H(s)$:

freqs(B,A,w)   Computes values of the transfer function $H(s) = B(s)/A(s)$, where **B** is the coefficient vector of $B(s)$ and **A** is the coefficient vector of $A(s)$. The vector **w** contains the frequency values in radians per second for which we want to evaluate $H(s)$. The vector of complex values of $H(s)$ is the same size as **w**.

It may require several trials to find an appropriate range of values for the frequency vector. In general, you want the frequency range to start at 0 and include all the critical information in the filter. Therefore, you want to be able to determine the filter type (lowpass, highpass, bandpass, bandstop) and the critical frequencies (cutoff, rejection).

The statements below determine and plot the magnitudes of the four example transfer functions.

```
%    These statements determine and plot the
%    magnitudes of four analog filters.
%
w1 = 0:0.05:5;
B1 = [0.5279];
A1 = [1,1.0275,0.5279];
H1s = freqs(B1,A1,w1);
%
w2 = 0:0.001:0.3;
B2 = [1,0,0];
A2 = [1,0.1117,0.0062];
H2s = freqs(B2,A2,w2);
```

```
%
w3 = 0:0.01:10;
B3 = [1.05,0];
A3 = [1,1.05,0.447];
H3s = freqs(B3,A3,w3);
%
w4 = 0:0.005:5;
B4 = [1,0,2.2359];
A4 = [1,2.3511,2.2359];
H4s = freqs(B4,A4,w4);
%
subplot(2,2,1),plot(w1,abs(H1s)),...
   title('Filter H1(s)'),xlabel('w, rps'),...
   ylabel('Magnitude'),grid,...
subplot(2,2,2),plot(w2,abs(H2s)),...
   title('Filter H2(s)'),xlabel('w, rps'),...
   ylabel('Magnitude'),grid,...
subplot(2,2,3),plot(w3,abs(H3s)),...
   title('Filter H3(s)'),xlabel('w, rps'),...
   ylabel('Magnitude'),grid,...
subplot(2,2,4),plot(w4,abs(H4s)),...
   title('Filter H4(s)'),xlabel('w, rps'),...
   ylabel('Magnitude'),grid
```

Figure 10.9 contains the plots of these filter magnitudes.

The phase of a filter can be determined using the **angle** function, which computes the phase of a complex number. Because the phase of a complex number is an angle in radians, the angle is only unique for a 2π interval. The **angle** function will return values between $-\pi$ and π. The **unwrap** function will detect 2π discontinuities in a vector of values and will replace the angles with equivalent values that do not have the discontinuities.

angle(X)	Computes the phase of the complex values in **x**. All angles are converted to equivalent values between $-\pi$ and π.
unwrap(X)	Removes 2π discontinuities in a vector **x**. This function is often used with the **angle** function, as in **unwrap(angle(X))**.

DIGITAL TRANSFER FUNCTIONS

Digital filter

A **digital filter** is defined by a transfer function $H(z)$, where $z = e^{j\omega T}$. The variable z can be written as a function of frequency (ω), or it can be written as a function of normalized frequency (ωT). If z is used as a function of frequency, then $H(z)$ is also a function of frequency. Because $H(z)$ is applied to input signals with a sampling time of T, the appropriate range of frequencies is from 0 to the Nyquist frequency, which is π/T rps or $1/(2T)$ Hz. If we assume that z is used as a function of normalized frequency, then $H(z)$ has a corresponding range of frequencies from 0 to π.

A general form of the transfer function $H(z)$ can be written in the following form:

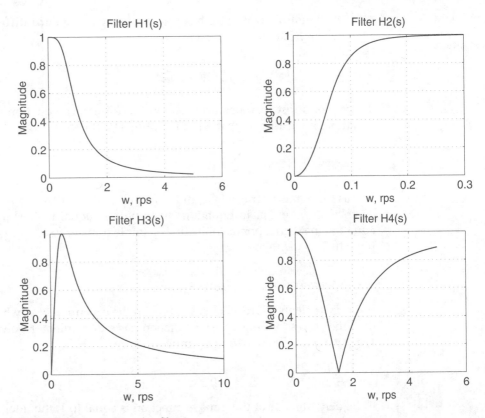

Figure 10.9 *Example analog filters.*

$$H(z) = \frac{B(z)}{A(z)}$$

$$= \frac{b_0 + b_1 z^{-1} + b_2 z^{-2} + \ldots + b_n z^{-n}}{a_0 + a_1 z^{-1} + a_2 z^{-2} + \ldots + a_n z^{-n}} \tag{10.2}$$

This transfer function corresponds to an nth-order digital filter. Some examples of specific transfer functions are the following:

$$H_1(z) = \frac{0.2066 + 0.4131 z^{-1} + 0.2066 z^{-2}}{1 - 0.3695 z^{-1} + 0.1958 z^{-2}}$$

$$H_2(z) = \frac{0.894 - 1.789 z^{-1} + 0.894 z^{-2}}{1 - 1.778 z^{-1} + 0.799 z^{-2}}$$

$$H_3(z) = \frac{0.42 - 0.42 z^{-2}}{1 - 0.0443 z^{-1} + 0.159 z^{-2}}$$

$$H_4(z) = \frac{0.5792 + 0.4425 z^{-1} + 0.5792 z^{-2}}{1 + 0.4425 z^{-1} + 0.1584 z^{-2}}$$

(It is also possible for a transfer function to include terms in the numerator with positive powers of z. We will discuss this case later in the chapter.)

A digital filter can also be specified using a **standard difference equation**, SDE, which has this general form:

$$y_n = \sum_{k=N_1}^{N_2} b_k x_{n-k} - \sum_{k=1}^{N_3} a_k y_{n-k} \qquad (10.3)$$

There is a direct relationship between the difference equation and the transfer equation, if we assume that N_1 in Equation (10.3) is equal to 0:

$$y_n = \sum_{k=0}^{N_2} b_k x_{n-k} - \sum_{k=1}^{N_3} a_k y_{n-k} \qquad (10.4)$$

In this form, the coefficients b_k and a_k from Equation (10.4) are precisely the same coefficients b_k and a_k in Equation (10.2), with a_0 equal to 1. Thus, the difference equation that corresponds to the first example transfer functions given after Equation (10.2) is the following:

$$y_n = 0.2066x_n + 0.4131x_{n-1} + 0.2066x_{n-2} \\ + 0.3695y_{n-1} - 0.1958y_{n-2}$$

If the coefficients a_k are all equal to 0, with the exception of a_0 which is equal to 1, then the corresponding transfer function has a denominator polynomial equal to 1, as shown in the following example:

$$y_n = 0.5x_n - 1.2x_{n-1} + 0.25x_{n-3} \\ H(z) = 0.5 - 1.2z^{-1} + 0.25z^{-3}$$

If the denominator of the transfer function is equal to 1, the filter is an **FIR** (finite impulse response) filter; if the denominator of the transfer function is not equal to a constant, the filter is an **IIR** (infinite impulse response) filter. Both types of filters are commonly used in digital signal processing.

In order to determine the characteristics of a system with a given transfer function, we need to plot the magnitude and phase of the transfer function. The MATLAB function **freqz** computes values of the complex function H(z):

[H,wT] = freqz(B,A,n)	Computes values of the transfer function $H(z) = B(z)/A(z)$, where **B** is the coefficient vector of $B(z)$ and **A** is the coefficient vector of $A(z)$. The integer n specifies the number of points for which we want to evaluate $H(z)$. The **n** values of $H(z)$ are evaluated at equally spaced points of normalized frequency in the interval $[0,\pi)$.

The coefficient vectors come directly from the transfer function. The number of points used in computing the transfer function determine the resolution. The resolution should be fine enough that you can determine the filter type (lowpass, highpass, bandpass, bandstop), and the critical frequencies (cutoff, rejection).

The next group of statements determine and plot the magnitudes of the four example transfer functions given at the beginning of this discussion.

```
%    These statements determine and plot the
%    magnitudes of four digital filters.
%
B1 = [0.2066,0.4131,0.2066];
A1 = [1,-0.3695,0.1958];
[H1z,w1T] = freqz(B1,A1,100);
%
B2 = [0.894,-1.789,0.894];
A2 = [1,-1.778,0.799];
[H2z,w2T] = freqz(B2,A2,100);
%
B3 = [0.42,0,-0.42];
A3 = [1,-0.443,0.159];
[H3z,w3T] = freqz(B3,A3,100);
%
B4 = [0.5792,0.4425,0.5792];
A4 = [1,0.4425,0.1584];
[H4z,w4T] = freqz(B4,A4,100);
%
subplot(2,2,1),plot(w1T,abs(H1z)),...
    title('Filter H1(z)'),...
    ylabel('Magnitude'),grid,...
subplot(2,2,2),plot(w2T,abs(H2z)),...
    title('Filter H2(z)'),...
    ylabel('Magnitude'),grid,...
subplot(2,2,3),plot(w3T,abs(H3z)),...
    title('Filter H3(z)'),...
    xlabel('Normalized Frequency'),
    ylabel('Magnitude'),grid,...
subplot(2,2,4),plot(w4T,abs(H4z)),..
    title('Filter H4(z)'),...
    xlabel('Normalized Frequency'),
    ylabel('Magnitude'),grid,pause
```

Figure 10.10 contains the plots of these filter magnitudes. Again, you can see that these four filters represent a lowpass filter, a highpass filter, a bandpass filter, and a bandstop filter.

The phase of a digital filter can be plotted using the **angle** function or the **unwrap** function. In addition, MATLAB also contains a function **grpdelay** that is used to determine the group delay of a digital filter. The **group delay** is a measure of the average delay of the filter as a function of frequency. It is defined as the negative first derivative of the filter's phase response. If $\theta(\omega)$ represents the phase response of the filter $H(z)$, then the group delay is

$$\tau(\omega) = -\frac{d\theta(\omega)}{d\omega}$$

The **grpdelay** function has three input arguments:

grpdelay(B,A,n)   Determines the group delay for a digital filter $H(z)$ defined by numerator coefficients **B** and denominator coefficients **A**. The integer **n** specifies the number of values of the group delay to determine over the range of normalized frequencies from 0 to π.

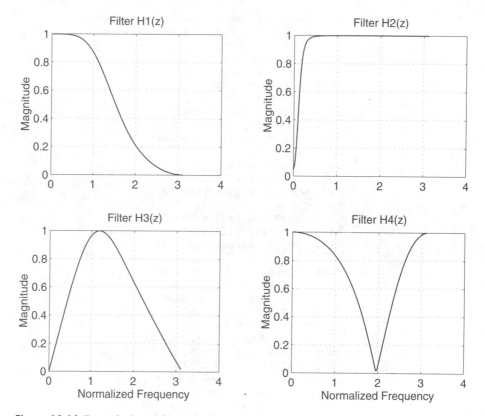

Figure 10.10 *Example digital filters.*

Because this function uses the **fft** function, it is desirable to select a value for **n** that is a power of 2.

PARTIAL FRACTION EXPANSIONS

Partial fraction expansion

In analyzing both analog and digital filters, we often need to perform a **partial fraction expansion** on the transfer function $H(s)$ or $H(z)$. This partial fraction expansion may be used to express the filter in a cascaded structure or in a parallel structure of subfilters. A partial fraction expansion may also be used to perform an inverse transformation on a frequency-domain function to obtain the corresponding time-domain function. MATLAB includes a function **residue** that performs a partial-fraction expansion (also called a residue computation) of the ratio of two polynomials B and A. Therefore, this function can be used with either $H(s)$ or $H(z)$ because both of these functions can be represented as the ratio of two polynomials. A precise definition of a partial fraction expansion is now needed in order to represent the most general case.

Let G be a ratio of two polynomials in the variable v. Because G may represent an **improper fraction**, we can also express G as a mixed fraction, as shown below;

$$G(v) = \frac{B(v)}{A(v)} \tag{10.5}$$

$$= \sum_{n=0}^{N} k_n v^n + \frac{N(v)}{D(v)} \tag{10.6}$$

If we then consider the proper fraction $N(v)/D(v)$, it can be written as a ratio of two polynomials in v. The denominator polynomial can be written as a product of linear factors with roots p_1, p_2, and so on. (The roots of the numerator are also called the **zeros** of the function, and the roots of the denominator are also called the **poles** of the function.) Each root of the denominator may represent a single root or a multiple root as shown below:

$$\frac{N(v)}{D(v)} = \frac{b_1 v^{n-1} + b_2 v^{n-2} + \ldots + b_{n-1} v + b_n}{(v - p_1)^{m1} (v - p_2)^{m2} \ldots (v - p_r)^{m\,r}}$$

This **proper fraction** can then be written as a sum of partial fractions. Single roots will correspond to one term in the partial fraction; a root with multiplicity k will correspond to k terms in the partial fraction expansion. This partial fraction expansion can then be written as

$$\frac{N(v)}{D(v)} = \frac{C_{11}}{v - p_1} + \frac{C_{12}}{(v - p_1)^2} + \ldots \frac{C_{1m1}}{(v - p_1)^{m1}}$$

$$+ \frac{C_{21}}{v - p_2} + \frac{C_{22}}{(v - p_2)^2} + \ldots \frac{C_{2m2}}{(v - p_2)^{m2}}$$

$$+ \ldots \tag{10.7}$$

$$+ \frac{C_{r1}}{v - p_r} + \frac{C_{r2}}{(v - p_r)^2} + \ldots \frac{C_{rmr}}{(v - p_r)^{mr}}$$

The `residue` function performs a partial fraction expansion. To interpret the output of the `residue` function, we use the notation presented for factoring a polynomial in Equations (10.5), (10.6) and (10.7).

`[r,p,k] = residue(B,A)`   Performs a partial fraction expansion of a ratio of two polynomials, B/A. The vector **B** contains the coefficients of the polynomial B, and the vector **A** contains the coefficients of the polynomial A. The **r** vector contains the coefficients C_{ij}, the **p** vector contains the values of the poles p_n, and the **k** vector contains the values of k_n.

It is important to recognize that a partial fraction expansion is generally not a unique expansion. There are often several different expansions that represent the same polynomial. Of course, the **residue** function will always give the same expansion for a given pair of numerator and denominator polynomials, but it may not be the only expansion for the polynomial.

To illustrate the use of the **residue** function, we now present several examples. First, consider the following polynomial:

$$F(z) = \frac{z^2}{z^2 - 1.5z + 0.5}$$

The MATLAB statement for computing the partial fraction expansion of this ratio of polynomials is the following:

```
%    Perform a partial fraction expansion.
B = [1,0,0];
A = [1,-1.5,0.5];
[r,p,k] = residue(B,A)
```

The values of the three vectors computed by the **residue** function are the - following:

$$\mathbf{r} = \begin{bmatrix} 2 \\ -0.5 \end{bmatrix} \quad \mathbf{p} = \begin{bmatrix} 1 \\ 0.5 \end{bmatrix} \quad \mathbf{k} = [1]$$

Thus, the partial fraction expansion is the following:

$$F(z) = \frac{z^2}{z^2 - 1.5z + 0.5}$$

$$= 1 + \frac{2}{z - 1.0} - \frac{0.5}{z - 0.5}$$

To double-check this expansion, you can combine the three terms over a common denominator or use the MATLAB functions for polynomial analysis presented in Chapter 3 to perform the combinations.

Consider the following function:

$$G(z) = \frac{z - 1}{z^2 + 4z + 4}$$

To use the **residue** function to factor this function, we use the following statements:

```
%    Perform a partial fraction expansion.
B = [1,-1];
A = [1,4,4];
[r,p,k] = residue(B,A)
```

The values of the three vectors computed by the **residue** function are the following:

$$\mathbf{r} = \begin{bmatrix} 1 \\ -3 \end{bmatrix} \quad \mathbf{p} = \begin{bmatrix} -2 \\ -2 \end{bmatrix} \quad \mathbf{k} = [\,]$$

Thus, the partial fraction expansion is the following:

$$G(z) = \frac{z - 1}{z^2 + 4z + 4}$$

$$= \frac{1}{z + 2} - \frac{3}{(z + 2)^2}$$

As a final example, consider the following function:

$$H(z) = \frac{z^{-2}}{1 - 3.5z^{-1} + 1.5z^{-2}}$$

To fit the general form presented, which uses positive powers in the polynomials, we multiply the numerator and denominator by z^2, giving the following equivalent form:

$$H(z) = \frac{1}{z^2 - 3.5z + 1.5}$$

To use the **residue** function to factor this function, we use the following statements:

```
%    Perform a partial fraction expansion.
B = [1];
A = [1,-3.5,1.5];
[r,p,k] = residue(B,A)
```

The values of the three vectors computed by the **residue** function are the following:

$$\mathbf{r} = \begin{bmatrix} 0.4 \\ -0.4 \end{bmatrix} \quad \mathbf{p} = \begin{bmatrix} 3 \\ 0.5 \end{bmatrix} \quad \mathbf{k} = [\,]$$

Thus, the partial fraction expansion is the following:

$$H(z) = \frac{1}{z^2 - 3.5z + 1.5}$$

$$= \frac{0.4}{z - 3} - \frac{0.4}{z - 0.5}$$

To write this using negative powers of z, we can multiply the numerator and denominator of each term by z^{-1}:

$$H(z) = \frac{0.4z^{-1}}{1 - 3z^{-1}} - \frac{0.4z^{-1}}{1 - 0.5z^{-1}}$$

Thus, the **residue** function can be used to determine terms with negative powers of z, which can be useful in performing inverse z transformations.

Practice!

For each of the following transfer functions, plot the magnitude response. Determine the transition band or bands for these filters. Use normalized frequency on the x-axis for the digital filters.

1. $H(s) = \dfrac{s^2}{s^2 + \sqrt{2}s + 1}$

2. $H(z) = \dfrac{0.707z - 0.707}{z - 0.414}$

3. $H(z) = -0.163 - 0.058z^{-1} + 0.116z^{-2} + 0.2\,z^{-3}$
   $\qquad + 0.116z^{-4} - 0.058z^{-5} - 0.163z^{-6}$

4. $H(s) = \dfrac{5s + 1}{s^2 + 0.4s + 1}$

10.3   Digital Filter Implementation

Difference equation

Analog filters are implemented in hardware using components such as resistors and capacitors. **Digital filters** are implemented in software; thus, this section refers specifically to digital filters. Recall from the previous section that a digital filter can be defined in terms of either a transfer function $H(z)$ or a standard difference equation. The input to the filter is a digital signal; the output is another digital signal. The **difference equation** defines the steps involved in computing the output signal from the input signal. This process is shown in the diagram in Figure 10.11, with x_n as the input signal and y_n as the output signal.

The relationship between the output signal y_n and the input signal x_n is described by the difference equation, as repeated in this general form of a difference equation:

$$y_n = \sum_{k=N_1}^{N_2} b_k x_{n-k} - \sum_{k=1}^{N_3} a_k y_{n-k} \tag{10.8}$$

Examples of difference equations are the following:

Figure 10.11 *Digital filter input and output.*

$$y_n = 0.04x_{n-1} + 0.17x_{n-2} + 0.25x_{n-3} + 0.17x_{n-4} + 0.04x_{n-5}$$

$$y_n = 0.42x_n - 0.42x_{n-2} + 0.44y_{n-1} - 0.16y_{n-2}$$

$$y_n = 0.33x_{n+1} + 0.33x_n + 0.33x_{n-1}$$

These three difference equations represent different filters with different characteristics. The output of the first filter depends only on past values of the input signal. For example, to compute y_{10}, we need values of x_9, x_8, x_7, x_6, and x_5. Then, using the difference equation, we can compute the value for y_{10}. This type of filter is an FIR filter (see the previous section), and the denominator of its transfer function $H(z)$ is equal to 1. The second filter requires not only past values of the input signal, but also past values of the output signal, in order to compute new output values. This type of filter is an IIR filter (also discussed in the previous section). The third filter is an FIR filter, because the output values depend only on input values. However, note that the subscripts in this third difference equation require that we be able to look ahead in the input signal. Thus, to compute y_5, we need values for x_6, x_5, and x_4. This look-ahead requirement is not a problem if we are computing the input signal values or if they are stored in a file. However, it can be a problem if the input values are being generated in real time by an experiment.

The simplest way to apply a digital filter to an input signal in MATLAB is with the **filter** function. The **filter** function assumes that the standard difference equation has the form

$$y_n = \sum_{k=0}^{N_2} b_k x_{n-k} - \sum_{k=1}^{N_3} a_k y_{n-k} \tag{10.9}$$

which also corresponds to the following transfer function form, which was discussed in the previous section:

$$H(z) = \frac{B(z)}{A(z)}$$

$$= \frac{b_0 + b_1 z^{-1} + b_2 z^{-2} + \ldots + b_n z^{-n}}{a_0 + a_1 z^{-1} + a_2 z^{-2} + \ldots + a_n z^{-n}}$$

Equation (10.9) is different from Equation (10.8) in that the first summation begins with $k = 0$ instead of $k = N_1$. With this definition, the **filter** function is the following:

filter(B,A,x)   Applies the digital filter $H(z) = B(z)/A(z)$ to the input signal x. The vector **B** contains the coefficients of the polynomial $B(z)$, and the vector **A** contains the coefficients of the polynomial $A(z)$.

To apply the first filter example in this section to a signal **x**, we could use the following statements:

```
%     Apply the filter defined by B and A to x.
B = [0.0,0.04,0.17,0.25,0.17,0.04];
A = [1];
y = filter(B,A,x);
```

To apply the second filter example to a signal **x**, we could use the following statements:

```
%     Apply the filter defined by B and A to x.
B = [0.42,0.0,-0.42];
A = [-0.44,0.16];
y = filter(B,A,x);
```

We cannot use the **filter** function to apply the third filter to a signal x_k because the difference equation does not fit the general form used by the **filter** function, Equation (10.9). The difference equation of the third filter requires that the first summation start with $k = -1$, not $k = 0$. In this case, we can implement the filter using vector arithmetic. Assuming that the input signal x is stored in the vector **x**, we can compute the corresponding output signal **y** using the following statements:

```
%     Apply a filter to x using a difference equation.
N = length(x);
y(1) = 0.33*x(1) + 0.33*x(2);
for n=2:N-1
    y(n) = 0.33*x(n+1) + 0.33*x(n) + 0.33*x(n-1);
end
y(N) = 0.33*x(N-1) + 0.33*x(N);
```

Note that we assume that the values of **x** for which we do not have a value (**x(-1)** and **x(N+1)**) are equal to 0. Another way to compute the signal **y** is the following:

```
%     Another way to apply the previous filter.
N = length(x);
y(1) = 0.33*x(1) + 0.33*x(2);
y(2:N-1) = 0.33*x(3:N) + 0.33*x(2:N-1) + 0.33*x(1:N-2);
y(N) = 0.33*x(N-1) + 0.33*x(N);
```

Any digital filter could be implemented using vector operations. However, the **filter** function generally provides a simpler solution.

The **filter** function can also be used with two output arguments and with three input arguments:

`[y,state] = filter(B,A,x)`	Applies the filter defined by the vectors **B** and **A** to the signal, giving the output signal **y**. The vector **state** contains the final set of **x** values used in the filter.
`y = filter(B,A,x,state)`	Applies the filter defined by the vectors **B** and **A** to the signal **x**, giving the output signal **y**. The vector **state** contains the initial set of values to use in the filter.

Thus, if we want to filter a vector **x2** that is another segment of the signal **x1**, we can specifiy that the initial conditions are the values in **state**. Then the output values will be computed as though **x1** and **x2** were one long vector instead of two separate vectors:

```
%   Steps to filter two segments of a signal.
[y1,state] = filter(B,A,x1);
y2 = filter(B,A,x2,state);
```

Finally, the **conv** function can be used to compute the output of an FIR filter. Because this function is restricted to FIR filters, we prefer to use the **conv** function for polynomial multiplication and the **filter** function for implementing filters. The **deconv** function can be used to compute the impulse response for an IIR filter, but it is generally used to perform polynomial division. The **conv** and **deconv** functions were discussed in Chapter 3 in the polynomial analysis section.

Practice!

The following transfer function has been designed to pass frequencies between 500 Hz and 1500 Hz in a signal sampled at 5 kHz:

$$H(z) = \frac{0.42z^2 - 0.42}{z^2 - 0.443z + 0.159}$$

Use the following signals as input to the filter. Plot the input and output of the filter on the same plot, and explain the effect of the filter on the magnitude of input signal.

1. $x_k = \sin(2\pi 1000kT)$
2. $x_k = 2\cos(2\pi 100kT)$
3. $x_k = -\sin(2\pi 2000kT)$
4. $x_k = \cos(2\pi 1600kT)$

10.4   Digital Filter Design

In this section, we present MATLAB functions for designing digital filters. The discussion is separated into two techniques for designing IIR filters and one for designing FIR filters.

IIR FILTER DESIGN USING ANALOG PROTOTYPES

MATLAB contains functions for designing four types of digital filters based on analog filter designs. **Butterworth** filters have maximally flat passbands and stopbands, **Chebyshev Type I** filters have ripple in the passband, **Chebyshev Type II**

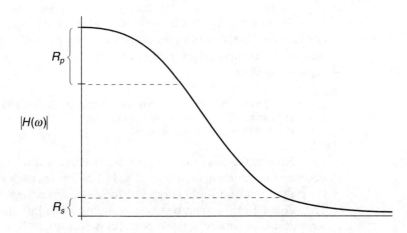

Figure 10.12 *Regions with ripple.*

filters have ripple in the stopband, and **elliptic** filters have ripple in both the pass-band and the stopband. However, for a given filter order, elliptic filters have the sharpest **transition** (narrowest transition band) of all these filters. The Chebyshev filters have a sharper transition than a Butterworth filter with the same design specifications. Figure 10.12 illustrates the definitions of the **passband ripple** (Rp) and the **stopband ripple** (Rs). The values of Rp and Rs are specified in decibels (where x in decibels is equal to $-20 \log_{10} x$). The MATLAB functions for designing these filters use a normalized frequency that is based on a scale with the Nyquist frequency equal to 1.0. (Note that this differs from the normalized frequency scale used by the `freqz` function.) The filter design functions compute vectors **B** and **A** that determine the transfer function $H(z)=B(z)/A(z)$ and the standard difference equation; the vectors **B** and **A** can also be used in the `freqz` function and the `filter` function.

To design a Butterworth filter, the following variations of the **butter** function compute the coefficients of an **N**th order filter $H(z) = B(z)/A(z)$:

`[B,A] = butter(N,Wn)`	Computes the coefficients of a lowpass Butterworth filter. **Wn** is the cutoff frequency in normalized frequency.
`[B,A] = butter(N,Wn,'high')`	Computes the coefficients of a high-pass Butterworth filter. **Wn** is the cutoff frequency in normalized frequency.
`[B,A] = butter(N,Wn)`	Computes the coefficients of a band-pass Butterworth filter. **Wn** is a vector containing the two cutoff normalized frequencies of the passband in ascending order.
`[B,A] = butter(N,Wn,'stop')`	Computes the coefficients of a band-stop Butterworth filter. **Wn** is a vector containing the two cutoff normalized frequencies of the stopband in ascending order.

To design a Chebyshev Type I filter, the following variations of the **cheby1** function compute the coefficients of an **N**th order filter $H(z) = B(z)/A(z)$:

`[B,A] = cheby1(N,Rp,Wn)`	Computes the coefficients of a low-pass Chebyshev Type I filter. **Rp** represents the passband ripple, and **Wn** is the cutoff frequency in normalized frequency.
`[B,A] = cheby1(N,Rp,Wn,'high')`	Computes the coefficients of a highpass Chebyshev Type I filter. **Rp** represents the passband ripple, and **Wn** is the cutoff frequency in normalized frequency.
`[B,A] = cheby1(N,Rp,Wn)`	Computes the coefficients of a bandpass Chebyshev Type I filter. **Rp** represents the passband ripple, and **Wn** is a vector containing the two cutoff normalized frequencies of the passband in ascending order.
`[B,A] = cheby1(N,Rp,Wn,'stop')`	Computes the coefficients of a stopband Chebyshev Type I filter. **Rp** represents the passband ripple, and **Wn** is a vector containing the two cutoff normalized frequencies of the stopband in ascending order.

To design a Chebyshev Type II filter, the following variations of the **cheby2** function compute the coefficients of an **N**th order filter $H(z) = B(z)/A(z)$:

`[B,A] = cheby2(N,Rs,Wn)`	Computes the coefficients of a low-pass Chebyshev Type I filter. **Rs** represents the stopband ripple, and **Wn** is the cutoff frequency in normalized frequency.
`[B,A] = cheby2(N,Rs,Wn,'high')`	Computes the coefficients of a highpass Chebyshev Type I filter. **Rp** represents the stopband ripple, and **Wn** is the cutoff frequency in normalized frequency.
`[B,A] = cheby2(N,Rp,Wn)`	Computes the coefficients of a bandpass Chebyshev Type I filter. **Rs** represents the stopband ripple, and **Wn** is a vector containing the two cutoff normalized frequencies of the passband in ascending order.

`[B,A] = cheby2(N,Rs,Wn,'stop')`	Computes the coefficients of a stopband Chebyshev Type I filter. R_p represents the stopband ripple, and W_n is a vector containing the two cutoff normalized frequencies of the stopband in ascending order.

To design an elliptic filter, the following variations of the `ellip` function compute the coefficients of an Nth order filter $H(z) = B(z)/A(z)$:

`[B,A] = ellip(N,Rp,Rs,Wn)`	Computes the coefficients of a lowpass elliptic filter. R_p represents the passband ripple, R_s represents the stopband ripple, and W_n is the cutoff frequency in normalized frequency.
`[B,A] = ellip(N,Rp,Rs,Wn,'high')`	Computes the coefficients of a highpass elliptic filter. R_p represents the passband ripple, R_s represents the stopband ripple, and W_n is the cutoff frequency in normalized frequency.
`[B,A] = ellip(N,Rp,Rs,Wn)`	Computes the coefficients of a bandpass elliptic filter. R_p represents the passband ripple, R_s represents the stopband ripple, and W_n is a vector containing the two cutoff normalized frequencies of the passband in ascending order.
`[B,A] = ellip(N,Rp,Rs,Wn,'stop')`	Computes the coefficients of a bandstop elliptic filter. R_p represents the passband ripple, R_s represents the stopband ripple, and W_n is a vector containing the two cutoff normalized frequencies of the stopband in ascending order.

To illustrate the use of these functions, suppose that we want to design a highpass Chebyshev II filter of order 6. We would also like to limit the passband ripple to 0.1, or 20 db. The filter is to be used with a signal sampled at 1 kHz; thus, the Nyquist frequency is 500 Hz. The cutoff is to be 300 Hz; thus, the normalized frequency is 300/500, or 0.6. The statements to design this filter and then plot the magnitude characteristics are the following:

```
%    Design highpass Chebyshev II filter.
[B,A] = cheby2(6,20,0.6,'high');
[H,wT] = freqz(B,A,100);
T = 0.001;
hertz = wT/(2*pi*T);
subplot(2,1,1),plot(hertz,abs(H)),...
   title('Highpass Filter'),...
   xlabel('Hz'),ylabel('Magnitude'),grid
```

The plot from these statements is shown in Figure 10.13. To apply this filter to a signal *x*, we could use the following statement:

```
y = filter(B,A,x)
```

The values of the vectors **B** and **A** also determine the filter's standard difference equation.

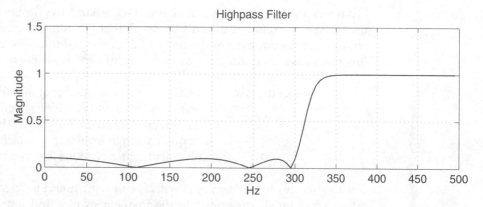

Figure 10.13 *Chebyshev Type II filter.*

DIRECT IIR FILTER DESIGN

MATLAB contains a function for performing **Yule-Walker filter** designs. This design technique can be used to design an arbitrarily shaped, possibly multiband, frequency response. The command to design a filter with this function is

`[B,A] = yulewalk(N,f,m)`	Computes the coefficients of an **N**th order IIR filter using vectors **f** and **m** that specify the frequency and magnitude characteristics of the filter of the frequency range from 0 to 1, which is 0 to the Nyquist frequency in normalized frequency.

The frequencies in **f** must begin with 0, end with 1, and be increasing. The magnitudes in **m** must correspond to the frequencies in **f** and represent the desired magnitude for each frequency. Thus, the following example designs a filter with two passbands and then plots the magnitude response in normalized frequency.

```
%    Design an IIR filter with two passbands.
m = [0,0,1,1,0,0,1,1,0,0];
f = [0,0.1,0.2,0.3,0.4,0.5,0.6,0.7,0.8,1];
[B,A] = yulewalk(12,f,m);
[H,wT] = freqz(B,A,100);
subplot(2,1,1),plot(f,m,'--',wT/pi,abs(H)),...
    title('IIR Filter with Two Passbands'),...
    xlabel('Normalized Frequency'),...
    ylabel('Magnitude'),grid
```

Figure 10.14 contains the plot from these statements.

DIRECT FIR FILTER DESIGN

FIR filters are designed using the **Parks-McClellan filter** design algorithm, which uses a **Remez exchange algorithm**. Recall that FIR filters require only a **B** vector because the denominator polynomial of $H(z)$ is equal to 1. Therefore, the MATLAB function **remez** computes only a single output vector, as shown in this statement:

B = remez(N,f,m)   Computes the coefficients of an **N**th order FIR filter using vectors **f** and **m**, which specify the frequency and magnitude characteristics of the filter of the frequency range from 0 to 1, which is 0 to the Nyquist frequency in normalized frequency.

The frequencies in **f** must begin with 0, end with 1, and be increasing. The magnitudes in **m** must correspond to the frequencies in **f** and represent the desired magnitude for each frequency. In addition, the number of points of **f** and **m** must be an even number. To obtain desirable filter characteristics with an FIR filter, it is not unusual for the filter order to become large.

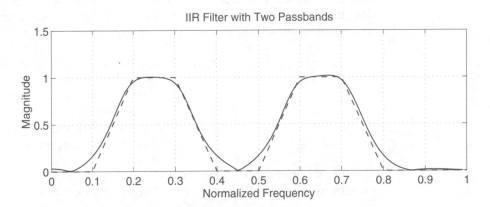

Figure 10.14 *Yule–Walker design method.*

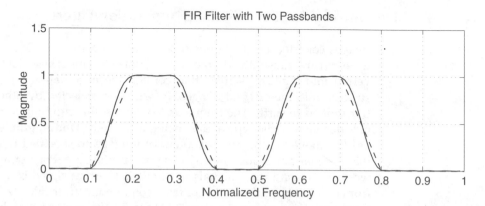

Figure 10.15 *Remez exchange design method.*

The following example designs an FIR filter with two passbands and then plots the magnitude response in normalized frequency.

```
%       Design an FIR filter with two passbands.
m = [0,0,1,1,0,0,1,1,0,0];
f = [0,0.1,0.2,0.3,0.4,0.5,0.6,0.7,0.8,1];
B = remez(50,f,m);
[H,wT] = freqz(B,[1],100);
subplot(2,1,1),plot(f,m,'--',wT/pi,abs(H)),...
    title('FIR Filter with Two Passbands'),...
    xlabel('Normalized Frequency'),...
    ylabel('Magnitude'),grid
```

Figure 10.15 contains the plot from these statements.

Additional variations of the **remez** function allow it to be used to design Hilbert transformers or differentiators. A weighting vector can also be used to give a weighting or priority to the values in each band defined by **f** and **m**.

Practice!

Use the MATLAB functions described in this section to design the following filters. Plot the magnitude of each filter to confirm that it has the correct characteristics.

1. Lowpass IIR filter with a cutoff of 75 Hz when used with a sampling rate of 500 Hz. (Use an order-5 filter.)

2. Highpass IIR filter with a cutoff of 100 Hz when used with a sampling rate of 1 kHz. (Use an order-6 filter.)

3. Lowpass FIR filter with a cutoff of 75 Hz when used with a sampling rate of 500 Hz. (Use an order-40 filter.)

4. Bandpass FIR filter with a passband of 100 to 200 Hz when used with a sampling rate of 1 kHz. (Use an order-80 filter.)

10.5   Problem Solving Applied: Channel Separation Filters

Images collected from spacecraft sent into deep space or from satellites circling the earth are transmitted to the earth in data streams. These data streams are converted into digitized signals that contain the information which can be reconstructed into the original images. Information collected by other sensors is also transmitted to earth. The frequency content of the information in the sensor signals depends on the type of data being measured. **Modulation techniques** can be used to move the frequency content of the data to specified frequency bands so that a signal can contain multiple signals at one time. For example, suppose that we want to send three signals in parallel. The first signal contains components from 0 to 100 Hz, the second contains components from 500 Hz to 1 kHz, and the third contains components from 2 kHz to 5 kHz. Assume that the signal containing the sum of these three components is sampled at 10 kHz. To separate these components after the signal is received, we need a lowpass filter with a cutoff at 100 Hz, a bandpass filter with cutoffs at 500 and 1 kHz, and a highpass filter with a cutoff at 2 kHz. The order of the filters should be large enough to generate narrow transition bands so that frequencies from one component do not contaminate other components.

1.   PROBLEM STATEMENT

Design three filters to be used with a signal sampled at 10 kHz. One filter is to be a lowpass filter with a cutoff of 100 Hz; another is to be a bandpass filter with a passband from 500 Hz to 1 kHz; another is to be a highpass filter with a cutoff of 2 kHz.

2.   INPUT/OUTPUT DESCRIPTION

There are no input values for this problem. The output values are the coefficient vectors that define the three filters $H_1(z)$, $H_2(z)$, and $H_3(z)$:

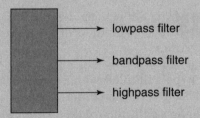

lowpass filter

bandpass filter

highpass filter

3.   HAND EXAMPLE

The sketch in Figure 10.16 shows the frequency range from 0 to the Nyquist frequency (5 kHz) with the three desired filters. We will use Butterworth filters in order to have filters with flat passbands and flat stopbands. We may need to experiment with the filter orders in order to be sure that the transition bands of the filters do not interfere with each other.

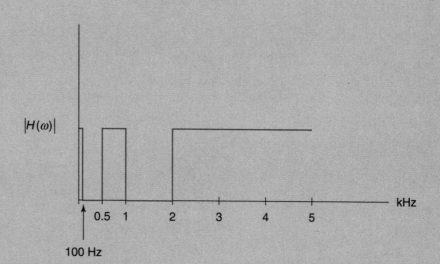

Figure 10.16 *Sketch of desired filters.*

4. MATLAB SOLUTION

The following MATLAB program determines the normalized frequency values (between 0 and 1, where 1 represents the Nyquist frequency) for the cutoff frequencies in the **butter** function. After computing the coefficients for the filters, we use the **freqz** function to plot the filter characteristics. Recall that the **freqz** function normalizes the frequencies to values between 0 and π, where π represents the Nyquist frequency. We will use Hz as the units for the frequency axis in order to easily verify the characteristics of the filters designed.

```
%    These statements design three digital filters
%    for use in a channel separation problem.
%
fs = 10000;          % sampling frequency
T = 1/fs;            % sampling time
fn = fs/2;           % Nyquist frequency
f1n = 100/fn;        % normalized lowpass cutoff
f2n = 500/fn;        % normalized bandpass left cutoff
f3n = 1000/fn;       % normalized bandpass right cutoff
f4n = 2000/fn;       % normalized highpass cutoff
%
[B1,A1] = butter(8,f1n);
[B2,A2] = butter(7,[f2n,f3n]);
[B3,A3] = butter(10,f4n,'high');
%
```

```
[H1,wT] = freqz(B1,A1,200);
[H2,wT] = freqz(B2,A2,200);
[H3,wT] = freqz(B3,A3,200);
%
hertz = wT/(2*pi*T);
subplot(2,1,1),...
    plot(hertz,abs(H1),'-',hertz,abs(H2),'--',...
    hertz,abs(H3),'-·'),...
    title('Channel Separation Filters'),...
    xlabel('Hz'),ylabel('Magnitude'),grid
```

5.   TESTING

The filter magnitudes for all three filters are shown on the same plot to verify
that the filters do not overlap each other, as shown in Figure 10.17.

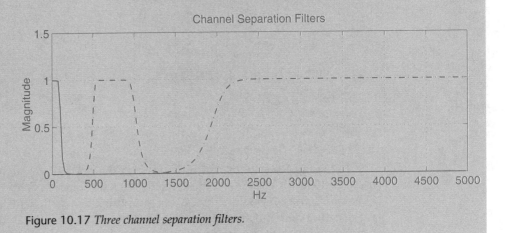

Figure 10.17 *Three channel separation filters.*

CHAPTER SUMMARY

A number of MATLAB functions for performing signal processing operations were
presented. The **fft** function was presented for analyzing the frequency content of
a digital signal. The **freqs** and **freqz** functions were discussed for computing the
frequency content of an analog or a digital filter from a transfer function. From the
complex signal that represents the frequency content, it is then straightforward to
compute and plot the magnitude and phase of the filter. The **filter** function can
be used to implement either an IIR or an FIR filter. Finally, a number of functions
were presented for designing IIR and FIR filters.

KEY TERMS

aliasing
analog filter
analog signal
bandpass filter
bandstop filter
Butterworth filter
Chebyshev filter
cutoff frequency
digital filter
digital signal
digital signal processing
discrete Fourier transform (DFT)
elliptic filter
fast Fourier transform (FFT)
FIR filter
frequency
frequency domain
frequency spectrum
group delay
Hertz

highpass filter
IIR filter
inverse Fourier transform
leakage
lowpass filter
Nyquist frequency
Parks-McClellan filter
passband
poles
rejection frequency
sampling frequency
sinusoid
standard difference equation
stopband
time domain
transfer function
transition band
Yule-Walker filter
zeros

MATLAB SUMMARY

This MATLAB summary lists all the commands and functions that were defined in this chapter. A brief description is included for each one.

COMMANDS AND FUNCTIONS

`butter`	designs a Butterworth digital filter
`cheby1`	designs a Chebyshev Type I digital filter
`cheby2`	designs a Chebyshev Type II digital filter
`ellip`	designs an elliptic digital filter
`fft`	computes the frequency content of a signal
`filter`	applies a digital filter to an input signal
`freqs`	computes the analog frequency content
`freqz`	computes the digital frequency content

grpdelay	measures the group delay of a digital filter
remez	designs an optimal FIR digital filter
residue	performs a partial-fraction expansion
unwrap	removes 2π discontinuities in a phase angle
yulewalk	designs an optimal IIR digital filter

Style NOTES

1.   We usually print frequency information only up to the Nyquist frequency because values above this are due to periodicity and not to higher frequency components in the signal.

DEBUGGING NOTES

1.   Use caution when determining a normalized frequency value. Remember that the **freqz** function assumes that the Nyquist frequency is π, whereas the filter design functions assume that the Nyquist frequency is 1.0.

PROBLEMS

Channel-Separation Filters. These problems relate to the channel-separation filter design problem. In these problems, we develop a computer simulation of this system.

1.   We first want to generate signals in the three bands described in this filter. We will do this using sums of sinusoids, all of which are sampled at 10 kHz. Signal 1 should contain a sum of sinusoids with frequencies at 25 Hz, 40 Hz, and 75 Hz. Signal 2 should contain a sum of sinusoids with frequencies at 600 Hz, 730 Hz, and 850 Hz. Signal 3 should contain a sum of sinusoids with frequencies at 3500 Hz, 4000 Hz, and 4200 Hz. Choose a variety of amplitudes and phase shifts for the sinusoids. Plot 500 points of Signal 1, Signal 2, and Signal 3.

2. Compute and plot the magnitude and phase of each of the three signals generated in Problem 1. Use Hz as the units for the x-axis in the plots. Make sure that the sinusoidal components appear where they would be expected.

3. Add the three time signals generated in Problem 1. Plot the time signal. Also plot the magnitude of the frequency content of the signal, using Hz as the units for the x-axis.

4. Apply the lowpass filter to the signal generated in Problem 3. Plot the output of the filter (time domain), and plot the magnitude of the frequency content of the output of the filter. Compare these plots to those generated in Problems 1 and 2. The time plot in this problem should be similar to the one generated in Problem 1 for Signal 1, with perhaps a phase shift. The magnitude plots should be very similar.

5. Repeat Problem 4 using the bandpass filter. Compare these plots to those generated in Problems 1 and 2. The time plot in this problem should be similar to the one generated in Problem 1 for Signal 2, with perhaps a phase shift. The magnitude plots should be very similar.

6. Repeat Problem 4 using the highpass filter. Compare these plots to those generated in Problems 1 and 2. The time plot in this problem should be similar to the one generated in Problem 1 for Signal 3, with perhaps a phase shift. The magnitude plots should be very similar.

Filter Characteristics. For each of the following filters, determine the passband(s), transition band(s), and stopband(s). Use 0.7 to determine cutoff frequencies, and use 0.1 to determine rejection frequencies.

7. $H(s) = \dfrac{0.5279}{s^2 + 1.0275s + 0.5279}$

8. $H(s) = \dfrac{s^2}{s^2 + 0.1117s + 0.0062}$

9. $H(s) = \dfrac{1.05s}{s^2 + 1.05s + 0.447}$

10. $H(s) = \dfrac{s^2 + 2.2359}{s^2 + 2.3511s + 2.2359}$

11. $H(z) = \dfrac{0.2066 + 0.4131z^{-1} + 0.2066z^{-2}}{1 - 0.3695z^{-1} + 0.1958z^{-2}}$

12. $H(z) = \dfrac{0.894 - 1.789z^{-1} + 0.894z^{-2}}{1 - 1.778z^{-1} + 0.799z^{-2}}$

10

13. $H(z) = \dfrac{0.42 - 0.42z^{-2}}{1 - 0.443z^{-1} + 0.159z^{-2}}$

14. $H(z) = \dfrac{0.5792 + 0.4425z^{-1} + 0.5792z^{-2}}{1 + 0.4425z^{-1} + 0.1584z^{-2}}$

15. $y_n = 0.04x_{n-1} + 0.17x_{n-2} + 0.25x_{n-3} + 0.17x_{n-4} + 0.04x_{n-5}$

16. $y_n = 0.42x_n - 0.42x_{n-2} + 0.44y_{n-1} - 0.16y_{n-2}$

17. $y_n = 0.33x_{n+1} + 0.33x_n + 0.33x_{n-1}$

18. $y_n = 0.33x_n + 0.33x_{n-1} + 0.33x_{n-2}$

Filter Design. The following problems use the filter design functions discussed in this chapter. Use Hz as the units for the x-axis in all plots of magnitude or phase.

19.   Design a lowpass filter with a cutoff frequency of 1 kHz when used with a sampling frequency of 8 kHz. Compare designs for the four standard IIR filter types with an order-8 filter by plotting the magnitude of the four designs on the same plot.

20.   Design a highpass filter with a cutoff frequency of 500 Hz when used with a sampling frequency of 1500 Hz. Compare designs using an order-8 elliptic filter to an order-32 FIR filter by plotting the magnitude of the two designs on the same plot.

21.   Design a bandpass filter with a passband of 300 Hz to 4000 Hz when used with a sampling frequency of 9.6 kHz. Compare designs using a Butterworth filter of order 8 to an FIR filter. Choose the order of the FIR filter so that the band of frequencies passed are similar. Plot the magnitude of the two designs on the same plot.

22.   Design a filter that removes frequencies from 500 Hz to 1000 Hz in a signal that is sampled at 10 kHz. Compare an elliptic filter of order 12 to an order-12 Yule-Walker filter design. Plot the magnitude of the two designs on the same plot.

23.   Design a filter that will eliminate frequencies between 100 and 150 Hz and between 500 and 600 Hz in a signal that is sampled at 2.5 kHz. Compare designs using an FIR filter and an IIR filter. Plot the magnitude of the two designs on the same plot.

24.   Design a highpass filter that will eliminate frequencies below 900 Hz in a signal that is sampled at 9.6 kHz. Compare elliptic filters of order 6, 8, and 10 by plotting the filter magnitudes on the same graph.

25. Design a bandpass filter that will pass frequencies between 1000 and 3000 Hz in a signal that is sampled at 10 kHz. Use a Chebyshev Type II filter, and choose the minimum order so that the transition bands are no more than 200 Hz on either side of the passband.

Filter Implementation. The following problems specify input signals to use to test the filters designed in problem 20.

26. Generate a signal that contains 1024 points of uniform noise with a mean of 0.5 and a variance of 1. Assume that this signal represents noise sampled at 1500 Hz. Compute and plot the FFT magnitude of this signal and verify that it contains frequencies at all frequencies from 0 to the Nyquist frequency at 750 Hz.

27. Run the signal generated in problem 26 through the elliptic filter designed in problem 20. Compute and plot the FFT magnitude of the output of the filter and verify that it removed frequencies below 500 Hz. Compare the FFT magnitude of the output signal to the FFT magnitude of the input signal.

28. Run the signal generated in problem 26 through the FIR filter designed in problem 20. Compute and plot the FFT magnitude of the output of the filter and verify that it removed frequencies below 500 Hz. Compare the FFT magnitude of the output signal to the FFT magnitude of the input signal.

29. Generate 1024 points of a sinusoid with a frequency of 550 Hz. Run the signal through the elliptic filter designed in problem 20. Plot the input and the output of the filter on the same plot. How many samples has the output been delayed from input?

30. Generate 1024 points of a sinusoid with a frequency of 550 Hz. Run the signal through the FIR filter designed in problem 20. Plot the input and the output of the filter on the same plot. How many samples has the output been delayed from input?

Courtesy of Phillips Laboratory/PAX.

GRAND CHALLENGE:
Enhanced Vehicle Performance

This telescope, located at the Starfire Optical Range at Phillips Laboratory in Albuquerque, New Mexico, is one of the world's largest telescopes. It has a 3.5-meter diameter primary mirror and is protected by a unique retracting cylindrical enclosure that allows it to operate in the open air. The telescope is capable of resolving basketball-sized objects 1,000 miles in space. It uses a laser guidestar technique that involves a laser fired toward space. Portions of that laser beam reflect back to earth, providing information that then is used in adaptive optical systems to correct for the distortions. Its applications include space object imaging, advanced tracking, and atmospheric physics. This research will provide information that will improve the guidance and control systems of spacecraft, including the Space Shuttle and satellites.

Control Systems

OBJECTIVES

The Student Edition of MATLAB has an extensive set of functions that are very useful for linear system and control system design and analysis. These functions, which are combined in the Signals and Systems Toolbox, have been selected from the Signal Processing Toolbox and the Control Systems Toolbox, which are available for the professional version of MATLAB. Many of the design and analysis tasks associated in linear systems and control systems involve matrix operations, complex arithmetic, root determination, model conversions, and plotting of complicated functions. As we have seen, MATLAB has been designed to make many of these operations easy to do. This chapter is divided into three topics: system modeling, model conversion functions, and analysis functions. Because linear-system theory and control-system theory are extensive fields of study, they cannot be addressed in depth in this chapter. Therefore, the information that follows assumes at least some familiarity with the topics.

11.1   System Modeling

Models

Linear and control system analysis and design begins with models of real systems. These **models**, which are mathematical representations of such things as chemical processes, machinery, and electrical circuits, are used to study the dynamic response of real systems. The mathematical techniques used by MATLAB to design and analyze these systems assume processes that are physically realizable, **linear and time-invariant** (LTI). Thus, the models themselves are similarly constrained: Nonlinear, time-varying systems either cannot be analyzed or must be approximated by LTI functions.

MATLAB uses models in the form of **transfer functions** or **state-space equations**, thus allowing both "classical" and "modern" control system design and analysis techniques to be used. Either model form can be expressed in continuous-time (analog) or discrete-time (digital) forms. Transfer functions can be expressed as a polynomial, a ratio of polynomials, or one of two factored forms: zero-pole-gain or partial-fraction form. State-space system models are particularly well-suited to MATLAB because they are a matrix-based expression.

To demonstrate the various ways models can be formulated, we use the classic example of a spring-mass-damper system, shown in Figure 11.1. In this system, a mass m is acted on by three forces: a time-dependent input force $u(t)$, a spring with spring constant k, and a viscous damper with damping constant b. The position of the mass as a function of time is represented by $x(t)$. Attached to the mass is a measurement potentiometer p, which provides an output voltage $y(t)$ that is proportional to $x(t)$. The equation of motion of the mass m is given by the second-order differential equation

$$mx'' + bx' + kx = u(t)$$

and the measurement equation for the potentiometer is

$$y(t) = px(t)$$

The equation for the potentiometer is an example of a situation in which the variable representing the dynamics of system (x in this case) is not the output variable

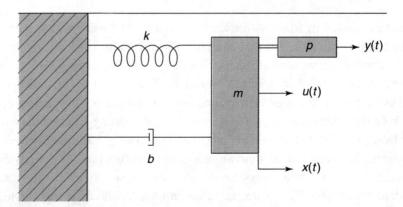

Figure 11.1 *Spring-mass-damper system.*

(y in this case). Together, these two equations provide a mathematical model of the **dynamic behavior** of the system. By integrating the equation of motion, using the techniques discussed in Chapters 7 or 9, we can determine the motion of the mass as a function of time. Such an analysis would therefore be called a time-domain analysis.

TRANSFER FUNCTIONS

The analysis of linear systems and control systems often involves determining certain dynamical properties, such as stability and frequency response, that cannot easily be determined using time-domain analyses. For these analyses, we often perform a Laplace transform on the time-domain equation so that we can analyze the system in the frequency-domain. The Laplace transform of our spring-mass-damper differential equation above is

$$(ms^2 + bs + k)x(s) = u(s)$$

where s is a complex variable ($\sigma + j\omega$), called the Laplace variable. (The complex variable s used in Chapter 10 in defining the Fourier Transform assumed that $\sigma = 0$.) This equation is easily rearranged to give a transfer function $H(s)$, which relates the output motion of the system $x(s)$ to the input force $u(s)$:

$$H(s) = \frac{x(s)}{u(s)} = \frac{1}{ms^2 + bs + k}$$

The transfer function for the potentiometer is simply

$$\frac{y(s)}{x(s)} = p$$

Block diagrams are frequently used to show how the transfer functions and the input and output variables of a system are related. Assuming for our spring-mass-damper example that $m = 1$, $b = 4$, $k = 3$, and $p = 10$, the block diagram in Figure 11.2 depicts the system. The first block represents the **plant model**, which is the part of the system that is controlled, and the second block represents the **measurement model**.

We can also combine the blocks into a single system model block as shown in Figure 11.3. This transfer function is expressed as a **ratio of two polynomials**, where the numerator polynomial is simply a scalar. For systems having a **single input** and a **single output (SISO)**, the form for writing transfer functions is

Ratio of two polynomials

$$H(s) = \frac{b_0 s^n + b_1 s^{n-1} + \ldots + b_{n-1}s + b_n}{a_0 s^m + a_1 s^{m-1} + \ldots + a_{m-1}s + a_m}$$

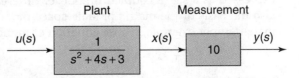

Figure 11.2 *Plant model and measurement model.*

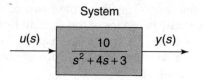

Figure 11.3 *System model.*

More generally, the numerator of this transfer function can be a three-dimensional matrix for **multi-input-multi-output (MIMO)** systems.

Very often, the numerator and denominator of a transfer function are factored into the **zero-pole-gain form**, which is

Zero-pole-gain form

$$H(s) = k\,\frac{(s - z_1)(s - z_2)\ldots(s - z_n)}{(s - p_1)(s - p_2)\ldots(s - p_m)}$$

For example, the zero-pole-gain form of the transfer function

$$H(s) = \frac{3s^2 + 18s + 24}{s^3 + 9s^2 + 23s + 15}$$

is

$$H(s) = 3\,\frac{(s + 2)(s + 4)}{(s + 1)(s + 3)(s + 5)}$$

This form is particularly useful, because it directly shows the roots of the numerator and denominator polynomials (the zeros and the poles of the system, respectively).

Finally, transfer functions can also be written in the **partial-fraction expansion**, or residue form, which is

Partial fraction expansion

$$H(s) = \frac{r_1}{s - p_1} + \frac{r_2}{s - p_2} + \ldots + \frac{r_n}{s - p_n} + k(s)$$

This form is useful in determining the inverse Laplace transform and for designing certain types of filters. For more on the use of the residue form, see the section on filter analysis in Chapter 10.

STATE-SPACE MODELS

In Chapter 8, we showed how a higher-order differential equation could be expressed as a set of coupled first-order differential equations. This technique is also the basis of the matrix or state-space model form. Using our earlier spring-mass-damper example, whose equation of motion was

$$mx'' + bx' + kx = u(t)$$

we can define

$$x_1 = x$$
$$x_2 = x'$$

Next, we rewrite the second-order differential equation as a set of coupled first-order differential equations

$$x_1' = x_2$$

$$x_2' = -\frac{k}{m}x_1 - \frac{b}{m}x_2 + \frac{u}{m} = -3x_1 - 4x_2 + u$$

and the measurement equation as

$$y = g(x,u) = 10x_1$$

State-space model

Using matrix notation, this system model can now be written as a **state-space model**

$$x' = Ax + Bu$$
$$y = Cx + Du$$

which, for this example, represents

$$\begin{bmatrix} x_1' \\ x_2' \end{bmatrix} = \begin{bmatrix} 0 & 1 \\ -3 & -4 \end{bmatrix}\begin{bmatrix} x_1 \\ x_2 \end{bmatrix} + \begin{bmatrix} 0 \\ 1 \end{bmatrix}u$$

$$y = \begin{bmatrix} 10 & 0 \end{bmatrix}\begin{bmatrix} x_1 \\ x_2 \end{bmatrix} + \begin{bmatrix} 0 \end{bmatrix}u$$

DISCRETE-TIME SYSTEMS

Many systems have variables that vary only at discrete times or are available for measurement or use only at discrete times. Some of these systems are analog systems whose continuous variables are sampled at regular time intervals; others may be digital systems whose quantized variables are similarly sampled.

Discrete-time systems are analyzed in a manner similar to continuous-time systems. The main difference is that they utilize the z-transform rather than the Laplace transform to derive transfer functions. The discrete-time variable z is mathematically related to the continuous-time Laplace variable s by the equation

$$z = e^{sT}$$

where T is the sampling time.

MATLAB represents discrete-time systems using the same forms that it does for continuous time systems: as polynomial, zero-pole-gain, and partial-fraction transfer functions, and as state-space equations. For example, the discrete-time version of a transform that is expressed as the ratio of two polynomials is

$$H(z) = \frac{b_0 z^n + b_1 z^{n-1} + \ldots + b_{n-1}z + b_n}{a_0 z^m + a_1 z^{m-1} + \ldots + a_{m-1}z + a_m}$$

The zero-pole-gain and partial-fraction discrete-time transfer function forms are similarly related to the continuous-time forms.

The state-space equations for discrete-time systems are also very similar to those for continuous systems:

$$x[n+1] = Ax[n] + Bu[n]$$
$$y[n] = Cx[n] + Du[n]$$

where n indicates the current sample and $n + 1$ indicates the next sample. Notice in the discrete-time form that $x[n + 1]$ replaces x' in the continuous-time form. This is because discrete-time systems use difference equations instead of differential equations. The equations for discrete-time systems compute the value of the state vector at the next sample time, rather than the derivative of the state vector at the current time, which continuous-time state-space equations compute.

In summary, there are several different forms of system models for both continuous-time and discrete-time systems. The next section presents MATLAB functions that can be used to convert from one model form to another.

11.2   Model Conversion

MATLAB has a number of functions that make it easy to convert from one model form to another and to convert continuous-time systems into discrete-time systems. These conversion functions and their uses are summarized in Table 11.1. We now present a discussion of each function, along with an example. *Because there are a number of variables in these models, we recommend that you use variable names that match the variables used in the general model forms.* This makes it easier to follow the code, and it also makes it easier to avoid errors.

Style

c2d Function. The **c2d** function converts the continuous-time state-space equation

$$x' = Ax + Bu$$

to the discrete-time state-space equation

$$x[n+1] = A_d x[n] + B_d u[n]$$

The function has two output matrices:

TABLE 11.1 Model Conversion Functions

Function	Purpose
c2d	continuous state-space to discrete state-space
residue	partial-fraction expansion
ss2tf	state-space to transfer function
ss2zp	state-space to zero-pole-gain
tf2ss	transfer function to state-space
tf2zp	transfer function to zero-pole-gain
zp2ss	zero-pole-gain to state-space
zp2tf	zero-pole-gain to transfer function

[Ad,Bd] = c2d(A,B,Ts)   Determines the matrices **Ad** and **Bd** of the discrete-time equation using the matrices **A** and **B** of the continuous-time state-space equation. **Ts** is the desired sample period.

The earlier continuous-time state-space plant equation

$$x' = Ax + Bu$$

where

$$A = \begin{bmatrix} 0 & 1 \\ -3 & -4 \end{bmatrix}, B = \begin{bmatrix} 0 \\ 1 \end{bmatrix}$$

can be converted to a discrete-time state-space equation with a sampling period of 0.1 seconds using these statements:

```
%    Convert continuous model to discrete model.
A = [0,1; -3,-4];
B = [0,1]';
[Ad,Bd] = c2d(A,B,0.1);
```

The values of the matrices computed by the **c2d** function are the following:

$$Ad = \begin{bmatrix} 0.9868 & 0.0820 \\ -0.2460 & 0.6588 \end{bmatrix}, \quad Bd = \begin{bmatrix} 0.0044 \\ 0.0820 \end{bmatrix}$$

Thus, the discrete-time state-space equation of the plant model is

$$x[n+1] = A_d x[n] + B_d u[n]$$

which represents

$$\begin{bmatrix} x_1 \\ x_2 \end{bmatrix}_{n+1} = \begin{bmatrix} 0.9868 & 0.0820 \\ -0.2460 & 0.6588 \end{bmatrix} \begin{bmatrix} x_1 \\ x_2 \end{bmatrix}_n + \begin{bmatrix} 0.0044 \\ 0.0820 \end{bmatrix} u_n$$

residue Function. The **residue** function converts the polynomial transfer function

$$H(s) = \frac{b_0 s^n + b_1 s^{n-1} + \ldots + b_{n-1} s + b_n}{a_0 s^m + a_1 s^{m-1} + \ldots + a_{m-1} s + a_m}$$

to the partial-fraction transfer function

$$H(s) = \frac{r_1}{s - p_1} + \frac{r_2}{s - p_2} + \ldots + \frac{r_n}{s - p_n} + k(s)$$

This function was discussed in detail in Section 10.2. Review that section for a complete discussion of the equations and notation. A summary of the function is presented here:

[r,p,k] = residue(B,A)   Determines the vectors **r**, **p**, and **k**, which contain the residue values, the poles, and the direct terms from the partial-fraction expansion. The inputs are the polynomial coefficients **B** and **A** from the numerator and denominator of the transfer function, respectively.

The partial-fraction expansion of this system transfer function

$$\frac{y(s)}{u(s)} = \frac{10}{s^2 + 4s + 3}$$

can be computed with these statements:

```
%    Compute partial fraction expansion.
B = [10];
A = [1,4,3];
[r,p,k] = residue(B,A);
```

The values of the matrices computed by the **residue** function are the following:

$$\mathbf{r} = \begin{bmatrix} -5 \\ 5 \end{bmatrix}, \quad \mathbf{p} = \begin{bmatrix} -3 \\ -1 \end{bmatrix}, \quad \mathbf{k} = [\,]$$

Thus, the partial-fraction expansion of our system polynomial transfer function is

$$H(s) = \frac{y(s)}{u(s)} = \frac{-5}{s+3} + \frac{5}{s+1}$$

ss2tf Function. The **ss2tf** function converts the continuous-time, state-space equations

$$x' = Ax + Bu$$
$$y = Cx + Du$$

to the polynomial transfer function

$$H(s) = \frac{b_0 s^n + b_1 s^{n-1} + \ldots + b_{n-1}s + b_n}{a_0 s^m + a_1 s^{m-1} + \ldots + a_{m-1}s + a_m}$$

The function has two output matrices:

[num,den] = ss2tf(A,B,C,D,iu)   Computes vectors **num** and **den** containing the coefficients, in descending powers of s, of the numerator and denominator of the polynomial transfer function for the **iu**th input. The input arguments **A,B,C**, and **D** are the matrices of the state-space equations corresponding to the **iu**th input, where **iu** is the number of the input for a multi-input system. In the case of a single-input system, **iu** is 1.

For example, the state-space equations for our system

$$\begin{bmatrix} x_1' \\ x_2' \end{bmatrix} = \begin{bmatrix} 0 & 1 \\ -3 & -4 \end{bmatrix} \begin{bmatrix} x_1 \\ x_2 \end{bmatrix} + \begin{bmatrix} 0 \\ 1 \end{bmatrix} u$$

$$y = \begin{bmatrix} 10 & 0 \end{bmatrix} \begin{bmatrix} x_1 \\ x_2 \end{bmatrix} + \begin{bmatrix} 0 \end{bmatrix} u$$

can be converted to a polynomial transfer function using the following statements:

```
%    Convert state-space model to transfer function.
A = [0,1; -3,-4];
B = [0,1]';
C = [10,0];
D = 0;
iu = 1;
[num,den] = ss2tf(A,B,C,D,iu);
```

The values of the vectors computed by the **ss2tf** function are the following:

$$\textbf{num} = \begin{bmatrix} 0 & 0 & 10 \end{bmatrix}, \quad \textbf{den} = \begin{bmatrix} 1 & 4 & 3 \end{bmatrix}$$

Thus, the transfer function is

$$\frac{y(s)}{u(s)} = \frac{10}{s^2 + 4s + 3}$$

ss2zp **Function.** The **ss2zp** function converts the continuous-time, state-space equations

$$x' = Ax + Bu$$
$$y = Cx + Du$$

to the zero-pole-gain transfer function

$$H(s) = k \frac{(s - z_1)(s - z_2) \dots (s - z_n)}{(s - p_1)(s - p_2) \dots (s - p_m)}$$

The function has three ouput matrices:

[z,p,k] = ss2zp(A,B,C,D,iu)   Determines the zeros (**z**) and poles (**p**) of the zero-pole-gain transfer function for the **iu**th input, along with the associated gain (**k**). The input matrices **A,B,C,** and **D** of the state-space equations correspond to the **iu**th input, where **iu** is the number of the input for a multi-input system. In the case of a single-input system, **iu** is 1.

For example, the state-space equations of the example system

$$\begin{bmatrix} x_1' \\ x_2' \end{bmatrix} = \begin{bmatrix} 0 & 1 \\ -3 & -4 \end{bmatrix}\begin{bmatrix} x_1 \\ x_2 \end{bmatrix} + \begin{bmatrix} 0 \\ 1 \end{bmatrix} u$$

$$y = \begin{bmatrix} 10 & 0 \end{bmatrix}\begin{bmatrix} x_1 \\ x_2 \end{bmatrix} + \begin{bmatrix} 0 \end{bmatrix} u$$

can be converted to a zero-pole-gain transfer function using these statements:

```
%     Convert state-space to zero-pole-gain model.
A = [0,1;-3,-4];
B = [0,1]';
C = [10,0];
D = 0;
iu = 1;
[z,p,k] = ss2zp(A,B,C,D,iu);
```

The values of the matrices computed the **ss2zp** function are the following:

$$\mathbf{z} = [\ ], \quad \mathbf{p} = \begin{bmatrix} -1 \\ -3 \end{bmatrix}, \quad \mathbf{k} = [10]$$

Thus, the zero-pole-gain transfer function is

$$\frac{y(s)}{u(s)} = \frac{10}{(s+1)(s+3)}$$

tf2ss Function. The **tf2ss** function converts the polynomial transfer function

$$H(s) = \frac{b_0 s^n + b_1 s^{n-1} + \ldots + b_{n-1}s + b_n}{a_0 s^m + a_1 s^{m-1} + \ldots + a_{m-1}s + a_m}$$

to the controller-canonical form state-space equations

$$x' = Ax + Bu$$
$$y = Cx + Du$$

The function has four output matrices:

[A,B,C,D] = tf2ss(num,den)   Determines the matrices A, B, C, and D of the controller-canonical form state-space equations. The input arguments **num** and **den** contain the coefficients, in descending powers of s, of the numerator and denominator polynomials of the transfer function that is to be converted.

The polynomial transfer function

$$\frac{y(s)}{u(s)} = \frac{10}{s^2 + 4s + 3}$$

can be converted to controller-canonical form state-space equations using these statements:

```
%    Convert transfer function to state-space.
num = 10;
den = [1,4,3];
[A,B,C,D] = tf2ss(num,den);
```

The values of the matrices computed by the **tf2ss** function are the following:

$$\mathbf{A} = \begin{bmatrix} -4 & -3 \\ 1 & 0 \end{bmatrix}, \quad \mathbf{B} = \begin{bmatrix} 1 \\ 0 \end{bmatrix}, \quad \mathbf{C} = [0 \quad 10], \mathbf{D} = [0]$$

Thus, the controller-canonical form state-space equations are

$$\begin{bmatrix} x_1' \\ x_2' \end{bmatrix} = \begin{bmatrix} -4 & -3 \\ 1 & 0 \end{bmatrix} \begin{bmatrix} x_1 \\ x_2 \end{bmatrix} + \begin{bmatrix} 1 \\ 0 \end{bmatrix} u$$

$$y = [0 \quad 10] \begin{bmatrix} x_1 \\ x_2 \end{bmatrix}$$

tf2zp Function. The **tf2zp** function converts the polynomial transfer function

$$H(s) = \frac{b_0 s^n + b_1 s^{n-1} + \ldots + b_{n-1}s + b_n}{a_0 s^m + a_1 s^{m-1} + \ldots + a_{m-1}s + a_m}$$

to the zero-pole-gain transfer function

$$H(s) = k \frac{(s - z_1)(s - z_2) \ldots (s - z_n)}{(s - p_1)(s - p_2) \ldots (s - p_m)}$$

The function has three output matrices:

[z,p,k] = tf2zp(num,den)   Determines the zeros (**z**), poles (**p**) and associated gain (**k**) of the zero-pole-gain transfer function using the coefficients, in descending powers of s, of the numerator and denominator of the polynomial transfer function that is to be converted.

The polynomial transfer function

$$\frac{y(s)}{u(s)} = \frac{10}{s^2 + 4s + 3}$$

can be converted to a zero-pole-gain transfer function using these statements:

```
%    Converts transfer function to pole-zero-gain.
num = 10;
den = [1,4,3];
[z,p,k] = tf2zp(num,den);
```

The values of the matrices computed by the `tf2zp` function are the following:

$$z = [\ ], \quad p = \begin{bmatrix} -3 \\ -1 \end{bmatrix}, \quad k = [10]$$

Thus, the zero-pole-gain transfer function is

$$\frac{y(s)}{u(s)} = \frac{10}{(s+3)(s+1)}$$

`zp2tf` Function. The `zp2tf` function converts the zero-pole-gain transfer function

$$H(s) = k \frac{(s-z_1)(s-z_2)\ldots(s-z_n)}{(s-p_1)(s-p_2)\ldots(s-p_m)}$$

into the polynomial transfer function

$$H(s) = \frac{b_0 s^n + b_1 s^{n-1} + \ldots + b_{n-1}s + b_n}{a_0 s^m + a_1 s^{m-1} + \ldots + a_{m-1}s + a_m}$$

The function has two output matrices:

`[num,den] = zp2tf(z,p,k)`	Determines the vectors **num** and **den** containing the coefficients, in descending powers of *s*, of the numerator and denominator of the polynomial transfer function. **p** is a column vector of the pole locations of the zero-pole-gain transfer function, **z** is a matrix of the corresponding zero locations, having one column for each output of a multi-output system, **k** is the gain of the zero-pole-gain transfer function. In the case of a single-output system, **z** is a column vector of the zero locations corresponding to the pole locations of vector **p**.

This zero-pole-gain transfer function

$$\frac{y(s)}{u(s)} = \frac{10}{(s+3)(s+1)}$$

can be converted into a polynomial transfer function using the following statements:

```
%    Converts zero-pole-gain to transfer function.
z = [];
p = [-3,-1]';
k = 10;
[num,den] = zp2tf(z,p,k);
```

The values of the matrices computed by the **zp2tf** function are the following:

$$\text{\textbf{num}} = [0 \quad 0 \quad 10], \quad \text{\textbf{den}} = [1 \quad 4 \quad 3]$$

Thus, the polynomial transfer function is

$$\frac{y(s)}{u(s)} = \frac{10}{s^2 + 4s + 3}$$

zp2ss Function. The **zp2ss** function converts the zero-pole-gain transfer function

$$H(s) = k \frac{(s - z_1)(s - z_2) \ldots (s - z_n)}{(s - p_1)(s - p_2) \ldots (s - p_m)}$$

to the controller-canonical form state-space equations

$$x' = Ax + Bu$$
$$y = Cx + Du$$

The function has four output matrices:

[A,B,C,D] = zp2ss(z,p,k)	Determines the matrices **A**, **B**, **C**, and **D** of the control-canonical form state-space equations. **p** is a column vector of the pole locations of the zero-pole-gain transfer function, **z** is a matrix of the corresponding zero locations, having one column for each output of a multi-output system, **k** is the gain of the zero-pole-gain transfer function. In the case of a single-output system, **z** is a column vector of the zero locations corresponding to the pole locations of vector **p**.

For example, the zero-pole-gain transfer function

$$\frac{y(s)}{u(s)} = \frac{10}{(s + 3)(s + 1)}$$

can be converted to the controller-canonical state-space representation using these statements:

```
%   Converts zero-pole-gain to state-space.
z = [];
p = [-3,-1]';
k = 10;
[A,B,C,D] = zp2ss(z,p,k);
```

The values of the matrices computed by the **zp2ss** function are the following:

$$\mathbf{A} = \begin{bmatrix} -4 & -1.7321 \\ 1.7321 & 0 \end{bmatrix}, \quad \mathbf{B} = \begin{bmatrix} 1 \\ 0 \end{bmatrix}$$

$$\mathbf{C} = [0 \quad 5.7735], \qquad \mathbf{D} = [0]$$

Thus, the control canonical form state-space equations are

$$\begin{bmatrix} x_1' \\ x_2' \end{bmatrix} = \begin{bmatrix} -4 & -1.7321 \\ 1.7321 & 0 \end{bmatrix}\begin{bmatrix} x_1 \\ x_2 \end{bmatrix} + \begin{bmatrix} 1 \\ 0 \end{bmatrix}u$$

$$y = [0 \quad 5.7735]\begin{bmatrix} x_1 \\ x_2 \end{bmatrix}$$

Practice!

For the polynomial transfer function

$$H(s) = \frac{s + 3}{s^2 + 4s - 12}$$

1. Use the **residue** function to find the partial fraction expansion.
2. Use the **tf2ss** function to convert the transfer function to continuous-time state-space equations.
3. Use the **c2d** function to convert the continuous-time state-space equations of problem 2 to discrete-time equations, using a sample period of 0.5 seconds.
4. Use the **tf2zp** function to convert the polynomial transfer function to a zero-pole-gain transfer function.
5. Use the **zp2ss** function to convert the zero-pole-gain function in problem 4 to the continuous-time state-space equations in problem 2.

11.3   Design and Analysis Functions

MATLAB has several functions that are useful for designing and analyzing linear systems. These functions can be used to study the response of systems in both the time domain and frequency domain. The functions that are described in this section are summarized in Table 11.2.

BODE PLOTS

This frequency-domain analysis tool consists of two separate plots of the amplitude ratio and the phase angle of a transfer function plotted versus the frequency of an input sinusoid. When plotted using the customary scales of amplitude ratio

TABLE 11.2 Design and Analysis Functions

Function	Purpose
bode	magnitude and phase frequency-response plots
nyquist	Nyquist frequency-response plot
rlocus	Evans root-locus plot
step	unit-step time response

Bode plots

in decibels and phase angle in degrees versus the $\log_{10}$ of frequency, these plots are referred to as **Bode plots**, after H. W. Bode, where the nondimensional **amplitude ratio (AR)** in decibels (dB) is defined as

$$AR_{dB} = 20 \log_{10} AR$$

Nichols plots

Nichols plots can also be generated by plotting the log of the amplitude versus the phase angle. Both plots are extremely useful for designing and analyzing control systems.

The **bode** function calculates the magnitude and phase frequency responses of continuous-time linear-time-invariant (LTI) systems for use in making Bode and Nichols plots. This function can be used in a variety of ways. If it is used without left-side arguments, it generates a Bode plot. It can also be used with output arguments as shown here:

[mag,phase] = bode(num,den,w)   Determines the magnitude and phase of the transfer function defined by the vectors **num** and **den,** which contain the coefficients of the numerator and denominator polynomials of the transfer function. The optional argument **w** specifies a user-specified input frequency vector **w**.

[mag,phase] = bode(A,B,C,D,iu,w)   Determines the magnitude and phase of the transfer function defined by the state space matrices **A**, **B**, **C**, and **D**. The optional argument **iu** specifies the input desired from a multi-input system; the optional argument **w** specifies a user-specified input frequency vector.

When used with multi-input systems, **bode(A,B,C,D)** produces a series of Bode plots—one for each input. A plot for a specific input **iu** of a multi-input system can be obtained using **bode(A,B,C,D,iu)**. Including a vector of user-specified frequency values **w** in the argument list will cause the **bode** function to calculate the system response at those frequencies. Note, however, that if **w** is included in the argument list of a state-space system, **iu** must also be included, even for a single-input system. A third output argument can also be specified to store the frequency values that correspond to the magnitude and phase values.

The Bode plot for the second-order system transfer function

$$\frac{x(s)}{u(s)} = \frac{10}{s^2 + s + 3}$$

can be generated with these statements:

```
%    Generate bode plot.
num = 10;
den = [1,1,3];
bode(num,den)
```

The plot generated is shown in Figure 11.4. The following statements produce the plots in Figure 11.5 for 100 logarithmically evenly spaced points between the frequencies 10^{-1} and 10^2 radians/second:

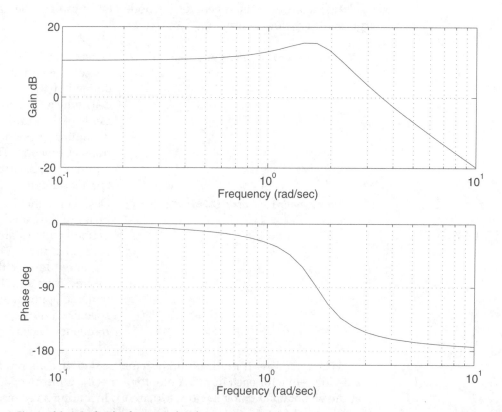

Figure 11.4 *Bode plot for second-order system.*

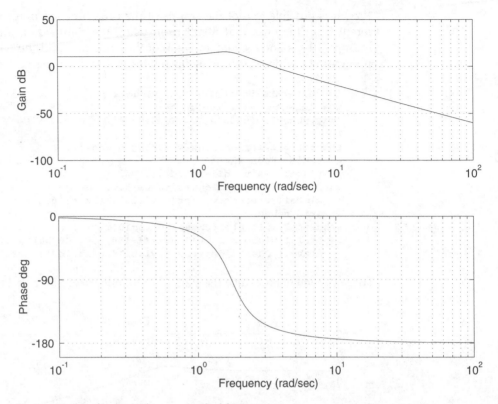

Figure 11.5 *Bode plot with user-specified frequencies.*

```
%    Generate bode plot at specified frequencies.
num = 10;
den = [1,1,3];
w = logspace(-1,2,100);
bode(num,den,w)
```

The state-space equations for the previous example are

$$\begin{bmatrix} x_1' \\ x_2' \end{bmatrix} = \begin{bmatrix} 0 & 1 \\ -3 & -1 \end{bmatrix} \begin{bmatrix} x_1 \\ x_2 \end{bmatrix} + \begin{bmatrix} 0 \\ 1 \end{bmatrix} u$$

$$y = \begin{bmatrix} 10 & 0 \end{bmatrix} \begin{bmatrix} x_1 \\ x_2 \end{bmatrix} + 0$$

Thus, the statements below will produce the same Bode plot as shown in Figure 11.4:

```
%    Generate Bode plot from state-space equations.
A = [0,1; -3,-1];
B = [0,1]';
C = [10,0];
D = 0;
bode(A,B,C,D)
```

It is possible to plot the results of the **bode** function in formats that are different from the ones that result from using the right-side arguments only. For example, the following statements plot the Bode plot and the Nichols plot of the previous state-space system, using 100 logarithmically spaced frequency values:

```
%    Generate Bode plot and Nichols plot.
w = logspace(-1,2,100);
[mag,phase] = bode(A,B,C,D,1,w);
%
subplot(2,1,1),semilogx(w,20*log10(mag)),...
    title('Bode Plot'),...
    ylabel('Gain, dB'),grid,...
subplot(2,1,2),semilogx(w,phase),...
    xlabel('Frequency, rps'),ylabel('Phase, degrees'),...
    grid,pause
subplot(2,1,1),plot(phase,20*log10(mag)),...
    title('Nichols Plot'),axis([-180,180,-20,20]),...
    xlabel('Phase, degrees'),ylabel('Gain, dB'),grid
```

These statements produce the plots shown in Figures 11.6 and 11.7.

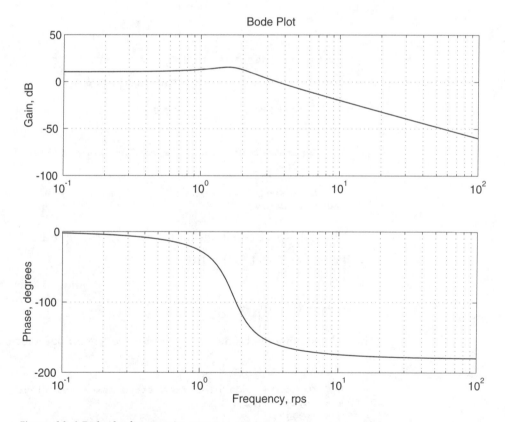

Figure 11.6 *Bode plot for a continuous state-space system.*

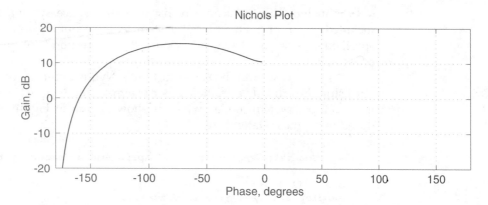

Figure 11.7 *Nichols plot for a continuous state-space system.*

NYQUIST PLOTS

The **nyquist** function is a frequency-domain analysis function that is similar to the **bode** function in that it uses exactly the same input arguments to produce frequency-response plots. The difference between the two functions is the output. The **Nyquist plot** is a single plot, as opposed to two plots for the Bode plot. It plots the real component of the open-loop transfer function versus the imaginary component for different values of frequency. It is also frequently referred to as a Nyquist path or a polar plot. The Nyquist plot is most often used for stability analysis for continuous-time, linear-time-invariant (LTI) systems. The various forms for its use are the following:

[re,im,w] = nyquist(num,den,w_in)   Determines the real and imaginary components of the transfer function defined by the vectors **num** and **den**, which contain the coefficients of the numerator and denominator polynomials. The optional argument **w_in** specifies a user-specified input frequency vector.

[re,im,w] = nyquist(A,B,C,D,iu,w_in)   Determines the real and imaginary components of the transfer function defined by the state-space matrices **A**, **B**, **C**, and **D.** The optional argument **iu** specifies the input desired from a multi-input system. The optional argument **w_in** specifies a user-specified input frequency vector.

When used with multi-input systems, **nyquist(A,B,C,D)** produces a series of Nyquist plots—one for each input. A plot for a specific input **iu** of a multi-input system can be obtained using **nyquist(A,B,C,D,iu)**. Including a vector of user-specified frequency values **w_in** in the argument list will cause the **nyquist** function to calculate the system response at those frequencies. Note, however, that if

w_in is included in the argument list of a state-space system, **iu** must also be included, even for a single-input system. A third output argument can also be specified to store the frequency values that correspond to the magnitude and phase values.

As is the case with the **bode** function, a Nyquist plot can be generated without using the left-side arguments. For example, the Nyquist plot of the spring-mass-damper system model, which is shown again in Figure 11.8, can be produced using these statements

```
%   Generate Nyquist plot of spring-mass-damper system.
num = 10;
den = [1,4,3];
subplot(2,1,1),nyquist(num,den),...
    title('Nyquist Plot'),grid
```

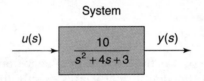

Figure 11.8 *System model.*

The resulting plot is shown in Figure 11.9. In this case, the function automatically selects the frequency range, whereas the next example uses a user-specified input frequency vector **w**:

```
%   Generate Nyquist plot of spring-mass-damper system.
num = 10;
den = [1,4,3];
w = logspace(0,1,100);
subplot(2,1,1),nyquist(num,den,w),...
    title('Nyquist Plot'),grid
```

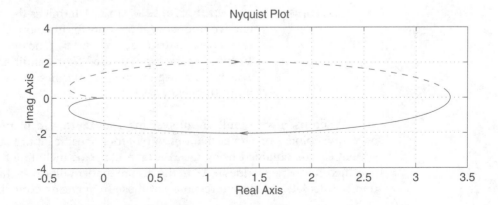

Figure 11.9 *Nyquist plot of spring-mass-damper system.*

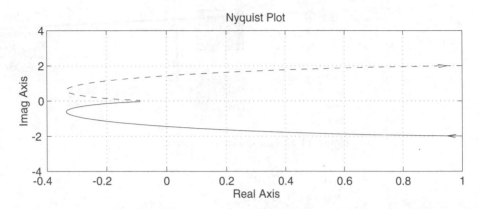

Figure 11.10 *Nyquist plot with user-specified frequencies.*

The resulting plot is shown in Figure 11.10 for 100 logarithmically evenly spaced points between the frequencies of 1 and 10 radians/second.

A Nyquist plot can also be generated using arguments that represent the continuous state-space system as demonstrated, using the state-space equations for the spring-mass-damper system, which produces the same Nyquist plot as shown in Figure 11.9:

```
%     Generate Nyquist plot of spring-mass-damper system.
A = [0,1; -3,-4];
B = [0,1]';
C = [10,0];
D = 0;
subplot(2,1,1),nyquist(A,B,C,D),...
    title('Nyquist Plot'),grid
```

ROOT-LOCUS PLOTS

Evans root locus

The root locus is an extremely useful analysis tool for single-input-single-output (SISO) systems. It is a graphical method that was developed by W. R. Evans for assessing the stability and transient response of a system and for determining, qualitatively at least, ways to improve the system performance. The **Evans root locus** is a plot of the location of the roots of the characteristic equation of a system. The roots of the characteristic equation determine the stability of the system and, generally, how the system will respond to an input. By analyzing the root-locus plot, the system designer can determine where to locate the roots and what changes may be needed in the transfer function to achieve the desired stability and response. When used in conjunction with frequency-response tools, such as Bode plots, the overall dynamic performance of a system can be thoroughly evaluated.

Figure 11.11 (a) is a commonly used block diagram that depicts a feedback control system. In this figure, $G(s)$ represents the forward-path transfer function, and $H(s)$ represents the feedback-path transfer function. The system closed-loop transfer function, shown in Figure 11.11 (b) is

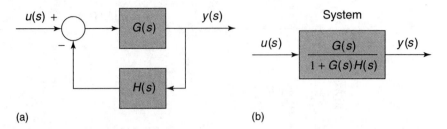

(a)   (b)

Figure 11.11 *Feedback control system.*

$$\frac{y(s)}{u(s)} = \frac{G(s)}{1 + G(s)H(s)}$$

The Evans root locus is obtained by setting the denominator of the closed-loop transfer function equal to 0, which gives the characteristic equation of the system:

$$1 + G(s)H(s) = 0$$

or

$$G(s)H(s) = -1$$

The roots of the characteristic equation are then computed as some parameter, usually the forward-path gain, is varied from 0 to infinity.

The **rlocus** function can be used to produce root-locus plots for both continuous-time and discrete-time systems. The forms for using **rlocus** are

[r,k] = rlocus(num,den,m)   Determines the root locations (**r**) and the corresponding gains (**k**) of the transfer function defined by the vectors **num** and **den** which contain the coefficients for the numerator and denominator polynomials of the open-loop transfer function $G(s)H(s)$. The optional input argument **m** allows a user-specified input gain vector.

[r,k] = rlocus(A,B,C,D,m)   Determines the root locations (**r**) and the corresponding gains (**k**) of the transfer function defined by the state-space matrices **A**, **B**, **C**, and **D**. The optional input argument **m** allows a user-specified input gain vector.

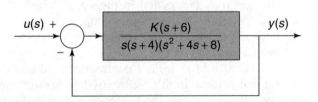

Figure 11.12 *Fourth-order control system.*

A root-locus plot can be quickly generated by using only the the right-side arguments shown in the list above. For example, the root-locus plot of the unity feedback fourth-order control system, shown in the block diagram in Figure 11.12, can be produced using the following statements:

```
%    Generate a root-locus plot.
num = [1,6];
p1 = [1,4,0];
p2 = [1,4,8];
den = conv(p1,p2);
subplot(2,1,1),rlocus(num,den),...
    title('Root Locus Plot'),grid
```

The root-locus plot is shown in Figure 11.13. In this case, the function automatically selects the values for the gain.

A root-locus plot can also be generated using arguments that represent the continuous state-space system. To illustrate, the root locus of the previous example can be produced by first using the conversion function **tf2ss** to obtain the state-space matrices **A,B,C**, and **D**, and then using the state-space argument for the **rlocus** function:

```
%    Generate root-locus plot.
[A,B,C,D] = tf2ss(num,den);
subplot(2,1,1),rlocus(A,B,C,D),...
    title('Root Locus Plot'),grid
```

These statements produce the same root-locus plot as shown in Figure 11.13. A plot of the individual pole locations for each gain value can then be generated with the statements

```
%  Plot the pole locations.
[r,k] = rlocus(A,B,C,D);
plot(r,'x'),title('Root Locus Plot'),...
    xlabel('Real Axis'),ylabel('Imag Axis'),grid
```

which produce the plot shown in Figure 11.14.

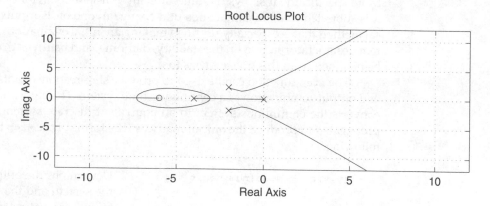

Figure 11.13 *Root locus plot.*

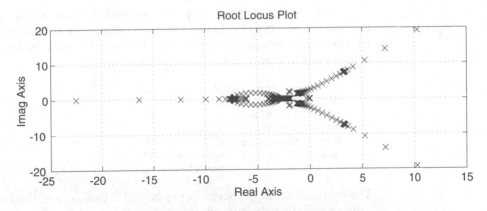

Figure 11.14 *Root locus plot with individual pole locations.*

Practice!

The following problems refer to this transfer function:

$$H(s) = \frac{s + 30}{s^2(s + 300)}$$

1. Generate a Bode plot.
2. Generate a Nyquist plot.
3. Generate a root-locus plot.

STEP RESPONSE

Step response

The **step response** generally shows how the system will respond to an input. More specifically, it shows the time-domain transient behavior of a system when it is subjected to an instantaneous unit change in one of its inputs. It is a graphical method that is especially useful in making an initial evaluation of a control system design. Information on the stability, damping, and bandwidth of a system can be obtained from this one analysis tool.

The **step** function can be used to produce step-response plots for each input and output combination of a continuous-time system. The algorithm used by **step** converts the continuous system to an equivalent discrete system, which is then propagated to produce the output matrices. The forms of the **step** function are the following:

`[y,x,t] = step(num,den,t_in)`   Determines the output matrix **y** of the system and the matrix **x** containing the values of the state vector of the equivalent discrete system, whose sampling period is the interval between the time values in output vector **t**. The transfer function is defined by the vectors **num** and **den**, which contain the coefficients for the numerator and denominator polynomials of the transfer function. Including a vector of user-specified time values **t_in** in the argument list will cause the step function to calculate the system response at only those times.

`[y,x,t] = step(A,B,C,D,iu,t_in)`   Determines the output matrix **y** of the system and the matrix **x** containing the values of the state vector of the equivalent discrete system, whose sampling period is the interval between the time values in output vector **t**. The transfer function is defined by the state space matrices **A**, **B**, **C**, and **D**.

When used with multi-input systems, `step(a,b,c,d)` produces a plot for each input and output combination of the system. Using `step(a,b,c,d,iu)` will produce a step-response plot from a selected input **iu** to all of the outputs of the system. Including a vector of user-specified time values **t_in** in the argument list will cause the step function to calculate the system response at only those times. Note, however, that if **t_in** is included in the argument list of a state-space system, **iu** must also be included, even for a single-input system.

A step-response plot can be generated without using the left-side arguments. For example, the step response of the second-order transfer function

$$\frac{y(s)}{u(s)} = \frac{5(s + 3)}{s^2 + 3s + 15}$$

can be produced using the statements

```
%   Generate a step response.
num = 5*[1,3];
den = [1,3,15];
subplot(2,1,1),step(num,den),grid,...
    title('Step Response for a Second-Order System')
```

which produce the plot shown in Figure 11.15. In this case, the function automatically selects the time values.

The following statements use a user-specified input time vector **t**

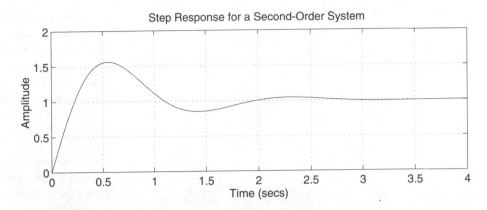

Figure 11.15 *Step response for a second-order system.*

```
%    Generate a step response.
num = 10;
den = [1,4,3];
t = 0:0.05:10;
subplot(2,1,1),step(num,den,t),grid,...
    title('Step Response for a Second-Order System')
```

and result in the plot shown in Figure 11.16 for 201 evenly spaced points between the times of 0 and 10 seconds.

A step-response plot similar to the plot in Figure 11.16 can also be generated using arguments that represent the continuous state-space system of the previous example using the **tf2ss** function:

```
%    Generate a step response.
num = 10;
den = [1,4,3];
[A,B,C,D] = tf2ss(num,den);
subplot(2,1,1),step(A,B,C,D),grid,...
    title('Step Response for a Second-Order System')
```

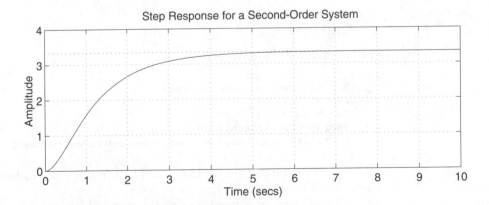

Figure 11.16 *Step response with user-specified times.*

11.4   Problem Solving Applied: Laser Beam Steering Mirror Control

Many laser systems use "steering mirrors," mirrors that can be moved quickly by a control system to redirect the laser beam. Engineers design the control systems by starting with the performance requirements. For example, the requirements might be that the mirror must be able to redirect the beam five degrees in less than a second and hold the beam at the new position with an accuracy of better than a thousandth of a degree. Candidate hardware for the steering mirror and its controller may then be selected and modeled so that designs can be developed for the system. The control system designs are analyzed using such things as root locus, Bode, and step-response plots to evaluate controller configurations and gain values. When a design is selected, the hardware is assembled and tested to see if the design specifications have been met.

1.   PROBLEM STATEMENT

A lead-lag compensation design is being evaluated for a steering mirror control system. The model of the control system design that is to be evaluated is shown in Figure 11.17. The block diagram shows the gain, the lead-lag compensator, the mirror plant, and the unity feedback path. Select a gain for the control system that will provide a stable, well-damped response.

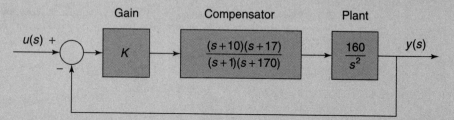

Figure 11.17 *Steering mirror control system diagram.*

2.   INPUT/OUTPUT DESCRIPTION

The analysis of the transfer function for this system will allow us to determine the desired gain. The root-locus plot represents the output of the program, as shown in the I/O diagram below:

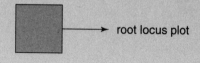

3.   HAND EXAMPLE

The best way to select the gain value is to use the root-locus plot and choose the closed-loop pole locations of the plant. The location of the plant's poles in the root-locus plot provide information on how the system should respond. Having selected the pole locations, we simply determine the associated gain value.

4.   MATLAB SOLUTION

We use the root locus-plot to see the locations of the poles as the gain changes. We can then select a location of the plant poles that we believe will provide a stable, well-damped system response and determine the gain that goes with those poles. The version of the root-locus function that we use has the form

```
[r,k] = rlocus(num,den,m)
```

because we would like to be able to see the root locations, select the input gain values, and use transfer functions rather than state-space equations for the inputs. To determine the values for the vectors **num** and **den**, we need the open-loop transfer function, which, for this system, is the product of the compensator and the plant-transfer functions. We could multiply the polynomials by hand, but it is quicker to use MATLAB statements to perform the polynomial multiplication. We then use the **rlocus** statement to plot the root locus to complete this step in the analysis.

```
%     These statements plot the root-locus information
%     for analyzing a steering mirror control system.
%
num = 160*conv([1,10],[1,17]);
den = conv(conv([1,1],[1,170]),[1,0,0]);
%
m = 1:100;
[r,k] = rlocus(num,den,m);
%
subplot(2,1,1), plot(r),...
    title('Steering Mirror Root Locus Plot'),...
    xlabel('Real Axis'),ylabel('Imag Axis'),grid
```

5.   TESTING

The resulting root-locus plot is shown in Figure 11.18. As seen in the plot, all of the closed-loop poles are to the left of the imaginary axis, which ensures that the system will be stable. The plant's closed-loop pole locations ($-28.9342 + 28.9028i$ and $-28.9342 - 28.9028i$) will provide a stable system response with good damping. The gain that is associated with these pole locations is 57.

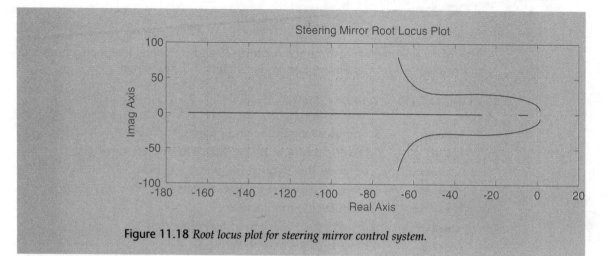

Figure 11.18 *Root locus plot for steering mirror control system.*

CHAPTER SUMMARY

Several model conversion and analysis functions for performing linear and control systems design and analysis were presented. Using the conversion functions, such as **c2d**, **tf2ss**, and so on, models can be converted from continuous-time to discrete-time equations, transfer functions to state-space equations, and many others. These conversion functions are useful when designing and analyzing systems using the analysis functions, by making it easy to convert a model that is expressed in one form to another form that the analysis function uses. The design and analysis functions—**bode, nyquist, rlocus**, and **step**—provide useful graphical information about the response of a system.

KEY TERMS

block diagram

Bode plot

measurement model

models

multi-input-multi-output (MIMO)

Nichols plot

Nyquist plot

partial-fraction expansion

plant model

root-locus plot

single-input-single-output (SISO)

state-space model

step response

transfer function

zero-pole-gain model

11

MATLAB SUMMARY

This MATLAB summary lists all the commands and functions that were described in this chapter. A brief description is also included for each one.

COMMANDS AND FUNCTIONS

bode	computes magnitude and phase response
c2d	converts continuous state-space to discrete state-space
nyquist	computes the Nyquist frequency response
residue	computes a partial-fraction expansion
rlocus	computes the root locus
ss2tf	converts state-space to transfer function
ss2zp	converts state-space to zero-pole-gain
step	computes the unit-step response
tf2ss	converts transfer function to state-space
tf2zp	converts transfer function to zero-pole-gain
zp2ss	converts zero-pole-gain to state-space
zp2tf	converts zero-pole-gain to transfer function

Style NOTES

1. For documentation purposes, use variable names that match the variables used in the general model forms.

DEBUGGING NOTES

1. Use variable names that match the variables used in the general model forms to avoid errors in translating the equations to MATLAB

PROBLEMS

Steering Mirror Control System. Assume that the design specifications for the steering mirror control system are

Bandwidth (-3dB): 10 Hz
Peak Overshoot: 20%
Settling Time: 0.5 seconds

1. Using the gain value of 57 determined in the Problem Solving Applied section, generate the open-loop Bode plot of the mirror control system. Find the crossover frequency, which is the frequency where the gain curve crosses the x-axis. Determine the phase margin at the crossover frequency by subtracting 180 degrees from the phase angle.

2. Generate the Nyquist plot and the Nichols plot for the open-loop mirror control system.

3. Compute the closed-loop transfer function for the mirror control system using the **conv** function. Generate the Bode plot for the closed-loop transfer function, plotting the frequency in Hz, and determine the closed-loop bandwidth. (The closed-loop bandwidth is the frequency where the gain curve drops below −3dB.) Does the control system meet the 10-Hz bandwidth requirement?

4. Plot the closed-loop step response for the mirror control system, and determine the peak overshoot and the settling time. The peak overshoot is the percent by which the peak value of the step response exceeds the final value. The settling time is the time that it takes for the step response to come within 5 percent of its final value. Have the peak overshoot and the settling time specifications been met?

5. Convert the closed-loop transfer function to state-space equations, and generate the Bode plot and step response of the mirror control system. Are the results the same as in Problem 4?

System Conversions. These problems use the conversion functions to convert a system from one form to another form. The problems refer to this set of system equations:

a. $$G(s) = 10 \frac{3s + 1}{s^5 + 7s^4 + 12s^2}$$

b. $$G(s) = \frac{s + 1}{s(s + 2)(s^2 + 4s + 8)}$$

c. $$G(s) = 15 \frac{s^2 + s + 10}{s^2 + 6s + 10}$$

d. $$G(s) = \frac{3}{s^3 + 6s^2 + {}^11s + 6}$$

e. $x' = Ax + Bu$
$y = Cx + Du$

$$A = \begin{bmatrix} 0 & 1 & 0 \\ 0 & 0 & 1 \\ -6 & -11 & -6 \end{bmatrix}, \quad B = [0 \ 0 \ 4]'$$

$$C = [1 \ 0 \ 0], \qquad D = [0]$$

6. Use the **tf2zp** function to convert transfer function (a) to the zero-pole-gain form.

7. Use the **conv** function and the **tf2zp** function to convert transfer function (b) to the zero-pole-gain form.

8. Use the **residue** function to convert transfer function (a) to partial-fraction form.

9. Use the **residue** function to convert transfer function (c) to partial-fraction form.

10. Use the **c2d** function and a sample period of 0.1 to convert the continuous-time state-space equations in (e) to discrete-time equations.

11. Use the **tf2ss** function to convert (d) to state-space equations and the **residue** function to convert (d) to partial-fraction form. Do you see any similarity between the two representations?

12. Use the **ss2tf** function to convert (e) to transfer-function form. Do you see any similarity with the results of problem 11?

13. Use the **ss2zp** function to convert (e) to zero-pole-gain form and then the **zp2ss** function to convert the result back to state-space form. What happened? What are the similarities with problems 11 and 12?

14. Use the **ss2zp** function to convert (e) to zero-pole-gain form and then the **zp2tf** function to convert the result to transfer-function form. Did you get the same results as in problem 13?

15. Use the **ss2tf** function to convert the state-space equations obtained in problem 14 to transfer-function form. Did you get transfer function (e)?

System Design and Analysis. These problems use the design and analysis functions presented in this chapter to provide further analysis of the system equations presented in the previous set of problems.

16. Generate the Bode and Nyquist plots for (a), using only the right-side arguments.

17. Generate the Bode and Nyquist plots for (b), using left and right-side arguments and a user-specified frequency range.

18. Generate the Bode and Nichols plots for (c) for a user specified range of frequencies.

19. Generate the Bode plot for the transfer function (d) and the state-space equations (e). Are they the same?

20. Generate the root-locus plots for (d) and (e). Are they the same?

21. Generate the root-locus plot for (c) using the left-side arguments, a user-specified set of gains and x's to mark the pole locations.

22. Generate the root locus plot for (a), and then use **tf2ss** to convert (a) to state-space equations. Generate the root-locus plot for the state-space equations. Are the plots the same?

23. Convert (b) to state-space equations, and generate the root-locus plot using the left-side arguments and a user-specified set of gains.

Appendix A
MATLAB *Function Summary*

This MATLAB summary lists all the functions that were defined in this text.

abs	computes absolute value or magnitude
acos	computes arccosine
all	determines if all values are true
ans	stores expression value
any	determines if any values are true
asin	computes arcsine
atan	computes 2-quadrant arctangent
atan2	computes 4-quadrant arctangent
axis	controls axis scaling
bode	computes magnitude and phase response
butter	designs a Butterworth digital filter
c2d	converts continuous state-space to discrete state-space
ceil	rounds towards ∞
cheby1	designs a Chebyshev Type I digital filter
cheby2	designs a Chebyshev Type II digital filter
clc	clears command screen
clear	clears workspace
clf	clears figure
clock	represents the current time
collect	collects coefficients of a symbolic expression
cos	computes cosine of angle
cumprod	determines cumulative products
cumsum	determines cumulative sums
date	prints current date
demo	runs demonstrations
det	computes the determinant of a matrix
diff	computes the differences between adjacent values; differentiates a symbolic expression
disp	displays matrix or text
dot	computes the dot product of two vectors

dsolve	solves an ordinary differential equation
eig	computes the eigenvalues and eigenvectors of a matrix
ellip	designs an elliptic digital filter
else	optional clause in **if** structure
elseif	optional clause in **if** structure
end	defines end of a control structure
eps	represents floating-point precision
exit	terminates MATLAB
exp	computes value with base e
expand	expands a symbolic expression
eye	generates identity matrix
ezplot	generates a plot of a symbolic expression
factor	factors a symbolic expression
fft	computes the frequency content of a signal
filter	applies a digital filter to an input signal
find	locates nonzero values
finite	determines if values are finite
fix	rounds towards zero
floor	rounds towards $-\infty$
for	generates loop structure
format 1	sets format to plus and minus signs only
format compact	sets format to compact form
format long	sets format to long decimal
format long e	sets format to long exponential
format loose	sets format to non-compact form
format short	sets format to short decimal
format short e	sets format to short exponential
fprintf	prints formatted information
freqs	computes the analog frequency content
freqz	computes the digital frequency content
function	generates user-defined function
grid	inserts grid in a plot
grpdelay	measure the group delay of a digital filter
help	invokes help facility
hist	plots histogram
horner	converts a symbolic expression into a nested form
i	represents the value $\sqrt{-1}$
if	tests logical expression
Inf	represents the value ∞
input	accepts input from the keyboard
int	integrates a symbolic expression

interp1	computes linear and cubic spline interpolation
inv	computes the inverse of a matrix
isempty	determines if matrix is empty
isnan	determines if values are **NaNs**
j	represents the value $\sqrt{-1}$
length	determines number of values in a vector
load	loads matrices from a file
log	computes natural logarithm
log10	computes common logarithm
loglog	generates a log-log plot
lu	computes the LU factorization of a matrix
max	determines maximum value
mean	determines mean value
median	determines median value
min	determines minimum value
NaN	represents the value Not-a-Number
numden	returns the numerator and denominator expressions
numeric	converts a symbolic expression to a number
nyquist	computes the Nyquist frequency response
ode23	computes a second/third-order Runge-Kutta solution
ode45	computes a fourth/fifth-order Runge-Kutta solution
ones	generates matrix of ones
pause	temporarily halts a program
pi	represents the value π
plot	generates a linear xy plot
poly2sym	converts a vector to a symbolic polynomial
polyfit	computes a least-squares polynomial
polyval	evaluates a polynomial
pretty	prints a symbolic expression in typeset form
print	print the graphics window
prod	determines product of values
qr	computes the QR factorization of a matrix
quad	computes the integral under a curve (Simpson)
quad8	computes the integral under a curve (Newton-Cote)
quit	terminates Matlab
rand	generates a uniform random number
randn	generates a Gaussian random number
rem	computes remainder from division
remez	designs an optimal FIR digital filter
residue	performs a partial-fraction expansion
rlocus	computes the root locus

`round`	rounds to nearest integer
`save`	saves variables in a file
`semilogx`	generates a log-linear plot
`semilogy`	generates a linear-log plot
`sign`	generates $-1,0,1$ based on sign
`simple`	shortens a symbolic expression
`simplify`	simplifies a symbolic expression
`sin`	computes sine of angle
`size`	prints row and column dimensions
`solve`	solves an equation
`sort`	sorts values
`sqrt`	computes square root
`ss2tf`	converts state-space to transfer function
`ss2zp`	converts state-space to zero-pole-gain
`std`	computes standard deviation
`step`	computes the unit step response
`subplot`	splits graphics window into subwindows
`sum`	determines sum of values
`svd`	computes the SVD factorization of a matrix
`sym2poly`	converts a symbolic expression to a coefficient vector
`symadd`	adds two symbolic expressions
`symdiv`	divides two symbolic expressions
`symmul`	multiplies two symbolic expressions
`sympow`	raises a symbolic expression to a power
`symsub`	subtracts two symbolic expressions
`symvar`	returns independent variable
`tan`	computes tangent of angle
`tf2ss`	converts transfer function to state-space
`tf2zp`	converts transfer function to zero-pole-gain
`title`	adds a title to a plot
`unwrap`	removes 2π discontinuities in a phase angle
`what`	lists variables
`while`	generates a loop structure
`who`	lists variables in memory
`whos`	lists variables in memory plus sizes
`xlabel`	adds x-axis label to a plot
`ylabel`	adds y-axis label to a plot
`yulewalk`	designs an optimal IIR digital filter
`zeros`	generates matrix of zeros
`zp2ss`	converts zero-pole-gain to state-space
`zp2tf`	converts zero-pole-gain to transfer function

Complete Solutions to Practice! Problems

SECTION 2.2, PAGE 36

1. 5 rows by 4 columns, or a 5 × 4 matrix
2. `G(2,2), G(4,1), G(4,2), G(4,4), G(5,4)`

SECTION 2.2, PAGE 38

1. 4 × 1
2. 2 × 3
3. 3 × 4
4. 1 × 3, 1 × 7
5. 5 × 1
6. 2 × 1

SECTION 2.2, PAGE 40

1. `[1.5, 0.5, 8.2, 0.5, -2.3]'`
2. `[10, 11, 12, 13, 14, 15]`
3. `[4, 5, 6, 7, 8, 9; 1, 2, 3, 4, 5, 6]`
4. `[0, 0.1, 0.2, 0.3, 0.4, 0.5, 0.6, 0.7, 0.8, 0.9, 1.0]`
5. `[0.5, 0.5, 2.4; 1.2, -2.3, -4.5]`
6. `[0.6,1.5,2.3,-0.5; 5.7,8.2,9.0,1.5; 1.2,-2.3,-4.5,50.5]`

SECTION 2.3, PAGE 54

1. `factor = 1 + b/v + c/(v*v);`
2. `slope = (y2 - y1)/(x2 - x1);`
3. `resistance = 1/(1/r1 + 1/r2 + 1/r3);`
4. `loss = f*p*(1/d)*(v*v/2);`

SECTION 2.3, PAGE 54

1. `[2, -2, 1, 1]`
2. `[0.6667, -0.5, -5, 0]`
3. `[12, -1, 10.2, 0]`
4. `[10 3 5.5 16]`
5. `[4 -1.3333 -3.3333 0]`

SECTION 3.1, PAGE 71

1. `-3`
2. `-2`
3. `-3`
4. `-2`
5. `-1`
6. `1`
7. `11`
8. `-1`

9.   `[5, 4, 3, 2, 1, 0, 1, 2, 3, 4, 5]`

10.   `[0, 0, 1, 1, 1, 2, 2, 1, 2, 3, 3, 4]`

SECTION 3.1, PAGE 73

1.   `motion = sqrt(vi^2 + 2*a*x);`

2.   `frequency = 1/sqrt((2*pi*c/L));`

3.   `range = 2*vi*vi*sin(b)*cos(b)/g;`

4.   `length = k*sqrt(1-(v/c)^2);`

5.   `volume = 2*pi*x*x*((1-pi/4)*y-(0.8333-pi/4)*x);`

6.   `center = 38.1972*(r^3 - s^3)*sin(a)/((r*r - s*s)*a);`

SECTION 3.1, PAGE 74

1.   `cosh(x)/sinh(x)`   2.   `1/cos(x)`

3.   `1/sin(x)`   4.   `ln(sqrt((x+1)/(x-1))`

5.   `log((1+sqrt(1-x*x))/x)`   6.   `asin(1/x)`

SECTION 3.1, PAGE 78

1.   r = 3.6056, θ = −0.5880   2.   r = 1, θ = −1.5708

3.   r = 2, θ = 3.1416   4.   r = 1.1180, θ = 1.1071

5.   a = 0.5403, b = 0.8415   6.   a = −0.7071, b = 0.7071

7.   a = −0.3331, b = 0.3729   8.   a = −3.500, b = 0.0000

SECTION 3.1, PAGE 82

```
f1 = [1, -3, -1, 3];
f2 = [1, -6, 12, -8];
f3 = [1, -8, 20, -16];
f4 = [1, -5, 7, -3];
f5 = [0, 0, 1, -2];
```

1.   `plot(x,polyval(f1,x))`

2.   `plot(x,polyval(f2-2*f4,x))`

3.   `plot(x,polyval(3*f5+f2-2*f3,x))`

4.   `plot(x,polyval(conv(f1,f3),x))`

5.   `plot(x,polyval(f4,x)./(x-1))`

6.   `plot(x,polyval(conv(f1,f2),x)./polyval(f5))`

SECTION 3.1, PAGE 86

1.   real roots: −1, 2, 4   2.   real roots: −2, −2

3.   no real roots   4.   real roots: −3, −1, 1, 2, 4

5.   real roots: 1, 3, 4   6.   real roots: 3, −2, −2

7.   real roots: 1   8.   real roots: −1

SECTION 3.2, PAGE 93

1.   `7`   2.   `[1, -1, -2]`

3.   `[0, -1, -2, 7]`   4.   `[3, 3.3333, 3]`

5.   `1.5`

6. `[1, 3 ,7; 2, 24, 28; 12, -24, -56]`
7. `[1, 3, 5, 21]`
8. `[1, -1, -2; 2, 3, 4; 6, 8, 7]`

SECTION 3.3, PAGE 99

1. true
2. true
3. true
4. false
5. true
6. true
7. true
8. false

SECTION 3.3, PAGE 101

1.
```
if abs(volt_1 - volt_2) > 10
    fprintf('%f %f \n',volt_1, volt_2);
end
```
2.
```
if log(x) >= 3
    time = 0;
    count = count + 1;
end
```
3.
```
if dist < 50 & time > 10
    time = time + 2;
else
    time = time + 2.5;
end
```
4.
```
if dist >= 100
    time = time + 2;
elseif dist > 50
    time = time + 1;
else
    time = time + 0.5;
end
```

SECTION 3.3, PAGE 103

1. `[1, 1, 1]`
2. `[1, 3, 6, 7, 8]'`
3. `1`
4. `0`
5. `[1, 1, 1]'`
6. `[1, 0, 1]`

SECTION 3.5, PAGE 108

1.
```
function s = step(x)
%   STEP  The step function is defined as 1
%         for x>=0, and 0 otherwise.
%
s = zeros(size(x));
set1 = find(x >= 0);
s(set1) = ones(size(set1));
```
2.
```
function r = ramp(x)
%   RAMP  The step function is defined as x
%         for x >= 0, and 0 otherwise.
%
```

```
      r = zeros(size(x));
      set1 = find(x >= 0);
      r(set1) = x(set1);
3.    function y = g(x)
      %    G  g is defined as 0 if x<0,
      %        sin(pi*x/2) if 0<=x<=1,
      %        and 1 otherwise.
      %
      y = zeros(size(x));
      set1 = find(x >= 0 & x <= 1);
      set2 = find(x > 1);
      y(set1) = sin(pi*x(set1)/2);
      y(set2) = ones(size(set2));
```

SECTION 3.6, PAGE 110

1. `x = rand(1,10)*10;`   2. `x = rand(1,10)*2 - 1;`
3. `x = rand(1,10)*10 - 20;`   4. `x = rand(1,10)*0.5 + 4.5;`
5. `x = rand(1,10)*2*pi - pi;`

SECTION 3.6, PAGE 111

1. `x = randn(1,1000)*sqrt(0.5) + 1;`
2. `x = randn(1,1000)*0.25 - 5.5;`
3. `x = randn(1,1000)*1.25 - 5.5;`

SECTION 3.7, PAGE 115

1. `[0,12,1,4; 5,9,2,3; 3,6,3,2; 1,3,4,1]`
2. `[1,4,0; 2,3,-1; 3,5,0; 0,0,3]`
3. `[3,0,-1,0; 0,5,3,4; 0,3,2,1]`
4. `[4,3,2,1; 1,2,3,4; 12,9,6,3; 0,5,3,1]`
5. `[0,3,3; 4,2,3; 1,0,0; -1,5,0]`
6. `[0,0; 4,5; 1,3; -1,3; 3,0; 2,0]`
7. `[0,1,3,0,3,0; 4,-1,2,5,3,0]`
8. `[1,3; 4,2; 3,9; 1,5; 2,4; 3,1; 6,12; 3,0]`
9. `[1,3,5,0; 0,6,9,12; 0,0,2,1; 0,0,0,4]`
10. `[1,3,5,0; 3,6,9,12; 0,3,2,1; 0,0,3,4]`
11. `[0,-1,0,0; 4,3,5,0; 1,2,3,0]`
12. `[0; 9; 3; 1]`

SECTION 3.8, PAGE 117

1. `1 8`   2. `1 7`
3. `9`   4. `1 1`
5. `0`   6. `4`

SECTION 4.1, PAGE 130

1. `[-14 62]`   2. `[9,-7,6; 7,-9,10]`
3. `[39; -25; 18]`   4. `[8,-4,2; -2,2,-2; 9,-3,0]`

SECTION 4.3, PAGE 136

1.   rank is 2, inverse does not exist   2.   **8**

3.   **0**   4.   **[-0.25,0.25; 0.625,-0.375]**

SECTION 4.3, PAGE 139

1.   **1.2583, 4, 8.7417**

2.   **[0.6623; -0.6053; 0.4415]**
      [-0.5547; 0.0000; 0.8321]
      [0.5036; 0.7960; 0.3358]

3.   **-4.2616e-15, -5.7732e-15, -4.9071e-14**

4.   **[0.8334, -2.2188, 4.4025;**
      -0.7617, 0.0000, 6.9584;
      0.5556, 3.3282; 2.9350]

SECTION 5.2, PAGE 157

1.   **[2,1]'**   2.   parallel lines

3.   same line   4.   close to same line or parallel lines

5.   **[-2,5,-6]'**   6.   **[9,-6,14]'**

7.   **[0.3055,-0.5636,1.0073]'**   8.   **[2,1,3,-1]';**

SECTION 6.1, PAGE 170

1.
```
t = 0:0.5:5;
temp = [72.5, 78.1, 86.4, 92.3, 110.6, 111.5, 109.3, ...
     110.2, 110.5, 109.9, 110.2];
new_t = 0:0.1:5;
temp_linear = interp1(t,temp,new_t,'linear');
temp_cubic = interp1(t,temp,new_t,'spline');
plot(new_t,temp_linear,new_t,temp_cubic,t,temp,'o')
```

2.   linear: **75.8600, 89.3500, 111.2480, 109.9240**
      cubic: **75.5360, 88.7250, 111.9641, 109.9081**

3.   linear: **0.6747, 1.6011, 1.7104, 1.8743**
      cubic: **0.5449, 1.5064, 1.7628, 2.1474**
   (These answers used only the first 6 points so that the
   independent variable would be increasing.)

SECTION 7.1, PAGE 189

1.   **0.0550**   2.   **0.5000**

3.   **0.3750**   4.   **0.2500**

SECTION 7.3, PAGE 198

Assume that **N** is the number of points in the original function (**N** = 201 for the answers here), **df1** contains the first derivative values, **df2** contains the second derivative values and **xf1** contains the x coordinates of the first derivative. Then, the points of local maxima and minima can be determined with these statements:

```
product = df1(1:N-2).*df1(2:N-1);
```

```
peaks = find(product<0);
minima = find(df2(peaks)>0.0001);
minx = xf1(peaks(minima));
maxima = find(df2(peaks)<0.0001);
maxx = xf1(peaks(maxima));
```

1. local maxima: **0.2000**
   local minima: **3.1000**
2. local maxima: none
   local minima: **-2**
3. local maxima: none
   local minima: **1**
4. local maxima: none
   local minima: none
5. local maxima: **-2 2**
   local minima: **-0.4 3.6000**

SECTION 8.2, PAGE 211

1.
```
function dy = ga(x,y)
%   GA   This function computes the values
%        of a differential equation.
%
dy = -y;

function dy = gb(x,y)
%   GB   This function computes the values
%        of a differential equation.
%
dy = (-x-exp(x))./(3*y.*y);
```
2.
```
[x,num_y] = ode23('ga',0,2,-3);
plot(x,num_y)
```
3.
```
[x,num_y] = ode23('ga',0,2,-3);
y = -3*exp(-x);
plot(x,num_y,x,y,'o')
```
4.
```
[x,num_y] = ode23('gb',0,2,3);
plot(x,num_y)
```
5.
```
[x,num_y] = ode23('gb',0,2,3);
y = (28-0.5*x.*x-exp(x)).^(1/3);
plot(x,num_y,x,y,'o')
```

SECTION 9.1, PAGE 229

1. `1/(x+4)/(x^2+8*x+16)`   2. `(x^2+8*x+16)*(x+4)^2`
3. `(x-2)/(x^2+8*x+16)`   4. `(x^2+8*x+16)^2`

SECTION 9.2, PAGE 230

1. (2,1)
2. parallel lines
3. same line
4. close to same line or parallel lines

5.   (−2,5,−6)
6.   (9,−6,14)
7.   (84/275,−31/55,277/275)
8.   (2,1,3,−1)

SECTION 9.3, PAGE 233

1.   `3*x^2-10*x+2`
      `6*x-10`
2.   `(2*x+4)*(x-1)+x^2+4*x+4`
      `6*x+6`
3.   `3/x-(3*x-1)/x^2`
      `-6/x^2+2*(3*x-1)/x^3`
4.   `2*(x^5-4*x^4-9*x^3+32)*(5*x^4-16*x^3-27*x^2)`
      `2*(5*x^4-16*x^3-27*x^2)^2+2*(x^5-4*x^4-9*x^3+32)`
          `*(20*x^3-48*x^2-54*x)`

SECTION 9.3, PAGE 234

1.   **0.0550**   2.   **0.5000**
3.   **0.3750**   4.   **0.2500**

SECTION 10.1, PAGE 248

Assume the following statements have been executed:

```
N = 128;
T = 0.001;
k = 0:N-1;
```

1.    ```
      f = 2*sin(2*pi*50*k*T);
      magF = abs(fft(f));
      hertz = k*(1/(N*T));
      plot(hertz(1:N/2),magF(1:N/2))
      ```
2.    ```
      g = cos(250*pi*k*T) - sin(200*pi*k*T);
      magG = abs(fft(g));
      hertz = k*(1/(N*T));
      plot(hertz(1:N/2),magG(1:N/2))
      ```
3.    ```
      h = 5 - cos (1000*k*T);
      magH = abs(fft(h));
      hertz = k*(1/(N*T));
      plot(hertz(1:N/2),magH(1:N/2))
      ```
4.    ```
      m = 4*sin(250*pi*k*T - pi/4);
      magM = abs(fft(m));
      hertz = k*(1/(N*T));
      plot(hertz(1:N/2),magM(1:N/2))
      ```

SECTION 10.2, PAGE 260

1.    ```
      w = 0:0.1:4;
      H = freqs([1,0,0],[1,sqrt(2),1],w);
      ```
      ```

```
plot(w,abs(H))
        transition band: 0.3 to 1 rps
```

2.  ```
    [H,wT] = freqz([0.707,-0.707],[1,-0.414],50);
    plot(wT,abs(H))
            transition band: 0.1 to 0.7 radians
    ```

3.  ```
    [H,wT] = freqz([-0.163,-0.058,0.116,0.2,0.116,-0.058,...
                    -0.163],1,50);
    plot(wT,abs(H))
            transition band: 0.3 to 0.9 radians, 1.1 to 1.7 radians
    ```

4.  ```
    w = 0:0.1:4;
    H = freqs([5,1],[1,0.4,1],w);
    plot(w,abs(H))
    ```
    If the magnitude values were scaled such that the peak value were at 1, then the transition band would be the following: 0.2 to 0.9 rps and 1.1 to 3.5 rps

SECTION 10.3, PAGE 263

Assume that the following statements have been executed:
```
T = 1/5000;
k = 0:100;
kT = k*T;
```

1.  ```
    x = sin(2*pi*1000*k*T);
    y = filter([0.42,0,-0.42],[1,-0.443,0.159],x);
    plot(kT,x,kT,y)
    ```
    amplitude of the input is multiplied by approximately 1.0

2.  ```
    x = 2*cos(2*pi*100*k*T);
    y = filter([0.42,0,-0.42],[1,-0.443,0.159],x);
    plot(kT,x,kT,y)
    ```
    amplitude of the input is multiplied by approximately 0.2

3.  ```
    x = -sin(2*pi*2000*k*T);
    y = filter([0.42,0,-0.42],[1,-0.443,0.159],x);
    plot(kT,x,kT,y)
    ```
    amplitude of the input is multiplied by approximately 0.2

4.  ```
    x = cos(2*pi*1600*k*T);
    y = filter([0.42,0,-0.42],[1,-0.443,0.159],x);
    plot(kT,x,kT,y)
    ```
    amplitude of the input is multiplied by approximately 0.7

SECTION 10.4, PAGE 269

1.  ```
    [B,A] = butter(5,75/250);
    [H,wT] = freqz(B,A,100);
    T = 1/500;
    plot(wT/(2*pi*T),abs(H))
    ```

2.  ```
    [B,A] = cheby2(6,20,100/500,'high');
    [H,wT] = freqz(B,A,100);
    T = 1/1000;
    plot(wT/(2*pi*T),abs(H))
    ```

3.  ```
    m = [1,1,1,1,0,0,0,0,0,0];
    f = [0,0.1,0.2,0.3,0.4,0.5,0.6,0.7,0.8,1];
    ```

```
          B = remez(40,f,m);
          [H,wT] = freqz(B,1,100);
          T = 1/500;
          plot(wT/(2*pi*T),abs(H))
4.        m = [0,0,1,1,0,0,0,0,0,0,0];
          f = [0,0.1,0.2,0.4,0.5,0.7,0.8,0.85,0.9,1];
          B = remez(80,f,m);
          [H,wT] = freqz(B,1,100);
          T = 1/500;
          plot(wT/(2*pi*T),abs(H))
```

SECTION 11.2, PAGE 292

```
1.    r =   0.3750
            0.6250
      p =   -6
             2
      k =   []
2.    a     -4      12
             1       0
      b =   1
            0
      c =   1       3
      d =   0
3.    ad = 0.7169     4.0027
           0.3336     2.0512
      bd = 0.3336
           0.0876
4.    z =   -3
      p =   -6
             2
      k =   1
5.    a =  -4.0000    3.4641
            3.4641       0
      b =   1
            0
      c =  1.0000    0.8660
      d =   0
```

SECTION 11.3, PAGE 302

```
1.    bode([1,30],[1,300,0,0]);
2.    nyquist([1,30],[1,300,0,0]);
3.    rlocus([1,30],[1,300,0,0]);
```

Index

MATLAB keywords and functions are entered in boldface.

Three easy ways to receive more information on MATLAB:

Fax this form to (508) 647-7101

Mail this form to The MathWorks, Inc., 24 Prime Park Way, Natick, MA 01760

@ Send e-mail to *info@mathworks.com* and request kit KP108

Send me a *free* copy of the *MATLAB®* Product Catalog.

This catalog provides information on MATLAB, Toolboxes, SIMULINK®, Blocksets, and more.

I am currently a MATLAB user: ☐ Yes ☐ No

My computer is: ☐ PC or Macintosh ☐ UNIX workstation

For the fastest response, fax to (508) 647-7101 or send e-mail to *info@mathworks.com* and request KP108.

NAME
_____

E-MAIL
_____

TITLE
_____

COMPANY/UNIVERSITY
_____

DEPT. OR M/S
_____

ADDRESS
_____

CITY/STATE/COUNTRY/ZIP
_____

PHONE
_____

FAX
_____

GRADUATION DATE IF APPLICABLE
_____

R-BK-ETR/411v0/KP108

NUMERIC DISPLAY FORMATS

MATLAB Command	Display	Example
format short	default	15.2345
format long	14 decimals	15.23453333333333
format short e	4 decimals	1.5235e+01
format long e	15 decimals	1.523453333333333e+01
format bank	2 decimals	15.23
format +	+, −, blank	+

ARITHMETIC OPERATIONS BETWEEN TWO SCALARS

Operation	Algebraic Form	MATLAB
addition	$a + b$	a + b
subtraction	$a - b$	a - b
multiplication	$a \times b$	a*b
division	$\dfrac{a}{b}$	a/b
exponentiation	a^b	a^b

ELEMENT-BY-ELEMENT OPERATIONS

Operation	Algebraic Form	MATLAB
addition	$a + b$	a + b
subtraction	$a - b$	a - b
multiplication	$a \times b$	a.*b
division	$\dfrac{a}{b}$	a./b
exponentiation	a^b	a.^b

LINE AND MARK OPTIONS FOR PLOTS

line type	indicator	point type	indicator
solid	–	point	.
dashed	–	plus	+
dotted	:	star	*
dash-dot	–.	circle	o
		x-mark	x

RELATIONAL OPERATORS

Relational Operator	Interpretation
<	less than
<=	less than or equal
>	greater than
>=	greater than or equal
==	equal
~=	not equal

LOGICAL OPERATORS

Logical Operator	Symbol
not	~
and	&
or	|

COMBINATIONS OF LOGICAL OPERATORS

A	B	~A	A | B	A & B
false	false	true	false	false
false	true	true	true	false
true	false	false	true	false
true	true	false	true	true

CONVERSION FORMULAS

Rectangular/polar

$$r = \sqrt{a^2 + b^2}, \; \theta = \tan^{-1}\frac{b}{a}$$
$$a = r \cdot \cos(\theta), \; b = r \cdot \sin(\theta)$$

Euler's Formulas

$$\sin(\theta) = \frac{e^{i\theta} - e^{-i\theta}}{2i}$$
$$\cos(\theta) = \frac{e^{i\theta} + e^{-i\theta}}{2}$$

Complex Numbers

$$a + ib = r\,e^{i\theta}$$

where $\quad r = \sqrt{a^2 + b^2}, \; \theta = \tan^{-1}\frac{b}{a}$

$\qquad\quad a = r \cdot \cos(\theta), \; b = r \cdot \sin(\theta)$